Table of Contents

1	**PREFACE**	3
2	**INTRODUCTION**	5
2.1	IMPORTANT NOTICE	8
2.2	REFERENCE VOLUMES	10
3	**HARMONIZATION**	11
3.1	OVERVIEW	11
4	**THE PLAY BY NUMBER SYSTEM**	12
4.1	MAPPING THE SCALES TO THE KEYBORD	12
4.2	NOTE NUMBER 1 – KEYBOARD RELATIONSHIP	14
4.3	NOTE NUMBER 1 – SCALE RELATIONSHIP	18
4.4	THE NUMBER SYSTEM AND ACCIDENTALS	18
4.5	THE NUMBER SYSTEM AND CHORDS	23
5	**THE ROMAN NUMBER SYSTEM**	28
6	**ROMAN NUMBER ANALYSIS**	33
7	**HARMONIZING A SIMPLE MELODY**	35
8	**REGISTRATION**	38
9	**ADVANCED HARMONIZATION OF -"JOY TO THE WORLD"**	39
9.1	STARTING WITH WHAT IS IN A HYMN BOOK	39
9.2	STARTING WITH A SIMPLE MELODY	42
9.3	JOY TO THE WORLD - ORIGINAL VERSION	45
9.4	JOY TO THE WORLD – MAKING THIS SOUND BEAUTIFUL – HARMONIZATION	46
9.5	INSERTING PASSING CHORDS INTO A PROGRESSION	66
9.6	CASE STUDY SUMMARY - HAS THE LIGHT BULB TURNED ON YET?	84
10	**HARK THE HERALD ANGELS SING – CASE STUDY**	87
11	**APPROACH TO COURSE**	109
12	**THE SECRETS TO THE NUMBERS**	110
12.1	THE 1 (I)	110
12.2	THE 2 (II)	110

12.3	The 4 and 5 (IV and V)	111
12.4	The 7 (VII)	113
12.5	The Major 7 (VII)	113
12.6	The 3 (III)	114
12.7	The 6 (VI)	114
13	**INTERVAL SIZING**	**115**
14	**THE DUALITY OF CHORDS**	**117**
14.1	Duality of Chords – "Over the Rainbow"	121
15	**AN INTRODUCTION TO PICTURE PASSING CHORDS**	**124**
15.1	The 7b5#5 Picture Chord	125
15.2	A Picture chord on the suspension	134
15.3	Chord Visual Analysis	137
16	**PROGRESSIONS**	**143**
16.1	Progression Sequence	144
16.2	Tone Sequence	145
16.3	Being neighborly	147
16.4	Build a progression	148
16.5	Add to a Progression	149
16.6	Build Forever	151
16.7	Voicing a Progression	152
16.8	Voice our progression	155
16.9	Voice the first chord in the progression (I).	156
16.10	Voice the second chord in the progression (MajVII).	158
16.11	Voice the third chord in the progression (III).	160
16.12	Voice the fourth chord in the progression (VI).	162
16.13	Voice the fifth chord in the progression (bII).	163
16.14	Voice the last chord in the progression (I).	164
17	**BEGIN YOUR ADVENTURE**	**166**
18	**NO BOUNDARIES**	**169**
19	**APPENDIX – ROMAN NUMBERS – ENHARMONIC SCALE NUMBERING**	**172**

1 Preface

Creative Music has developed a revolutionary method enabling keyboard musicians to quickly harmonize a line of notes with infinite chord changes. Imagine being able to play a different chord on every melody note! Whether or not it is gospel, jazz, contemporary etc., Creative Music has published five volumes (1200 pgs) of instructional material that illustrates pictorially in color with easy-to-follow printed text instructions, of how to harmonize music of your choice with advanced voicings. The system is such that no two musicians will come up with the same resulting harmonization.

Their patent pending technology has been internationally acclaimed by users who virtually witness that the new learning premise is categorically reinventing and rejuvenating how music should be taught henceforth. The initial distribution of "The Adventures in Harmony Course" has set off a sustained frenzy of international sales orders from both professional and amateur performers. As a subsequent result, Creative Music now uniquely occupies and satisfies a new segment of music artisans that have not yet been fully recognized because their departure from long-standing static methodology to a fluid self-styled mode where discovery and reaching for higher individual performance plateaus is beyond the scope of ordinary expectation.

The users of The Adventures in Harmony course materials have been consistently reporting how the patent pending system has enhanced their ability to easily create, on the fly, complex chord harmonies and exciting progressions. The new learning principal is presented in an easy-to-follow format and goes against the grain of traditional music instruction.

Our mission at gospel-chords.com Creative Music Ventures LLC., is to focus on quickly getting the musician to the end-result of playing beautiful advanced harmonies, without being burdened by the intricacies and complications of music theory. We want to give the musician a path of least resistance to reach this goal as quickly as possible. We have already done all the dirty work and analysis of chord structures, harmonies, progressions and their interrelationships. We have filtered all that down to a methodology that you can use, to consistently and easily achieve beautiful harmonization in your own music without being bogged down a fishing though the previous 1500 years of music theory.

Music education has not changed in the last century, and Creative Music is on the forefront of turning that around. The "Adventures in Harmony Course" is re-inventing how music has been taught for the last century. Our instructional method goes against the grain of all past music education teaching methodologies. In fact we are proud of

Adventures in Harmony – Introduction to the System

this "invention/discovery" and the internals of our system and technique are proprietary and were developed through years of computer analysis and modeling.

Gregory Moody Creative Music's founder is an accomplished musician and software engineer, who comes from a family lineage of musicians, i.e., his world famous cousin NEA jazz master; flute, tenor and alto saxophonist, James Moody.

A word from Gregory Moody:

"The Adventures in Harmony Course" consist of hundreds of chord voicings that have been computer engineered and modeled using proprietary computer algorithms. The fascinating thing is that these chords can be fit together in any order similar to kids LEGO™ building blocks to create an infinite possibility of chord progressions and harmonizations. Playing by number is not just for kids, the entire system is based on numbers; if you can count to 21 you can master this system. In following our system, it is nearly impossible to put together chords and create chord progressions that are not pleasing.

Even the most novice musician is able to quickly create complex lush harmonies and progressions. The complete course consists of over 1200 pages of detailed instruction spread over seven volumes.

To accompany the written material is 4 hours of video instruction on DVD. Students will find just the right mix of theory and instruction presented at a level that is sure to spawn creativity. This is not your typical "copy what I do" music course. In this course, there are no progressions or songs to remember. This is because the student is applying our techniques to music of their choosing to create their own unique harmonization. By using the course materials, students will be able to quickly turn their single finger melodies into colorful harmonizations.

For further information, visit their website at www.gospel-chords.com

2   Introduction

Harmonization is where you take something as simple as a single note, one finger melody, and turn that into a song where you are playing more than one finger at a time. Re-harmonization is where you take an existing song and play it with completely different chords, perhaps for the purpose of giving it a more soulful and contemporary feel

If you have any music reading knowledge or experience, I'm sure that you know that music from a church hymnal that is played as it is written is boring and plain. Have you ever been in a church service where the organist or pianist is reading the music from the hymnal, but you know darn well, that what they are playing is not what is written in the hymnal, and wondered where is the beautiful music that they are playing coming from? They are re-harmonizing as they play!

With the Adventures in Harmony Play by Number System, you are going to discover that the process of harmonization is something that you will be able to do almost instantly after the completion of the course.

Have you ever listened to a piece of music that you have never heard before, but is being performed by an artist that you are familiar with, and you were immediately able to identify the artist and say "Hey, that's , Stevie Wonder or that's Ray Charles." You were able to do this because you recognized that artists harmonizations. Musicians tend to have favorite harmonization's; ones that they tend to use very often. It is the musicians' harmonization's, that defines the musician and who they are. It is the harmonization that defines the artists' style, and gives you the ability to recognize them, even though you may have never heard the song.

With the Adventures in Harmony Play by Number System, you will have the ability to be YOU, an individual, and have your own unique harmonizations. The chords that you will be playing won't be those simple plain sounding chords, they will be those contemporary, and soulful chords that you always wanted to know how to play. You will no longer have to try and be somebody else, or always asking somebody else for chords. With the Adventures in Harmony Play by Number System, people are going to be coming to YOU, and asking YOU….."Hey man what are those changes!"

Adventures in Harmony – Introduction to the System

Many musicians fall into the following trap where they hear some beautiful chord changes and right away they are asking "Hey…What are those chord changes? What are those notes? Can I have that?"

Please don't go down that road because it's really not helping you. In fact, that's a much harder road to travel:

1) You have now forced yourself with the task of having to memorize a sequence of notes and changes, and depending on how good your memory is, who knows how long that is going to take.

2) Now you are becoming a robot, if you are not already one, where you are playing something the same way over and over from something that you have memorized. Now how boring is that it listen to!

3) And even worse, you are playing somebody else's chord changes! Stop being somebody else. Stop playing chords that you probably don't even know what they are; or how the chords or changes were put together. You are really going nowhere with this.

4) What's usually the case is that the person you are asking "Hey, what are those changes," probably couldn't tell you, because they don't remember what they just played, only because they made it up as they were playing! Now think about it, why would you want to play somebody else's chord changes, those chord changes define who they are, wouldn't you rather play your own chord changes!

The Adventures in Harmony Play by Number System is going to expose how you can be YOU, an individual, playing your own beautiful chord changes!

There are NO progressions to memorize in the Adventures in Harmony Play by Number System. That's because you are going to be creating your own progressions as you play. Your music playing is about to move to the next level. This will truly be the most amazing music lesson you have ever had!

With the Adventures in Harmony Play by Number System, we want to give you the ability to harmonize as you play, and be free to choose where you want to go musically depending on the mood.

The entire course has over one thousand advanced voicing's, and we mean those voicing's that are going to turn heads!

Adventures in Harmony – Introduction to the System

We are going to show you step-by-step how to use these voicing's in your favorite music.

If you purchase any of our DVD video course material, you will see that this is not your typical show off music course where something is played and they expect you to just watch and mimic and copy.

In the course, we will explain every single chord transition, every note in every chord as well as the how and why. And in our DVD video course material when something is shown on the keyboard, there are going to be no fingers in the way if you are trying to look at the keys. You are going to get a clear unobstructed view using our computerized virtual keyboard system where you can see the notes being played with no fingers on the keyboard!

The information that you are going to get in this course on advanced harmonization and passing chords has never before appeared in print. This is information that is usually only passed on among musicians by word of mouth. And it's usually only among musicians in that "trusted circle," and that trusted circle usually doesn't include you!

It is our intent to expose it all in this course. What is talked about in this course applies not only to organ but also piano.

Musicians have even referred to some aspects of this course as the "Keyboard Musicians Missing Manual"

This is the manual that didn't come with your Keyboard. These are the music lessons you can't just sign-up for at the local music store.

In this course, we will take you step-by-step, with an example of starting from a simple one-note melody to a full-blown contemporary version with those beautiful chords changes.

2.1 IMPORTANT NOTICE

This course is not intended to replace a formal course in music theory. Our intent is to give you a process that you can use to quickly create advanced voicings. We have taken the formal "notion" of music theory and broken it down, simplified it, and presented many of the formal concepts in our "own way."

We did not want to bog you down to the extent that the material becomes too technical. All of the chord spelling and scales in this course are going to be the enharmonic spelling. i.e. The note (Gb) will always be called a (Gb), even if we are in the (D) scale, where that same (Gb) would formally be called an (F#). We have done this to simplify the material, these details are not important for you to play the actual note. We have also extended this enharmonic naming to our chord names. The chord names in this course are sufficient for anybody advanced musical knowledge to understand their meaning.

Our goal is to get you to that end result quickly, which is the ability to create and play the advanced voicings.

If you are looking for something formal, then this is not the course for you, but if you are looking to play quickly and take a short cut, then you are in the right place!

This manual is the introduction for the Adventures in Harmony Course.

We fully describe the Adventures in Harmony Play by Number System.

This tutorial contains samples voicings from many of our course reference volumes:

In this tutorial you will see that everything we say about the course is true.

1) You are going to see that you will never play a song the same way twice!
2) You are going to see that you can create and insert passing chords on the fly as you play.
3) You are going to see that you can play beautiful chords from a simple single note melody.
4) You are going to see that you can make up and create passing chord progressions as you play.

5) You are going to see that there are NO progressions to memorize... because you are making them up as you play.

You will discover that this will truly be the most amazing music lesson you've ever had.

This introductory material contains voicings from many different voicing reference manuals that are available separately. We have over 1200 voicings. The melody voicing reference manuals are interchangeable. The voicing process is the same; no matter which voicing reference you use. Your result may simply be a different chord.

The core of this tutorial is presented as a case study, where we take a simple piece of music, analyze it step-by-step, and show you the different things that you can do to it to make it sound contemporary. Every note, every chord and chord change is explained, the how, why and all the possibilities.

In this introductory tutorial, we will harmonize the first phrase of the hymn "Joy to the World" and turn it into a beautiful progression with many possibilities. The case studies will help you become proficient in the process of advanced harmonization.

We are going to help you take your playing to the next level.

2.2 Reference Volumes

The following additional chord voicing reference volumes are available to apply the techniques you will learn in this volume. The chord voicings that are used in this introductory volume are from these references:

VOLUME I – Handbook of Harmony - This Volume

VOLUME II - The Tritone and Beyond - Explore the b9, m3, b5 (Tritone) and the #5

VOLUME III – Part 1 - Harmonization on the Melody – Tones 1-4

  Advanced Voicings for Melody and Suspension Harmonization

VOLUME III – Part 2 - Harmonization on the Melody – Tones 5-Maj7

  Advanced Voicings for Melody and Suspension Harmonization

VOLUME IV - Mastering Chord Suspensions

  Additional advanced Instruction for Volumes III and V

VOLUME V – Black Gospel Chords

  Advanced Two Handed Voicings

VOLUME VI - The Chords Naming System

  Learn to instantly create any chord; Even if you have never played it before. Throw away your chord dictionaries. Learn to name any chord by simply looking at the notes in the chord.

VOLUME VII - In Scale Harmonization

   Substitution and Passing Chord Reference

Adventures in Harmony DVD – 4.5 Hours

   Additional video instruction to complement the written material

Our reference volumes contain over 12000 advanced chords and voicings that are detailed note-by-note in all twelve keys. These chord references are available from CREATIVE MUSIC VENTURES at the following address:

www.gospel-chords.com

3 Harmonization

3.1 Overview

When you are harmonizing a piece of music, you actually have a couple of options available depending on what you are starting with and what you are trying to accomplish.

Your starting point may be just a single note melody that you want to harmonize and add fullness, giving it that full soulful contemporary sound.

Perhaps you have the full music notation in front of you, such as something from a hymnal and you want to re-harmonize it. That essentially means that you want to change the existing chords perhaps to chords that are more soulful or contemporary sounding.

You may wish to harmonize only the chord changes, for example, when you are simply providing accompaniment when you are backing up a singer, or accompanying other instruments. Or you can harmonize directly on the melody when you are in the lead or want to make a strong statement. You can also do some combination of both where you are harmonizing the melody and the chord changes.

In the simplest case, the process of harmonization is where we take something as simple as a single note, one finger melody, and turn that into a song where we are playing more than one finger at a time. As an example, this may consist of a multi-note chord in the right hand, and one or more notes played in the left-hand or foot, that function as the bass.

The process of harmonization is a form of music analysis. To perform the analysis we use Roman numbers to make notations on the music. These Roman numbers indicate the structure of a piece of music. The first step in playing with a soulful sound is to determine what the Roman numbers are for the music that you want to play.

We will show you how you can easily look at a piece of music and determine what the Roman numbers are, or if you don't have music, it is still simple to determine what the Roman numbers are based on the notes that you are playing. As we promised we are going to explain every detail! There is no other course that will give you these details! We are going to tell you both the how and why!

4 The Play by Number System

In our Play by Number System, all of the notes of the major scale are numbered. When playing a note or chord using the Play by Number System, we indicate which notes to play on the keyboard by their corresponding number in the scale. Later in the course we will see how we can use the number system in the song writing and progression creation process.

There are seven notes in any major scale and we will number them one through seven. However in our Play by Number System we don't stop counting at seven, we just continue counting eight, nine, ten, etc. When we get to note number eight, which really corresponds to the first note in the scale again. We essentially start back at the beginning of the scale again.

4.1 Mapping the Scales to the Keybord

In Figure 4-1 we show the numbering for the notes in the (C) Scale. The first note of the (C) Scale is number (1); the second note is number (2), etc. When we get to (B) the seventh note in the scale, you will see that the scale then repeats and starts at (C) again, but the numbering continues.

C Scale															
Note	C	D	E	F	G	A	B	C	D	E	F	G	A	B	C
Number	1	2	3	4	5	6	7	8	9	10	11	12	13	14	15

Figure 4-1 - Number System for the C Scale

In our Play by Number System, we use these numbers to indicate which keys to play on the keyboard. This numbering will give us proper orientation when playing multiple notes and chords. For example, if we asked you to play the notes (C) and (D) together, you would have no idea which (C) and (D) we were talking about. It could be the (C) and (D) that you see in Figure 4-2, or it could be the (C) and (D) that you see in Figure 4-3.

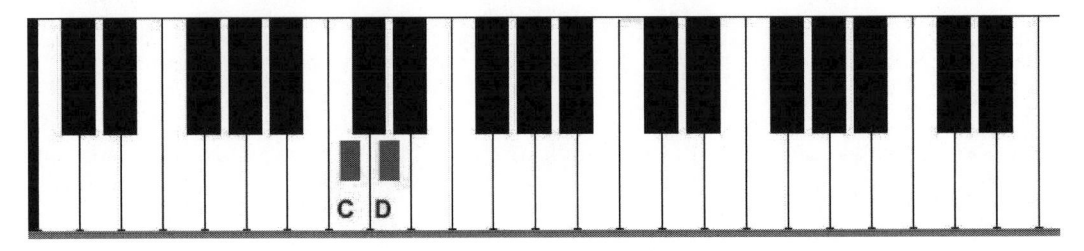

Figure 4-2

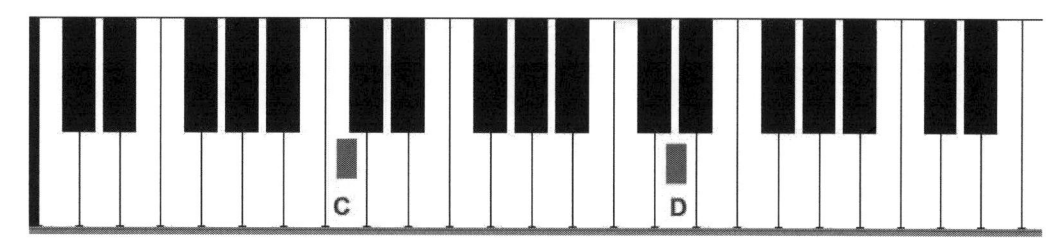

Adventures in Harmony – Introduction to the System

Figure 4-3

It could even be (C) and (D) reversed as you see in Figure 4-4. You can clearly see that you would have no idea which (C) and (D) we were talking about, and also you would have no idea of the ordering of the notes. You don't know if we meant (D) and (C), or (C) and (D).

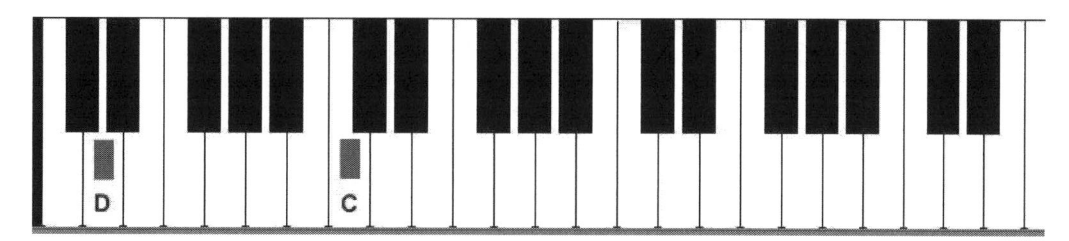

Figure 4-4

We resolve this problem by numbering the keys on the keyboard to correspond to the number of the note in the corresponding scale. This numbering is something that you should do mentally in your head because the numbering is different for every scale. For example, in the (C) scale, the (C) is number (1), but in the (F) scale the F is number (1). Figure 4-5 shows an example numbering of the notes on the keyboard for the (C) scale.

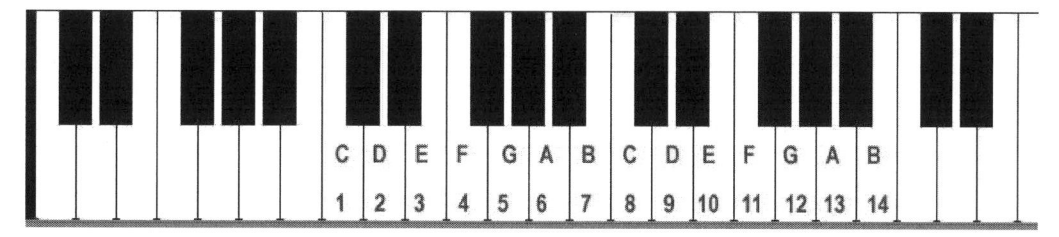

Figure 4-5

4.2 Note Number 1 – Keyboard Relationship

When numbering the notes on the actual piano, you can start numbering anywhere you want as long as you start on the note corresponding to the name of the scale, and that you number that note number (1). In this example since we are talking about the (C) scale, the (C) is number (1).

Now if we asked you to play notes (1) and (2) of the (C) scale, it is quite clear which (C) and (D) we were talking about Figure 4-6. If we asked you to play notes (1) and (9) of the (C) scale, Figure 4-6, which are also (C) and (D), musically that (C) and (D) make a very different sound than (1) and (2) Figure 4-6.

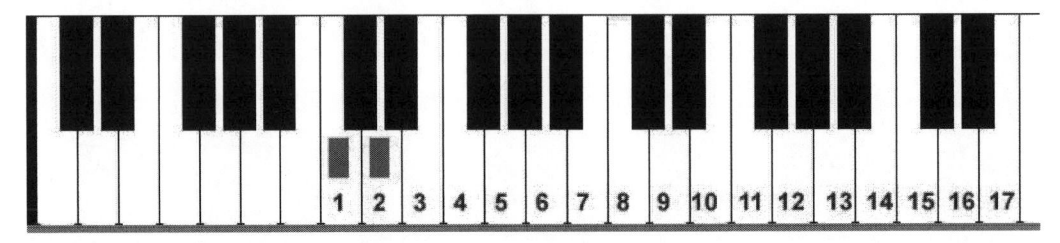

Figure 4-6 (1) and (2) in the C scale (C and D)

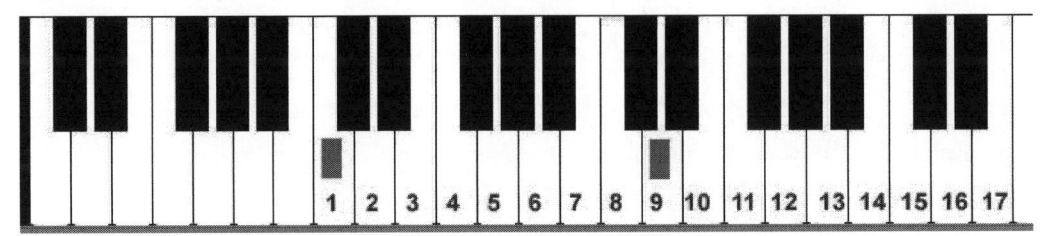

Figure 4-7- (1) and (9) in the C scale (C and D)

When numbering the keys on the keyboard according to a scale, using (C) as an example, we know the keyboard has many (C)'s on it Figure 4-8. You can make any (C) on the keyboard number (1). You could have made any of the (C)'s in Figure 4-8, number (1), and started numbering from there.

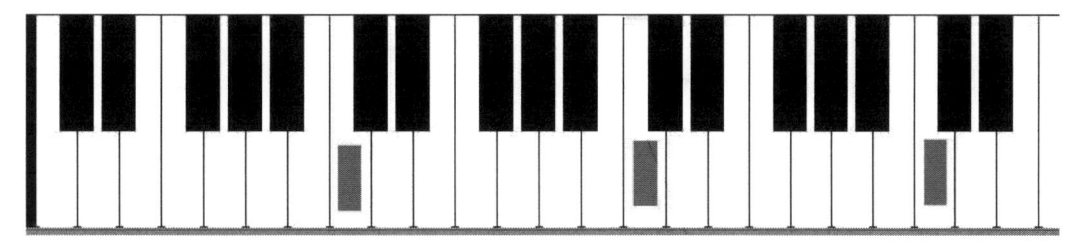

Figure 4-8

As an example, in Figure 4-9 we have started numbering from one of the other (C)'s on the keyboard.

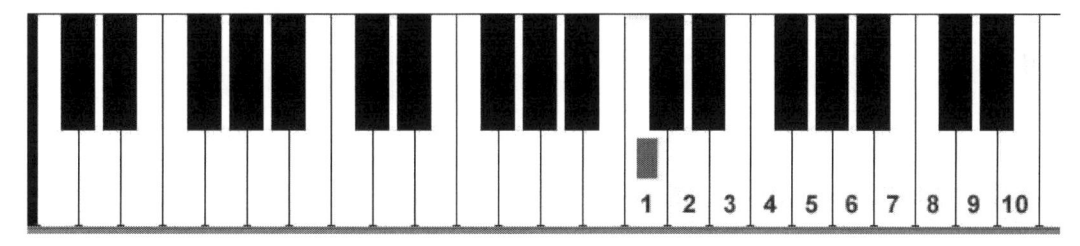

Figure 4-9

We are simply trying to establish a starting reference point for us to indicate which notes to play.

Examples:

If we asked you to play (1) and (8) in the C Scale, we are really asking you to play two (C)'s. In the (C) Scale, numbers (1) and (8) both correspond to (C)'s Figure 4-10 and Figure 4-11.

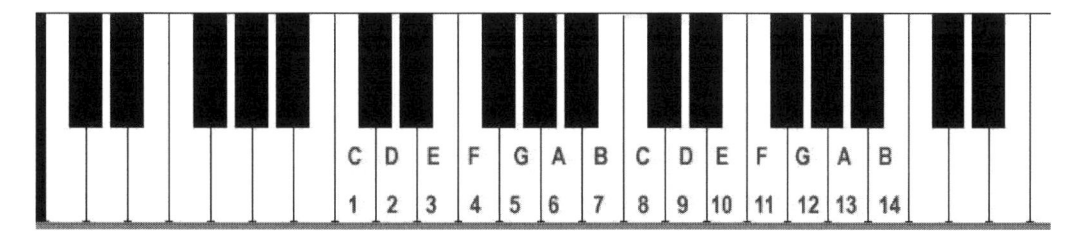

Figure 4-10

C Scale															
Note	C	D	E	F	G	A	B	C	D	E	F	G	A	B	C
Number	1	2	3	4	5	6	7	8	9	10	11	12	13	14	15

Figure 4-11

We are really just asking you to play any (C) on the keyboard and then play the (C) that is an octave above that (C). Playing (1) and (8) on the actual keyboard as in Figure 4-12 or Figure 4-13 are both correct.

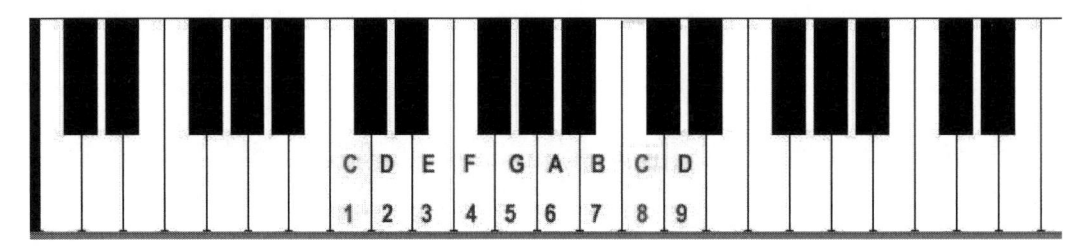

Figure 4-12

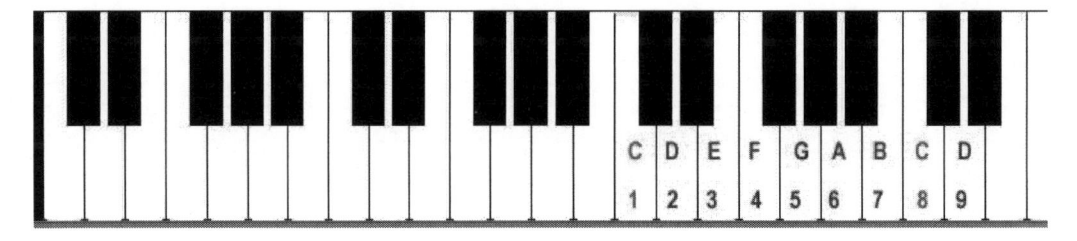

Figure 4-13

When we indicate the numbers of notes to play, just make sure that when you actually play the notes, that they do not sound too muddy because they is being played too low on the keyboard, or too high on the keyboard.

For example, if we asked you to play a chord consisting of the (1), (3) and (5) in the (C) Scale don't play it on the keyboard as indicated in Figure 4-14. It sounds way too low and muddy there.

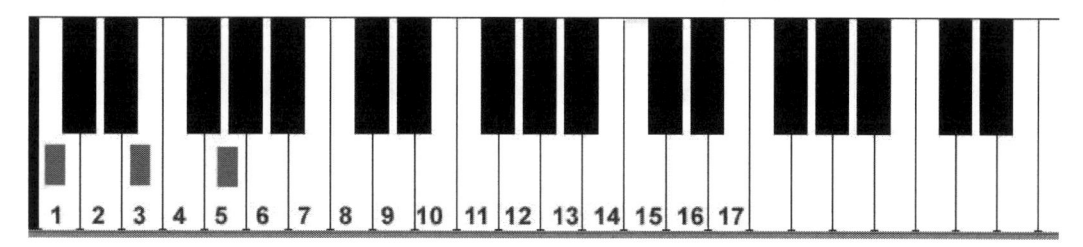

Figure 4-14

Choose a (C) that is at a higher position on the keyboard and start counting from there as in Figure 4-15.

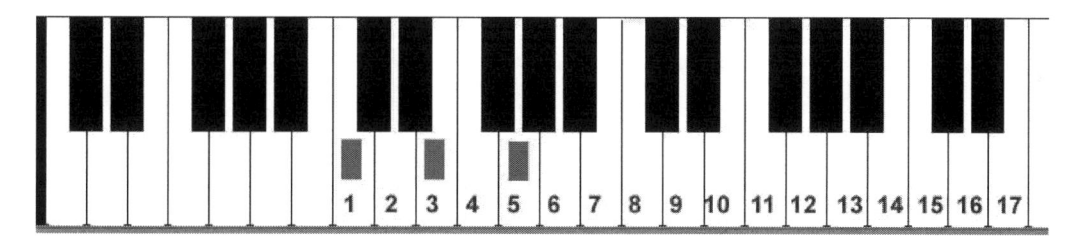

Figure 4-15

When playing with two hands on the keyboard, each hand has its own separate count. The numbers for the notes that you play with the left hand start at number (1). If we were in the (C) scale and you could be told to play (1) and (5) with the left hand and (2) and (5) with your right hand you would be playing (C) and (G) with the left hand and (D) and (G) with the right hand (Figure 4-16).

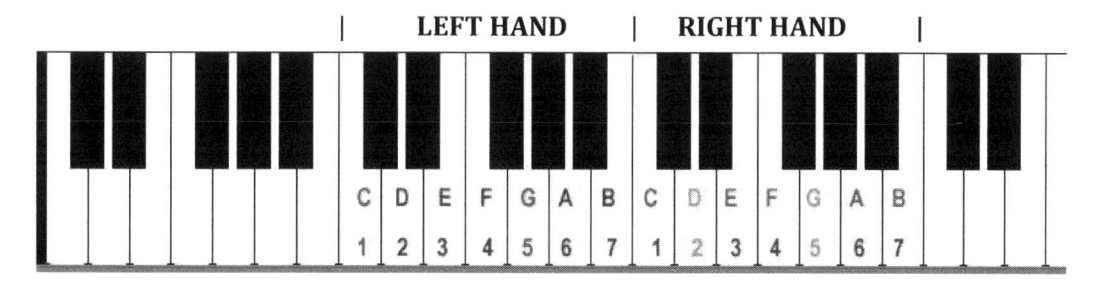

Figure 4-16

4.3 Note Number 1 – Scale Relationship

Do not make the mistake in thinking that note number (1) is always a (C). (C) is note number (1) in these examples only because we are using the (C) scale as an example.

The note numbers are always relative to the current scale.

If we were in the (F) scale, then note number (1) would be (F), and note number (2) would be (G), etc. The numbers are always relative to the current scale. Figure 4-17 shows the (F) scale on the keyboard. Note number (1) always corresponds to the note representing the name of the scale or key.

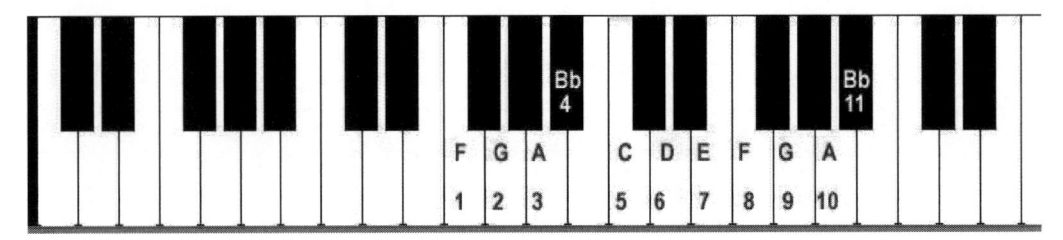

Figure 4-17

The following are the notes and their numbers in the (F) scale.

4.3.1 Key of F

F Scale															
Note	F	G	A	Bb	C	D	E	F	G	A	Bb	C	D	E	F
Number	1	2	3	4	5	6	7	8	9	10	11	12	13	14	15

4.4 The Number System and Accidentals

We can also use the Play by Number System to represent notes known as accidentals. Accidentals are the notes that are not part of the major scale.

The (C) scale consists of the following notes Figure 4-18 and Figure 4-19.

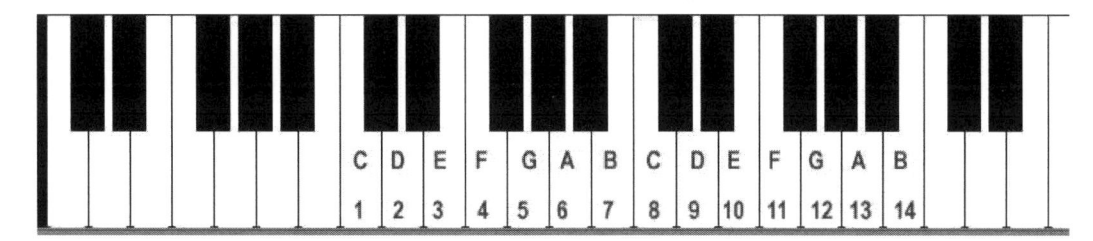

Figure 4-18 - The numbering for the (C) Scale

C Scale															
Note	C	D	E	F	G	A	B	C	D	E	F	G	A	B	C
Number	1	2	3	4	5	6	7	8	9	10	11	12	13	14	15

Figure 4-19 – The numbering for the (C) Scale

On the keyboard there are twelve unique notes before they start to repeat (Figure 4-20).

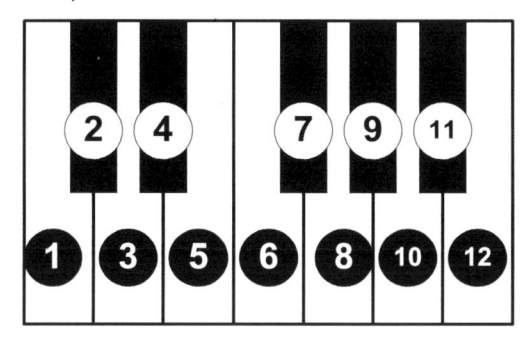

Figure 4-20

When we number the notes of a major scale, you will notice that we only numbered seven of the twelve possible notes. This is because there are only seven notes in any major scale.

If we use the (C) scale as an example, you will notice that there are four notes that have no numbers assigned to them (Figure 4-21). This presents a problem if we need to refer to these notes.

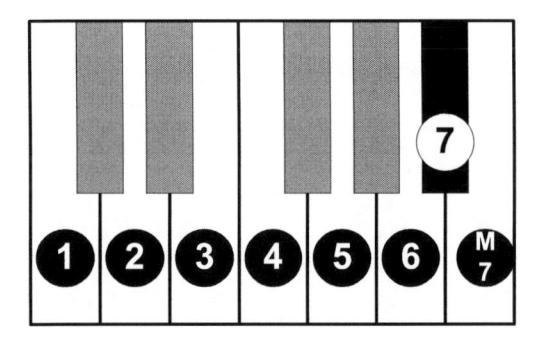

Figure 4-21

The way we will handle this problem, is by referring to these notes (labeled A, B, C and D) (Figure 4-22), by how they are related to the notes that are near them that already have numbers.

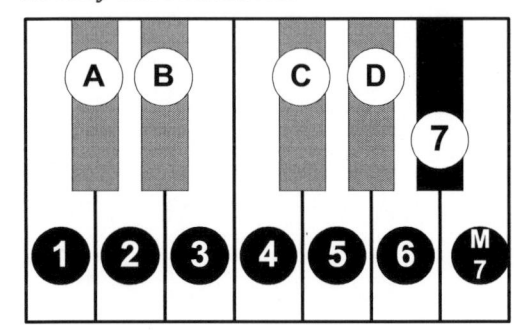

Figure 4-22

We are going to use the terms flat and sharp or the symbols b or # to refer to these notes that are not part of the major scale. If an unnumbered note is located to the right of a note that is numbered, we will refer to the unnumbered note as being a sharp (#, or +), and if an unnumbered note is located to the left of a note that is numbered, we will refer to that unnumbered note as being flat (b, - or m). Let's look at an example to get you used to this concept.

If we had to refer to the note labeled (C) (Figure 4-22), we could call this note a b5, -5, or m5 because it is located to the immediate left of the (5). We could also refer to this same note as a (+4), or (#4) because it is to the immediate right of the (4).

If we had to refer to note labeled (B) (Figure 4-22), we could call this note a b3, -3, or m3 because it is located to the immediate left of the (3). We could also refer to this same note as a (+2), or (#2) because it is to the immediate right of the (2).

Don't make the mistake and assume that just because a note number has a (#) or (b) symbol next to it that is its one of the black keys on the keyboard. It's just a coincidence and it happens to fall this way when we look at the (C) scale. For example the (#5) is the note labeled (D) in Figure 4-23, is a black key, but if we were in the key of (Db), the (#5) would be a white key.

If we look at what the rogue notes that are in the (Db) scale (Those labeled A, B, C, and D in Figure 4-23), you will see that they are all white notes. The (b5) in the key of (Db) is a (G) and a (#5) is an (A).

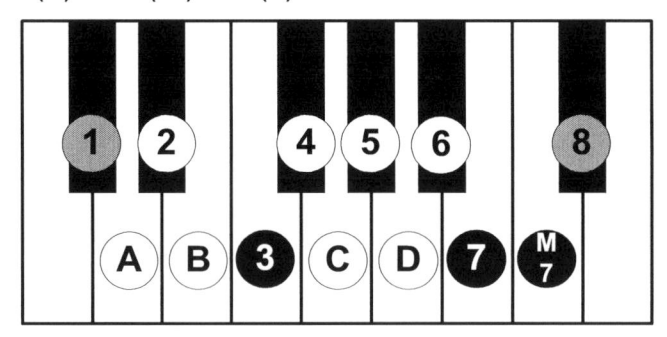

Figure 4-23

Now that we understand the concept of how to refer to the notes that are not numbered in the major scale, let me tell you what the actual names are in practice, because there is a convention. For example, there is no such thing as a (+1) or a (#1), this note is always referred to as a (b9).

Using the above as an example, let's summarize and see what the conventional names are in general.

Label	Non Conventional names	Conventional names
A	+1, #1, b2, -2, -9	b9
B	+2, #2, b3, -10, m10	#9, b10, -3, m
C	+4, #4, -5, b12, -12	b5
D	b6, -6, -13, b13	#5, +5

As an example of using the table above, whenever you are writing down or referring to the note numbers that make up a chord, you would never refer to the note at location (C) in (Figure 4-23), as any of the following (+4, #4, -5, b12, -12), you would always refer to this note as the (b5). When referring to the notes in a scale, use the conventional names in the right column.

If we wanted to refer to the (Ab) note in the (C) scale (Figure 4-24), that note would be called the (+5), (#5).

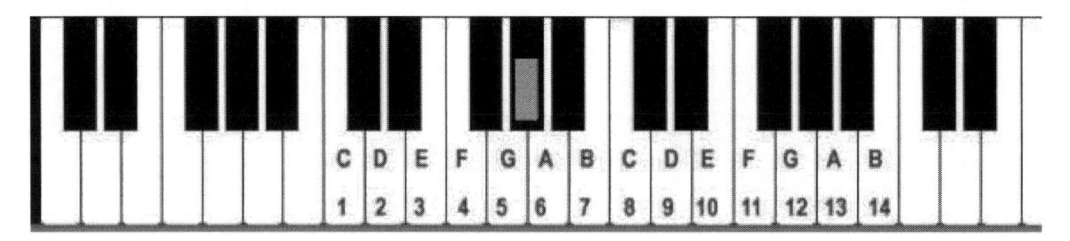

Figure 4-24

Do not make the mistake and think that all notes that are suffixed with a (b), i.e. (Ab), are accidentals, or that the black keys are accidentals. For example, the following notes are in the (F) scale.

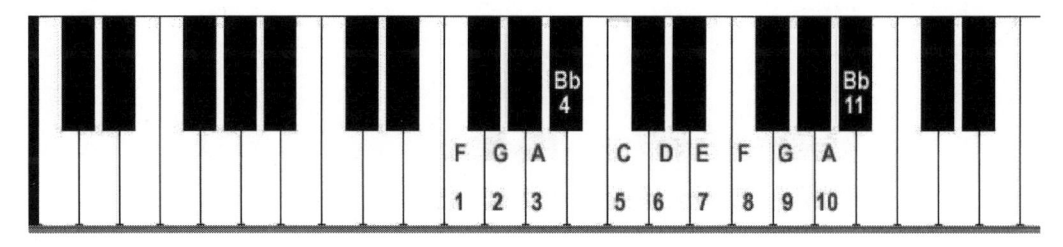

Figure 4-25 The F Scale

The following are the notes and their numbers in the (F) scale.

4.4.1 Key of F

F Scale															
Note	F	G	A	Bb	C	D	E	F	G	A	Bb	C	D	E	F
Number	1	2	3	**4**	5	6	7	8	9	10	**11**	12	13	14	15

The (Bb) is not an accidental in the key of (F). The (Bb) occurs in the (F) scale naturally. If we were trying to refer to the (B) in the key of (F), the (B) would be an accidental. The

(B) does not naturally occur in the (F) scale. So, if we wanted to refer to the (B), we would call that note a (b5). It is a (b5) because if we took the (5) which is a (C) and flatted it, we would be on the (B).

4.5 The Number System and Chords

Each chord in the Adventures in Harmony Play by Number System has the following information areas:

The name of the chord is indicated at the top of every page. In this example, the chord is a **minor add 6, 9**. Notice that we do not indicate which kind of **minor add 6, 9**, i.e., an (**A minor add 6, 9**) or a (**Bb minor add 6, 9**). This is because the information that follows, is going to tell you how to construct the **minor add 6, 9** in all 12 keys.

The Left Hand bass note indicated, tells you that for this example, the note that you should play as the bass note in your left hand and or in the bass pedal with your foot. In this example, you should play an (E) as the bass with your left hand and or foot. This bass note, also further qualifies the full name of the chord for the example given. Therefore, the full name of the chord in the picture is an (**E minor add 6, 9**). The picture visually indicates which notes to play to construct an (**E minor add 6, 9**).

The bass note is ALWAYS the root of the chord, and the bass note tells you what scale you need to be in, to create the chord using the Adventures in Harmony Play by Number System. Remember, the note that names the scale is always numbered number (1). Therefore the bass is always number one. So, in this example to create this (E) chord, we use the (E) scale, and (E) is note number (1) in the (E) scale.

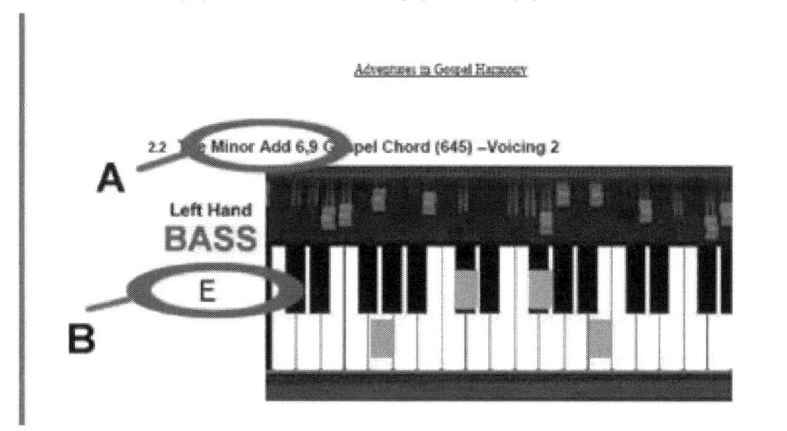

The table that follows indicates which notes numbers in the scale are needed to create the chord. Use this table to create the chord in ANY key. Therefore, to create the chord

(**E minor add 6, 9**), that means (E) is the bass note. Remember the bass note is always note number (1), and it tells us which scale we are in. The table indicates 'Left Hand,' note number (1), note number (1) in the (E) scale is (E). The table indicates 'Right Hand,' note numbers (-3, 6, 9 and 12). Those are the note numbers from the (E) scale that you are going to play. The 3rd of (E) is (Ab), so the -3 is ½ step lower at (G). The 6th of (E) is (Db), the 9th of (E) is (Gb) and the 12th of (E) is (B).

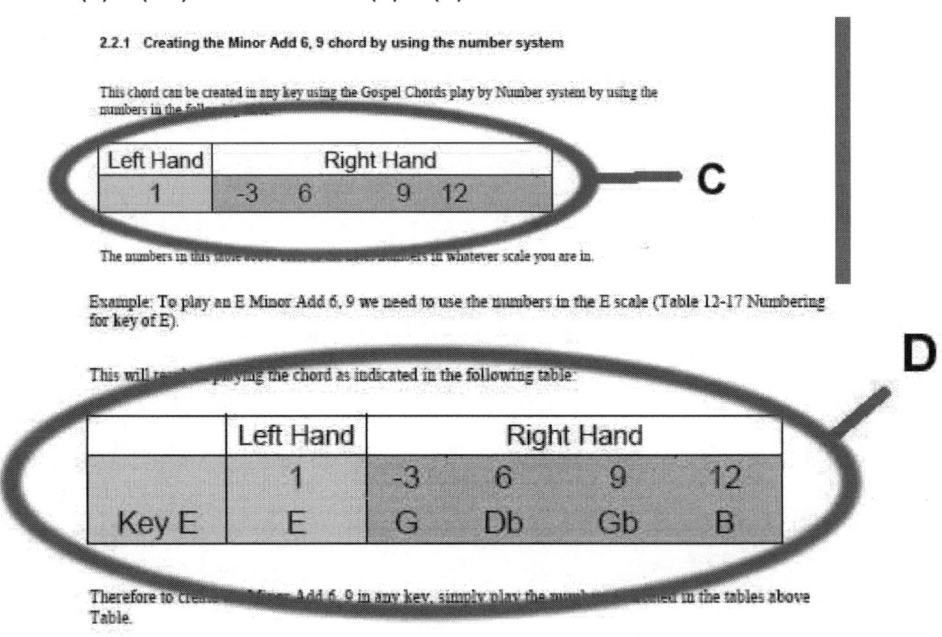

2.2.1 Creating the Minor Add 6, 9 chord by using the number system

This chord can be created in any key using the Gospel Chords play by Number system by using the numbers in the following table:

Left Hand	Right Hand			
1	-3	6	9	12

C

The numbers in this table are to be used as note numbers in whatever scale you are in.

Example: To play an E Minor Add 6, 9 we need to use the numbers in the E scale (Table 12-17 Numbering for key of E).

This will result in playing the chord as indicated in the following table:

	Left Hand	Right Hand			
	1	-3	6	9	12
Key E	E	G	Db	Gb	B

D

Therefore to create a Minor Add 6, 9 in any key, simply play the numbers indicated in the tables above Table.

In the table above, the note letters listed in the 2nd row are obtained by matching the numbers to the notes for the key of (E).

E Scale															
Note	E	Gb	Ab	A	B	Db	Eb	E	Gb	Ab	A	B	Db	Eb	E
Number	1	2	3	4	5	6	7	8	9	10	11	12	13	14	15

Numbering for key of E

Note: The scales in this course may be enharmonic (alternate) spellings. i.e. in the key of (E), the (Gb) is officially named (F#) instead of (Gb).

Note: The chord chart indicates to play a (-3), but scale tables do not show the accidentals, i.e. (b , #, -). If you look above at (3) in the (E) scale, you see an (Ab), you just have to lower it ½ step down to a (G) to make it a (-3).

NOTE: The chords pictured at the top of every page in the reference books correspond to songs written in the key of (Db). Therefore, if you have already written down the Roman numbers for the notes in the song, you can immediately play it in the key of (Db) by looking at the pictures to obtain the proper chord. If you need the chord in another key, refer to the tables at the bottom of the page. Do not refer to the picture at the top of the page.

If you needed this chord in the key of (C), that means the chord would be an (**Eb minor add 6, 9**). This also means that (Eb) would be the bass note that is played in your left hand and or foot. This also means that (Eb) is note number (1). So, to figure out the rest of the notes in the right hand, you are going to play the note numbers (-3, 6, 9 and 12). Those notes would be a (Gb), (C), (F) and (Bb).

4.5.1 Key of Eb

Eb Scale															
Note	Eb	F	G	Ab	Bb	C	D	Eb	F	G	Ab	Bb	C	D	Eb
Number	1	2	3	4	5	6	7	8	9	10	11	12	13	14	15

Numbering for Key of Eb

The Adventures in Harmony Play by Number System will represent all chords as described above. Each chord will be illustrated as indicated by the earlier figure. **Error! Reference source not found.** shows an example of an (**E minor add 6, 9**) chord. It tells us that the bass is played with the left hand and that the bass note is (E). The number of the bass note is (1). It also tells us that the right hand consists of the (-3, 6, 9 and 12) of the (E) scale.

You will also notice in our chord reference material that all chords are detailed note-by-note in all 12 keys. The table at the bottom of the following figure contains the notes for the pictured chord in all keys.

Adventures in Harmony – Volume III

4.10 The (-III) m add 6,9 (645)

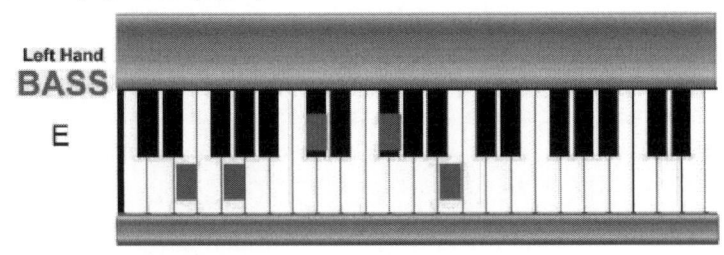

Left Hand
BASS
E

4.10.1 When to use this chord.

When the current melody note of your song is a (VII), play a (-III) m add 6,9 chord.
1. A (VII) melody note in the key of (Db) is a (B).
2. A (-III) chord in the key of (Db) is an (E).
3. Play E m add 6,9 ((-III) m add 6,9)

4.10.2 Creating the m add 6,9 chord by using the number system

This chord can be created in any key by using the numbers in the following table:

Bass	Left and Right Hand				Tension	Open
1	-3	6	9	5	0.75	5.33

The numbers in the table above, refer to the note numbers for whatever scale you are in.

Example: To play an E m add 6,9 chord, we need to use the numbers in the E scale.

This following table contains the proper [m add 6,9] to be played for a song in any key.

Song Key	Chord Key	Bass	Left and Right Hand			Name
		1	-3	6	9 5	m add 6,9
Db	Key E	E	G	Db	Gb B	E m add 6,9
C	Key Eb	Eb	Gb	C	F Bb	Eb m add 6,9
B	Key D	D	F	B	E A	D m add 6,9
Bb	Key Db	Db	E	Bb	Eb Ab	Db m add 6,9
A	Key C	C	Eb	A	D G	C m add 6,9
Ab	Key B	B	D	Ab	Db Gb	B m add 6,9
G	Key Bb	Bb	Db	G	C F	Bb m add 6,9
Gb	Key A	A	C	Gb	B E	A m add 6,9
F	Key Ab	Ab	B	F	Bb Eb	Ab m add 6,9
E	Key G	G	Bb	E	A D	G m add 6,9
Eb	Key Gb	Gb	A	Eb	Ab Db	Gb m add 6,9
D	Key F	F	Ab	D	G C	F m add 6,9

Figure 4-26

Adventures in Harmony – Introduction to the System

When we refer to chords in a particular key, chords are referred to by Roman Numbers and notes are referred to by decimal numbers. We have Roman Numbers I through Maj VII (I, II, III, IV, V, VI and Maj VII) that represent chords for each of the notes in the major scale. For example a (G) chord is the [V] chord in the key of (C), the [VI] chord in the key of (C) is an (A) chord.

We can also have accidentals on the Roman Numbers. A [#V] chord in the key of (C) would be an (Ab) chord. When we use Roman Numbers to represent chords, the Roman Numbers do not go above [VII]. We would not refer to a chord as a [IX] chord; it would be a [II] chord.

Note: There are two sevenths in any scale the Dominant 7th and the Major 7th. If the major 7th is not explicitly stated, then it is understood that we are referring to the Dominant 7th. The Major 7th is the note that occurs naturally in the major scale. For example, (B) is the major 7th in the (C) scale. The Dominant 7th is ½ step below the major 7th. The (Bb) is the Dominant 7th in the key of (C).

Go ahead and play the chord indicated on the sample page in **Error! Reference source not found.**. Play the (-3), (6), (9) and (12) with your right hand. Remember, these numbers are relative to the (E) Scale. Don't forget to play the bass note with your left hand and foot. Now isn't that one pretty!

(E min add 6,9)

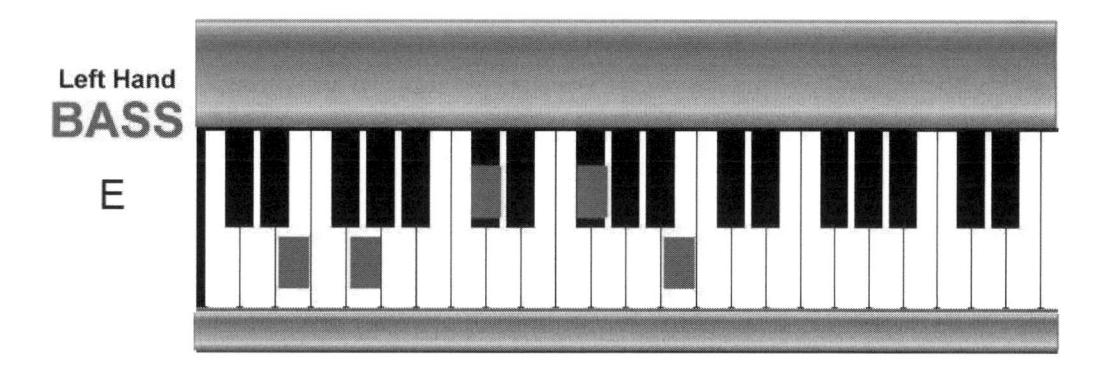

Left Hand
BASS
E

The Roman numbers for all 12 scales may be found in the Appendix

5 The Roman Number System

In this section we are going to discuss all of the steps necessary to prepare a piece of music for this advanced harmonization process. The goal is to get what is known as the Roman number analysis for the song. The Roman number analysis is a shorthand representation that tells us the structure of a song. It tells us the sequence of chords in a song. Playing the sequence of chords that correspond to a song is essentially the same thing as playing the song. Playing this sequence alone for any song is enough to back up a singer. When this sequence of chords is written on a piece of paper, it is called a Lead Sheet.

Each note in a scale has a group of chords associated with it. In looking at the seven notes associated with the (C) Major Scale (Figure 5-1), each one of those notes has a group of chords associated with it, and we refer to those chords by Roman number.

C Scale							
Note	C	D	E	F	G	A	B
Number	1	2	3	4	5	6	7

Figure 5-1

In using the (C) scale as an example Figure 5-1, the Roman numbers for the chords of the (C) scale are as follows:

C Scale							
Note	C	D	E	F	G	A	B
Number	I	II	III	IV	V	VI	VII

Figure 5-2

When we do Roman number analysis, you must remember that we are not talking about individual notes, we are now talking about chords. What you see above, is the Roman numbering for the chords in the (C) scale.

So if a song is written in the key of (C), we can use Figure 5-2, and make the following statements about that song:
- The [II] Chord is some kind of (D) Chord, i.e. D minor, D13, etc.

- The [V] Chord is some kind of (G) Chord
- (B) is the [VII] Chord
- (C) is the [I] Chord

The chords of a song written in any key are represented by Roman numbers I-Maj VII. We simply have to map the Roman numbers to the actual chord names, depending on what key we are in. Remember the numbering and notes in Figure 5-1 and Figure 5-2 are only for a song written in the key of (C).

If a song is written in the key of (C), and that song has a (G) chord in it, we call that the [V] chord. If that song has an (A) chord in it, we call that the [VI] chord.

So in the key of (C), when we say play the [V] chord, that means play the chord corresponding to the 5th note of the (C) scale; that would be a (G) chord. In the key of (C), when we say play the [II] chord, that means play the chord that corresponds to the 2nd note of the (C) Scale; that would be a (D) Chord.

The Roman number system is important because musicians use this system to talk about music to one another, and we are going to use this system when we talk about passing chords and creating contemporary sounding versions of your favorite songs.

The major scale in any key has seven notes associated with it. When we talk about chords and progressions, those notes are referred to using Roman numerals. Each one of these notes in the scale has a group of chords associated with it. Table 5-1 is an example of the (C) Scale and the seven Roman numerals associated with each note.

C Scale							
Note	C	D	E	F	G	A	B
Number	I	II	III	IV	V	VI	VII

Table 5-1

From now on, when we say the [II] chord, we are referring to the chords associated with the note labeled [II] in the current scale.

In this example, since we are dealing with the key of (C), the [II] chord would be a (D) Chord, the [V] chord would be a (G) Chord, and the [VII] chord is a (B) Chord, etc.

We can even use the Roman numeral to refer to a specific kind of chord. In this example in the key of (C), we can talk about the [V] minor chord, which would be a (G) minor. We can talk about the [II] 7 chord which would be a D7. We can talk about the [III] dim7 which would be an Edim7.

If we refer to the [V] chord, and don't specify the type of [V] chord (major, minor, diminished, etc.) then we are referring to any type of [V] chord or in this specific case, any type of (G) chord.

We can even use the Roman numbers to refer to chords that are not in the scale of the current major key! We all know that there is no (Gb) in the key of (C), but we can still talk about a (Gb) chord, we would call that a [bV] chord.

Just as there is no (E) in the key of (Db), we can still talk about an (E) chord, we would call that a [bIII] chord. An (A) chord in the key of (Db), would be a [#V] chord. A (D minor) in the key of (Db) would be a [bII] minor chord (Table 5-2).

Db Scale												
Note	Db	D	Eb	E	F	Gb	G	Ab	A	Bb	B	C
BucketNumber	I	bII	II	bIII	III	IV	bV	V	#V	VI	VII	MajVII

Table 5-2

Why would we ever want to talk about those chords that are not in the key? You are going to find out that those chords are the most beautiful chords ,and are part of those sweet soulful and contemporary movements that we are going to tell you how to create.

As another example, suppose we were in the (Db) scale, Table 5-3, what would be the [V] chord? The [V] chord would be some kind of (Ab) chord. The [III] minor chord would be some kind of (F) minor.

Db Scale							
Note	Db	Eb	F	Gb	Ab	Bb	C
Number	I	II	III	IV	V	VI	VII

Table 5-3

What would be the [–III] (bIII) chord? That would be some kind of (E) Chord. What would be the [–III]-7 (-IIIm7)? That would be an Em7 (E-7, Emin7). To read and interpret the Roman numbers, simply replace the Roman number with the actual note depending on what scale you are in.

Any chord that's part of a progression or song can be referred to by its Roman number. For example in the key of (Db), if you see the following sequence of chords (Eb), (Ab), followed by (Db), we would call that a [II]-[V]-[I] progression. We simply replaced the actual chord names with their corresponding Roman numbers for the indicated key or scale.

Another example in the key of (Db), if you see the following sequence of chords, (E), (F), followed by an (A), we would call that a [bIII]-[III]-[#V] progression. Don't let the accidentals through you off. The [bIII] in the key of (Db) is an (E), and the [#V] is an (A).

These Roman numbers give us a shorthand way to refer to a series of chords that is not key specific.

If we said play [II]-[V]-[I], we are telling you to play the [II] chord followed by the [V] chord followed by the [I] chord, but play it in any key that you want.

Therefore, if you were in the key of (C), you would play a (D) chord followed by a (G) chord followed by a (C) chord (Table 5-1). If you were in the key of (Db), you would play an (Eb) chord followed by an (Ab) chord followed by a (Db) chord (Table 5-3).

This Roman number system also allows you to instantly transpose a song to any key instantly.

I am sure, you have all seen church organ and piano players that are looking at the hymn book of when they play a song, but you know that what they are playing is not what is written in the hymn book. When you play what is written in the hymn book, you get that boring "church music" sound. So where is all that other beautiful music coming from? It's coming from the Roman number system. When they look at the music in the hymn book all they see in their heads mentally is the Roman number version of the song, they are not reading the notes!

Adventures in Harmony – Introduction to the System

An entire song may be reduced to something as simple as a series of Roman numbers:

As an example the first line of the song "Joy to the World" can be reduced to the following!

[I] – [IV] – [I] – [V] – [I]

Now it's a lot easier to read those numbers than the actual music!

The above Roman numbers would refer to the following chord sequence in the key of (Db).

(Db) – (Gb) – (Db) – (Ab) – (Db)

It is from these Roman numbers that you are able to create beautiful contemporary versions of any music. And that's what we are going to show you how to do in this course Adventures in Harmony.

6 Roman Number Analysis

As we told you earlier, after doing the Roman number analysis for a song, the sequence of Roman numbers is called a lead sheet. When you play the sequence of chords on the lead sheet, musicians call this "playing the changes."

You are essentially playing the song without the melody. This is fine, in the case where you have a singer or choir that will be singing the melody. You are simply backing up the choir or singer, and you are allowing the singer or choir to take the lead. This gives the singer and or choir the freedom to show off.

As long as you are playing the changes, you are playing the song. It is the changes that define the song; the melody is simply the icing on the cake.

The lead sheet has many powerful applications among musicians:

If you are not good at reading music, and you are not one of those people who can sit down with any piece of music and play it instantly, then a lead sheet is for you. As long as you are "playing the changes" that's fine. If you can reduce a complicated piece of music down to a sequence of Roman numbers, then you are fine. You have essentially reduced the music down to a sequence of numbers, i.e. [I], [VII], [III], [VI]. This is probably much easier to play than trying to read the music.

The other interesting thing about the lead sheet is that it allows you to instantly play a piece of music in any key. You can simply mentally translate the Roman numbers to whatever key you wish to play in. For example if you are looking at the following sequence, [I] [VII] [III] [VI], if you had to play in the key of (C), you would play the following sequence of chords, (C), (B), (E) and (A).

C Scale							
Note	C	D	E	F	G	A	B
Number	I	II	III	IV	V	VI	VII

If you had to play in the key of (Db) you would play the following sequence of chords, (Db), (C), (F) and (Bb).

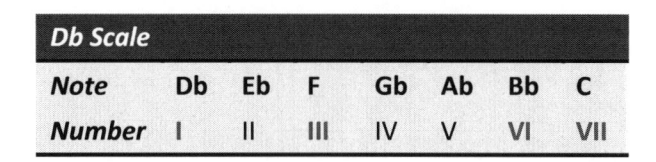

Db Scale							
Note	Db	Eb	F	Gb	Ab	Bb	C
Number	I	II	III	IV	V	VI	VII

At this point you are probably thinking that you don't know your scales, and that it will take you forever to learn them. And how the heck are you going to be able to figure out "... What is the [II] of some key, or what is the [VI] of some key."

Don't worry; there is a short cut for figuring out what the note is for any Roman number or note number, in any key. This trick is something that we will present to you in a later chapter.

We are sure that after we tell you how to do it, you can master it in less than one hour, and you will have no problem answering these questions immediately.

> What is the [IV] of Ab?
> What is the [V] of E?
> What is the [II] or A?

Later in this course, we are going to use a similar concept of mapping numbers to notes as a way of presenting to you the advanced voicings for chords. The only difference is that we are going to use regular numbers instead of Roman numbers.

7 Harmonizing a Simple Melody

Most music can be harmonized using the (I), (IV) and (V) major chords of current scale. Let's take a look at what this really means and why and how it works.

Examples:

In the key of (C), the [I], [IV] and [V] major chords would be (**C Major**), (**F Major**) and (**G Major**).

In the key of (F), the [I], [IV] and [V] major chords would be (**F Major**), (**Bb Major**) and (**C Major**).

In the key of (Db), the [I], [IV] and [V] major chords would be (**Db Major**), (**Gb Major**) and (**Ab Major**).

Let's take a closer look at the [I], [IV] and [V] chords in the key of (C).

In the key of (C), the (I) chord; (**C Major**) consists of the notes (C), (E), and (G). The (IV) chord, (**F Major**) consists of the notes (F), (A) and (C) and finally the (V) chord, (**G Major**) consists of the notes (G), (B) and (D).

In using the (I), (IV) and (V) chords, and in looking at the notes that make up all of those chords, you will notice that those chords use every single note in the scale. Using the (C) scale as an example, the (C) Scale consists of the notes (C), (D), (E), (F), (G), (A) and (B) (Figure 7-1) .

C Scale							
Note	C	D	E	F	G	A	B
Number	I	II	III	IV	V	VI	VII

Figure 7-1

If you look at Figure 7-2, you will see that all of the notes of the (C) Scale are used when using just those three chords. The [I], [IV] and [V] chords use all the notes in the (C) Scale! So we really don't need any other chords besides the [I], [IV] and [V].

Chord Number	Chord Name	NOTES		
I	C Major	C	E	G
IV	F Major	F	A	C
V	G Major	G	B	D

Figure 7-2 - I, IV and V in the Key of C

Figure 7-2 is simply telling us that by using only the [I], [IV] and [V] chords, that these are enough chords to harmonize a song or melody that use the notes of the (C) Major scale. Therefore whenever we have a melody that is in key of (C), we can harmonize that melody with the chords (C), (F) and (G).

As another example, if we are in the key of (Db), then the [I], [IV] and [V] chords would be (Db), (Gb) and (Ab) (Figure 7-3).

Chord Number	Chord Name	NOTES		
I	Db Major	Db	F	Ab
IV	Gb Major	Gb	Bb	Db
V	Ab Major	Ab	C	Eb

Figure 7-3 the I, IV and V in the Key of Db

After a song has been broken down to Roman numbers, by doing the Roman number analysis, then the fun begins. Then you are ready to use the Adventures in Harmony Play by Number System to create those beautiful chord changes

Adventures in Harmony – Introduction to the System

In the next section we will go through the process of harmonizing an actually melody.

You are going to be playing the advanced substituted chord voicings and passing chords.

You are going to see how you can really never play a song the same way twice.

You are going to see how you can insert an infinite number of beautiful passing chords to make your playing sound beautiful.

You may find yourself in this situation many times where you have no music for a particular song, but you have picked out or know what the one finger melody is for the song and you need to know what chords go with the melody.

We will lead you step-by-step through the process of determining the chords that can be played with a melody note.

8 Registration

If you happen to be on a Hammond Organ, may we suggest that you play both hands on the same manual and use the following registration:

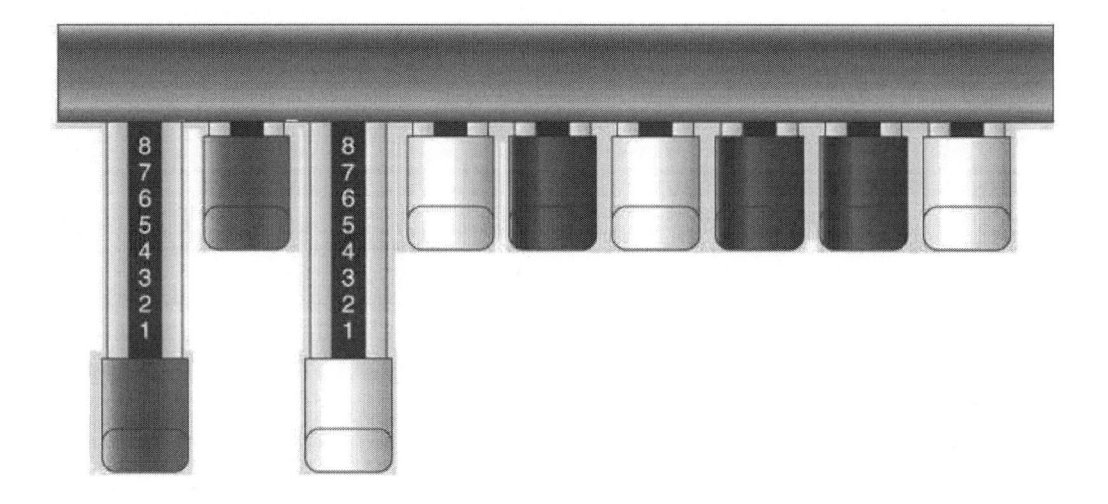

Play the bass with your left hand on the lowest possible octave and you may also play the bass with your foot.

9 Advanced Harmonization of -"Joy to the World"

9.1 Starting with what is in a hymn book

For those of you that can read music, this may be a starting point in your advanced harmonization process. If you cannot read music this section may still be of interest.

You have a hymn book with the written music, but you know if you play what is written in the hymn book, you are going to get nothing more than boring "church music," with those simple chords.

How do people look at what is written in the hymn book and then play all those beautiful contemporary chords?

Let's see a real example of how this is done.

When looking at music written in a hymn book, most of what is written on the page is really not important.

In fact, you are not even going to be playing what is written on the page.

You may consider the written hymn as a sort of "cheat sheet" for when you are playing the advanced contemporary version.

Figure 9-1 is an example of how the first line of the hymn "Joy to the World" appears in most hymnals.

Figure 9-1 Joy to the World

For those of you that cannot read music, we have a shorthand version of this written out in pictures in Section 9.3.

Our goal is to turn this hymn into a Lead Sheet. Remember, a Lead Sheet is essentially a very compact shorthand notation for a song. Let's go through the steps necessary to reduce this single line down to a lead sheet. We are essentially doing a Roman number analysis that we learned earlier in the course.

Step 1 – The most important thing for you to focus on in playing the advanced harmony for any song, is the bass and melody. All the other notes are not important. Those other notes are just somebody else's harmonization of the song, and we know we don't want to play it like that!!

So let's take a look at how the song looks when we strip out everything except the bass and melody (Figure 9-2).

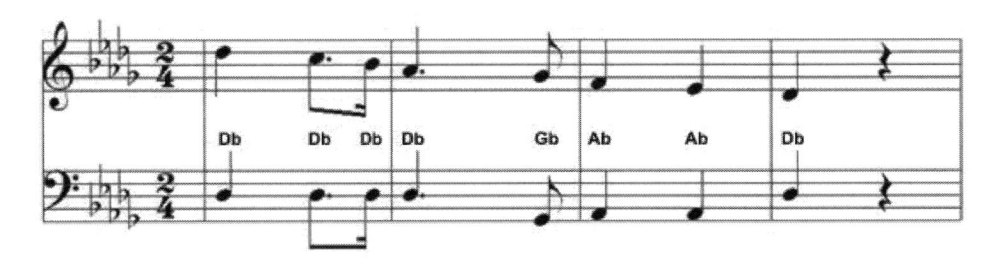

Figure 9-2 Joy to the World - Bass and Melody

In Figure 9-2 we have labeled all of the bass notes in the song. Those bass notes tell us what the basic harmonization is for the song. For this song we see that the basic simple chords are (Db), (Gb) and (Ab). Now let's translate this into the Roman numbers as we learned earlier in the course.

If you can read music, you need to not only see the notes as notes, but also start seeing them as numbers.

This song is written in the key of (Db), so the Roman number for (Db) in the (Db) scale is [I], the Roman number for (Gb) in the key of (Db) is [IV] and the Roman number for (Ab), in the key of (Db) is [V] (Table 9-1).

Db Scale							
Note	Db	Eb	F	Gb	Ab	Bb	C
Number	I	II	III	IV	V	VI	VII

Table 9-1

If you were looking at an actual hymn book to play this song, Figure 9-3 is a representation of the mental image you should have in your head when looking at the music.

Figure 9-3

So in replacing the bass note names with the Roman numbers we can see that this first line of the hymn" Joy to the World", is an [I] - [IV] - [I] - [V] - [I] progression.

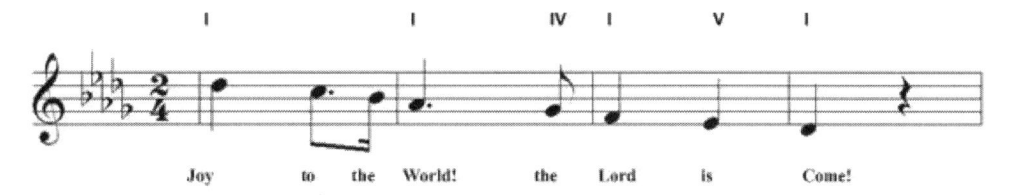

Figure 9-4 Joy to the World I-IV-I-V-I Progression

From all the music in the hymnal for the first phrase of "Joy to the World," the only thing that is important is that this phrase has a [I] - [IV] - [I] - [V] - [I] progression. What you see in Figure 9-4, is all you need to play an advanced contemporary version of "Joy to the World!"

If you really wanted to take a short-cut, the only thing that is important is the Roman numbers that appear on this lead sheet. Figure 9-5 is an example "Lead Sheet" for the first line of the song, as you can see there is not even any music on it. The only thing that is important is the chord changes and where they occur.

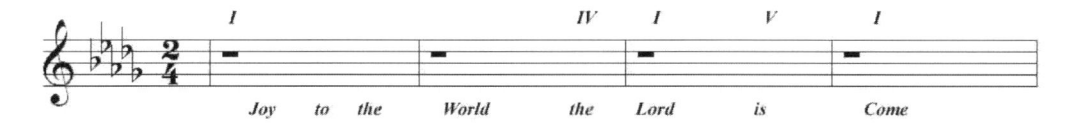

Figure 9-5

If you wanted to turn this into something with lots of color and passing chords, then the Roman numbers [I] - [IV] - [I] - [V] - [I] in Figure 9-5 is a starting point for us to take this to the next level.

So in looking at the hymnal the only thing you should really see in looking at the first phrase is [I] - [IV] - [I] - [V] - [I]   Figure 9-5. You will then use those Roman numbers to play the advanced voicings that you will learn later in this course.

Later in this section we are going to take that lead sheet and turn it into a beautiful contemporary version of "Joy to the World." Let's take a quick look at how we can arrive at this same place if we had no music and only had the one finger melody that we picked out on the keyboard (Section 9.2).

9.2 Starting With a Simple Melody

Our goal is to figure out the harmonization of a song if all we have is the simple one finger melody, and then turn it into a contemporary sounding version.

We are going to start out with a simple one-finger melody of "Joy to the World"

For those of you that can't read music, we have labeled all of the notes in the first phrase of "Joy to the World." Figure 9-6.

We are now going to figure out what the basic harmonization is, and then turn it into an advanced contemporary harmonization.

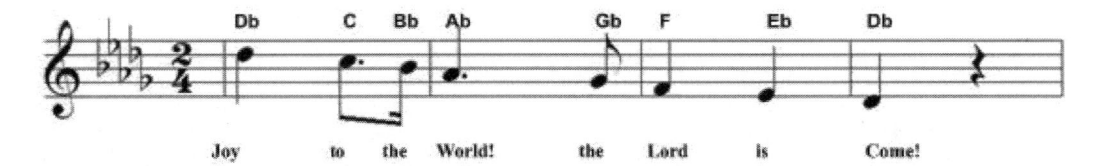

Figure 9-6

Earlier in the course, we learned that most praise and worship music can be harmonized with the basic [I], [IV] and [V] chord. We see that this song is written in the key of Db, so let's look at the [I], [IV], and [V] chord in the key of (Db) and the notes that make up those chords (Table 9-2).

Chord Number	Chord Name	NOTES		
I	Db Major	Db	F	Ab
IV	Gb Major	Gb	Bb	Db
V	Ab Major	Ab	C	Eb

Table 9-2 [I], [IV] and [V] Chords of (Db)

We are going to harmonize on the words "Joy", and then "World", and then all of the words "the Lord is come." That means those are the words in the song that we are going to make our chord changes on.

Remember it is really up to you what words you harmonize on, if you wanted to, you could harmonize on every single word.

9.2.1 Harmonize the Simple Melody

We will now do an actual simple harmonization

We then look at the note that we want to harmonize in our song, and then see where we find that note in the Table 9-2. Refer to Figure 9-6 in following the steps below to harmonize "Joy to the World."

1. The first word we want to harmonize on is "Joy," and we see that the note for the word "Joy" is a (Db). We then look in Table 9-2 and see which chord numbers have a (Db) as a note. We see that Chord number [I] and [IV] both have a (Db). So we have a choice when we harmonize to play a [I] (Db) chord or a [IV] (Gb) chord. We are going to choose the [I] Chord. So we have just harmonized the first measure with the [I] Chord. We are going to see later how sweet this song sounds when we do the contemporary version and we use the [IV] chord (Gb) on the first measure of our song.

2. The next word we want to harmonize on is "World," and we see that the note for the word "World" is (Ab). We then look in Table 9-2 and see which chord numbers have an (Ab). We see that Chord number [I] and [V] both have an (Ab). So we have a choice when we harmonize to play a [I] (Db) chord or a [V] (Ab) chord. We are going to choose the [I] Chord. So we have just harmonized the word "World" with the [I] Chord.

3. The next word we want to harmonize on is "the," and we see that the note for the word "the" is (Gb). We then look in Table 9-2 and see which chord numbers have a (Gb). We see that Chord number [IV] is the only one that has a (Gb). So we have just harmonized the word "the" with the [IV] Chord (Gb).

4. The next word we want to harmonize on is "Lord," and we see that the note for the word "Lord" is (F). We then look in Table 9-2 and see which chord numbers have an (F). We see that Chord number [I] is the only one that has an (F). So we have just harmonized the word "Lord" with the [I] Chord (Db).

5. The next word we want to harmonize on is "is," and we see that the note for the word "is" is (Eb). We then look in Table 9-2 and see which chord numbers have an (Eb). We see that Chord number [V] is the only one that has an (Eb). So we have just harmonized the word "is" with the [V] Chord (Ab).

6. The next word we want to harmonize on is "come," and we see that the note for the word "come" is (Db). We then look in Table 9-2 and see which chord numbers have a (Db). We see that Chord number [I] and [IV] both have a (Db). So we have a choice when we harmonize to play a [I] (Db) chord or a [IV] (Gb) chord. We are going to choose the [I] Chord. So we have just harmonized the word "come" with the [I] Chord.

We have now just arrived at the same harmonization as we did when we had the written music (Figure 9-6).

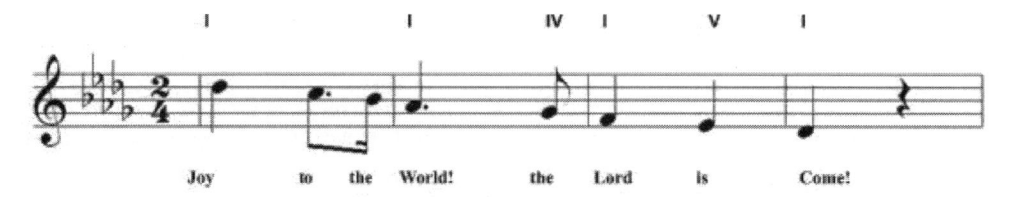

Figure 9-4 Joy to the World I-IV-I-V-I Progression

As we indicated in the last section, these Roman numbers are enough to do an advanced contemporary Harmonization using what you have learned in the Adventures in Harmony Course. Now the FUN will begin. We are now going to turn this plain Jane version of "Joy to the World" into something that will turn heads.

9.3 Joy to the World - Original Version

Below is the plain harmonization of "Joy to the World." This version closely corresponds to what you will find in most hymnals. In the next several sections, we are going to take this simple harmonization and turn it into something beautiful. We are going to lead you step-by-step using all of the tools in the Adventures in Harmony Course.

Play through these chords changes (1-7) so that you can hear the original plain version.

We have written the Roman numbers next to the words.

DON'T FORGET TO PLAY THE BASS WITH YOUR LEFT HAND AND OR FOOT!!!

Chord	TONE	Left Hand BASS	Chord / Word
Chord 1 **Joy**	I	Db	[Db] Maj — Joy
Chord 2 **To**	I	Db	[Db] Maj — to
Chord 3 **The World**	I	Db	[Db] Maj — the-world
Chord 4 **The**	IV	Gb	[Gb] Maj — The

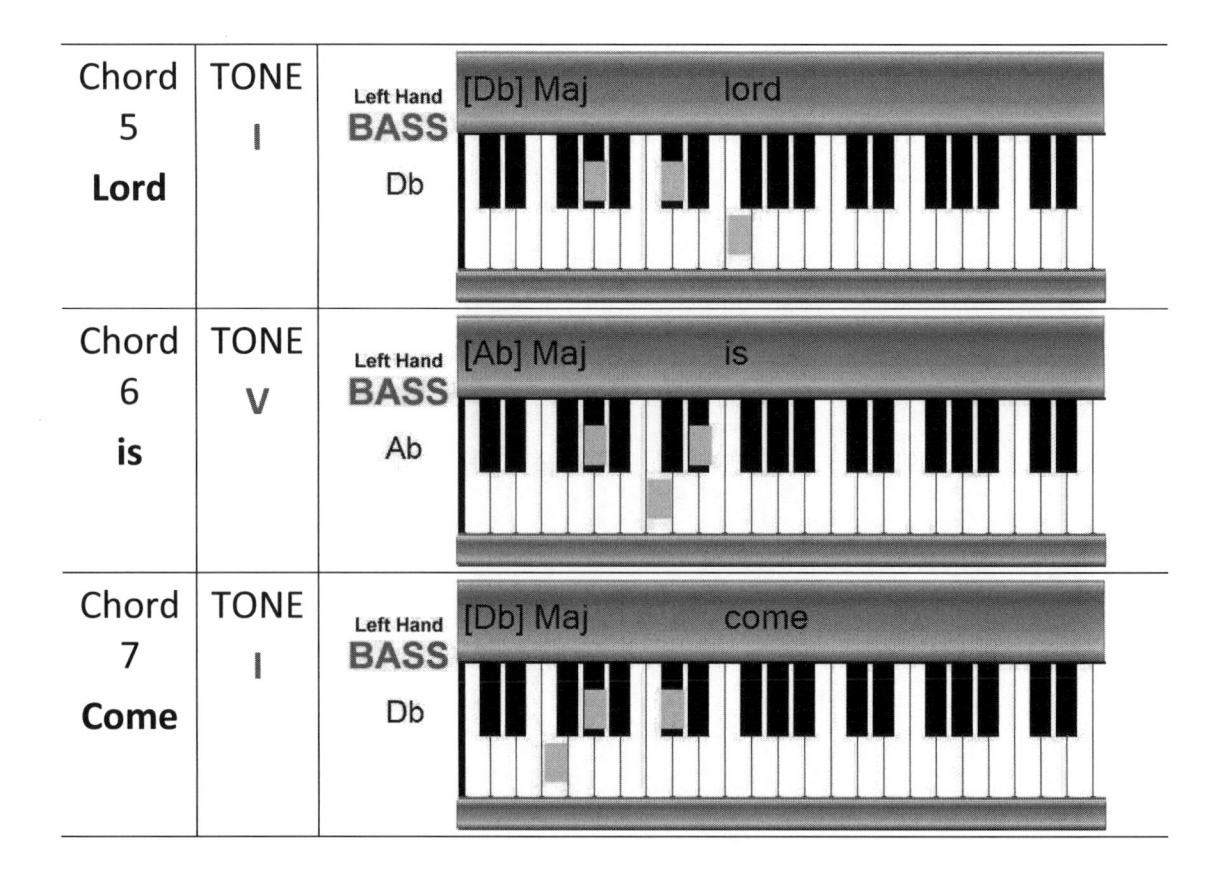

Chord 5 **Lord**	TONE I	Left Hand BASS Db	[Db] Maj — lord
Chord 6 **is**	TONE V	Left Hand BASS Ab	[Ab] Maj — is
Chord 7 **Come**	TONE I	Left Hand BASS Db	[Db] Maj — come

9.4 Joy to the World – Making this sound beautiful – Harmonization

Now that we know we are dealing with a [I] - [IV] - [I] - [V] - [I] progression we can now begin to enhance this by inserting advanced contemporary voicings and passing chords. READY!!

All you need in front of you at the piano and or organ are the Roman numbers.

I   I   IV   I   V   I

Joy   to   the   World!   the   Lord   is   Come!

Figure 9-5 Joy to the World – Adventures in Harmony!

We are going to harmonize on the words "Joy", "World", "the", "Lord", "is" and "Come." That means we are going to make our chord changes on those words.

Adventures in Harmony – Introduction to the System

The next step in the process in to convert (substitute) all the simple plain chords to their advanced contemporary versions. It's really up to you which chords you convert. You can change just one or you can change all of them.

In the Adventures in Harmony Course there are advanced contemporary voicings for each of the twelve scale positions. The seven in scale voicings for Roman numbers [I] through [Maj VII] and the five out of scale voicings for Roman numbers [bII], [-III], [bV], [#V] and [VII] corresponding to accidentals.

When playing Joy to the World in Figure 9-5, when you get to the Roman number [I], simply substitute one of the advanced voicing that you learned for the Roman number [I]. When you get to the Roman number [IV], simply substitute one of the advanced voicings that you learned for Roman number [IV], and finally when you get to the Roman number [V], simply choose one of the advanced voicings that you learned for the Roman number [V].

It does not matter which one of the advanced voicings that you pick for each one of the Roman numbers.

It is impossible to play a wrong chord if you follow the system. After a while you may even have favorites. For example every time you see the Roman number [V], you may have some favorites that you like to play.

You will never play a song the same way twice because you have so many options to choose from for each Roman number.

Each one of the advanced contemporary voicings has its unique characteristic sound and or function. Some of the voicings are ones that you would end a song on, some of them are ones that create tension or suspense, and some are sad.

Now let's actually do this and see what interesting sounds and progressions we can create for "Joy to the World." Remember in the examples in this course, you are going to be hearing my harmonizations and what I think sounds good. If the harmonization that I picked doesn't sound good to you, then in this course you are going to be able to pick another one that is pleasing to you! Everyone has their own personal taste, and harmonization is a major factor in why people have different tastes in music. The reason why you like, or don't like a particular musician is that you probably like or dislike their choices in harmonization.

9.4.1 Joy to the World - Contemporary Version 1

Below is the first pass of the contemporary harmonization of "Joy to the World."

All we have done is changed all of the simple chords to one of their many advanced voicings available in one of the "Adventures in Harmony – Core References."

In the Adventures in Harmony course, each tone of the scale, in Roman numbers, has its own set of contemporary voicings for you to choose from! There are over 1200+ advanced voicings in the complete course!

Play through these chord changes so that you can hear the new and improved contemporary sound, then below we will discuss each chord numbered 1-6, where it came from and why we are playing it.

We have written the Roman numbers next to the words.

DON'T FORGET TO PLAY THE BASS WITH YOUR LEFT HAND AND OR FOOT!!!

Chord	TONE	Left Hand BASS	Chord
Chord 1 **Joy to the**	IV	Gb	GbMaj9 Chord (699)
Chord 2 **World**	III	F	Fm7#5 Chord (273)
Chord 3 **The**	bIII	E	Em add 6 9 Chord (644)

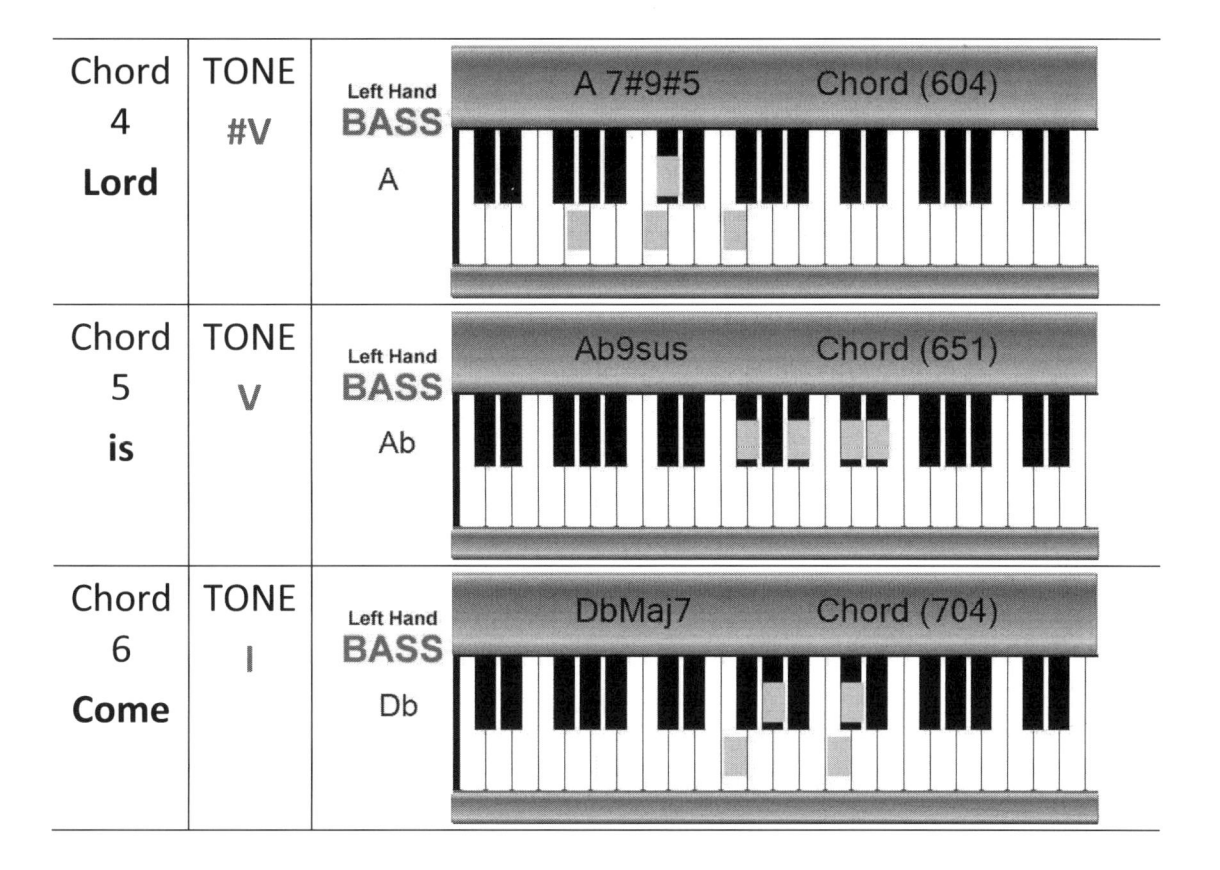

Chord	TONE			
Chord 4 **Lord**	#V	Left Hand BASS A	A 7#9#5	Chord (604)
Chord 5 **is**	V	Left Hand BASS Ab	Ab9sus	Chord (651)
Chord 6 **Come**	I	Left Hand BASS Db	DbMaj7	Chord (704)

9.4.1.1   Detailed Analysis - Chord 1

At this point you may be asking yourself where the heck did this [IV] (Gb) chord come from for harmonizing on the words "Joy to the." You are probably thinking that this is supposed to be a [I] chord (Db) from looking at our original Roman numbers for this song Figure 9-7.

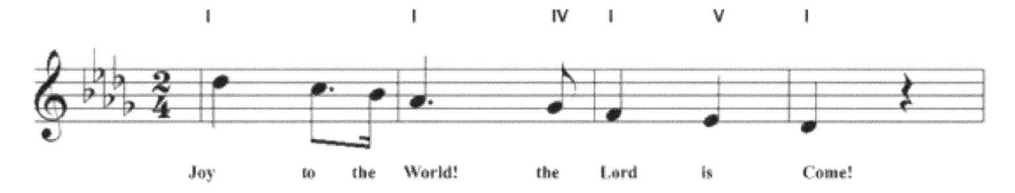

Figure 9-7

You are correct, we did say that this was the place for a Roman number [I] chord, but remember back in Section 9.2 when we harmonized on the melody note (Db), and we also said that it could be a [IV] Chord.

The first word we want to harmonize on is "Joy," and we see that the note for the word "Joy" is a (Db). We then look in Table 9-2 and see which chord numbers have a (Db) as a note. We see that Chord number [I] and [IV] both have a (Db). So we have a choice when we harmonize to play a [I] (Db) chord or a [IV] (Gb) chord. We are going to choose the [IV] Chord. So we have just harmonized the first measure with the [IV] Chord. Listen to how sweet this song sounds when we do the contemporary version and we use the [IV] chord (Gb) on the first measure of our song.

Here we decided to be a little different and make it a Roman number [IV] just to show you that it doesn't matter which one you choose. Look at the trick that we just learned. Whenever we see a Roman number [I] Chord, we can also play a [IV] Chord. In other words, in the key of (Db), whenever you see a (Db) chord you can play a (Gb) chord! And now you even know why!!! There are lots of tricks and tips in the course.

So now that we have decided to play a [IV] chord, we simply open one of our chord references "Adventures in Harmony – In Scale Harmonization - Substitution and Passing Chords", and turn to the chapter on Harmonizing on the [IV] Chord and choose one of the many contemporary voicings available. It really doesn't matter which one you choose. It's 100% up to you depending on what the mood is and what kind of contemporary voicing you want to play. In the "Adventures in Harmony – In Scale Harmonization - Substitution and Passing Chords", we selected "The Maj9 Chord (699)" for Chord number 1.

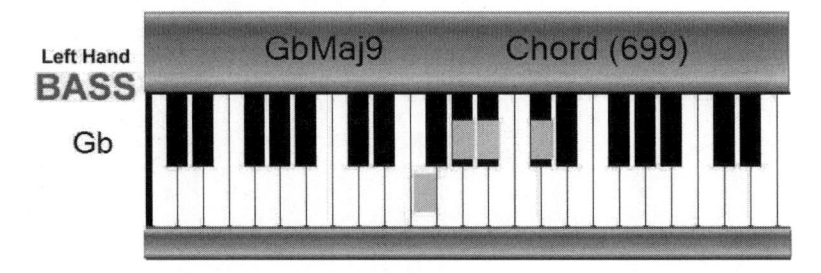

Figure 9-8 Chord 1 (GbMaj 9) "Joy"

This happens to be the one that we like for this example, if you don't like it; there are many others for you to choose from!

9.4.1.2   Detailed Analysis - Chord 2-4

For Chords 2-4, we did something a little different, and we didn't follow our Roman numbers again. If we followed our Roman numbers for the words "World", "the", and

Adventures in Harmony – Introduction to the System

"Lord" we would have picked from the contemporary voicings for the [I] and [IV] only, and I just thought that's way too long and too much of listening to the I chord, even though we have lots of voicings to choose from.

```
      I        I      IV  I    V     I
  Joy  to the World!  the Lord is  Come!
```

So we are going to do something a little different here and harmonize directly on the melody note. That means that the melody note is going to be on top of our voicing. When you harmonize on the melody is sends a stronger message to your listeners that you are playing "Joy to the World," since they hear the melody since it's the top note.

In the Adventures in Harmony Course, there are different voicings for each tone when you are harmonizing directly on the melody. To harmonize on the melody you will need one of the reference volumes for melody harmonization.

We are harmonizing on the melody notes (Ab), (Gb), (F) which correspond to the words "World","the", and "Lord." These melody notes (Ab), (Gb) and (F) correspond to the [V], [IV] and [III].

The (Ab) note for the word "World" is the [V]; the (Gb) note for the word "the" is the [IV], and the (F) note for the word "Lord" is the [III].

Originally when we harmonized on the bass this would have been the [I], [IV] and [I], and that probably would have sounded too boring because that's just too much of just the [I] and the [IV] since the beginning of the phrase.

So harmonizing on the melody is just another option that's available. We are going to expose it all!

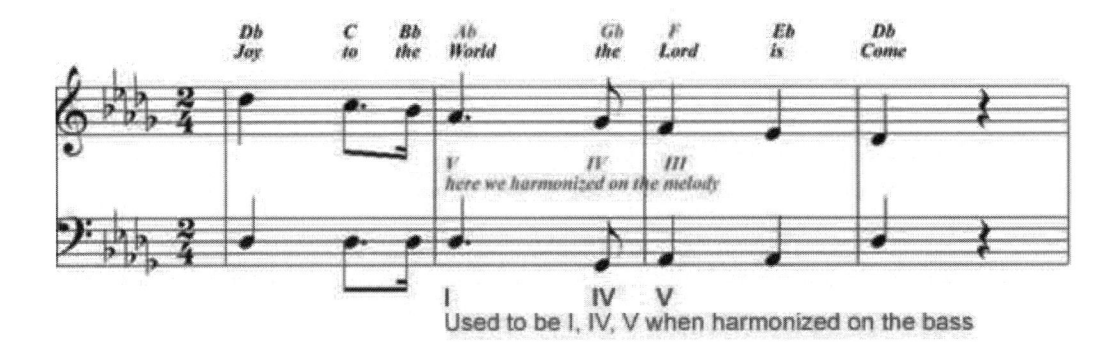

As we said before, there are different advanced voicings for harmonization directly on the melody, we simply select one of the contemporary voicing's that we learned for melody harmonization for the [V], [IV] and [III]. We can choose any of the references available for melody harmonization. Some of the options are the Volume, "Adventures in Harmony – Harmonization on the Melody," or "Preaching Chords – Special Edition."

9.4.1.2.1   Detailed Analysis - Chord 2

So now that we have decided to harmonize directly on the (Ab) melody note, a [V], we simply open our reference "Adventures in Harmony – Harmonization on the Melody", and turn to the chapter on Harmonizing on the [V], and select one of the advanced voicing's available.

In the "Adventures in Harmony – Harmonization on the Melody", in the section on "Melody Harmonization on the V", we selected "The **[III] minor 7#5** Chord (273)" for this chord. Let's look at this a little more carefully. Its telling us in order to harmonize on a [V] in the melody (Ab), we need to play a **[III] minor 7#5**. Remember we learned how to read this notation earlier (**[III] minor 7#5**). A [III] in the scale of (Db) is an (F). So it's telling us to play an (**F minor 7#5**). Don't let the fact that we looked up a [V] confuse you; that [V] was a melody note, but we are going to be playing a [III] in the bass (F). So that's how we got Chord number 2 for the word "World" in our contemporary version of "Joy to the World!"

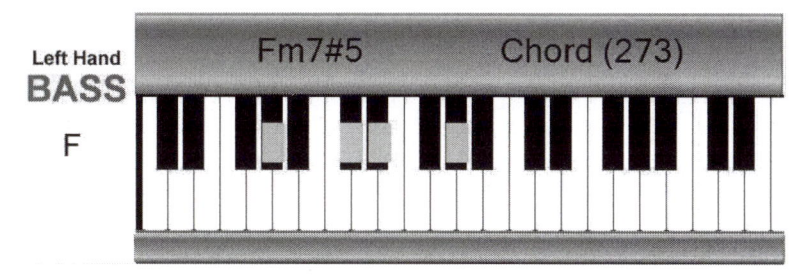

Figure 9-9 Chord 2 (Fmin7#5) "World"

We told you, we explain it all!!!!

When you start using voicings that harmonize directly on the melody note, you are really into some advanced transitions and you will get the most colorful movements.

We did the exact same thing for Chords 3 and 4 to harmonize directly on the melody notes (Gb) and (F), which are the [IV] and [III], let's take a look.

9.4.1.2.2 *Detailed Analysis - Chord 3*

To harmonize directly on the (Gb) melody note, a [IV], we simply open our reference "Adventures in Harmony – Core Reference –Volume – Harmonization on the Melody", and turn to the chapter on Harmonizing on the [IV], and select one of the voicing's available.

In the "Adventures in Harmony – Core Reference –Volume – Harmonization on the Melody", in the section on "Melody Harmonization on the IV", we selected "The **[bIII] minor add 6, 9** Chord (644)" for this chord. Again, look at this a little more carefully. It's telling us in order to harmonize on a [IV] in the melody (Gb), we need to play a **[bIII] minor add 6, 9**. Remember we learned how to read this notation earlier (**[bIII] minor add 6, 9**). A [bIII] in the scale of (Db) is an (E). So it's telling us to play an E minor add 6, 9. Don't let the fact that we looked up a [IV] confuse you, again that [IV] was a melody note, but we are going to be playing a [bIII] in the bass (E). So that's how we got Chord number 3 for the word "the" in our contemporary version of "Joy to the World!"

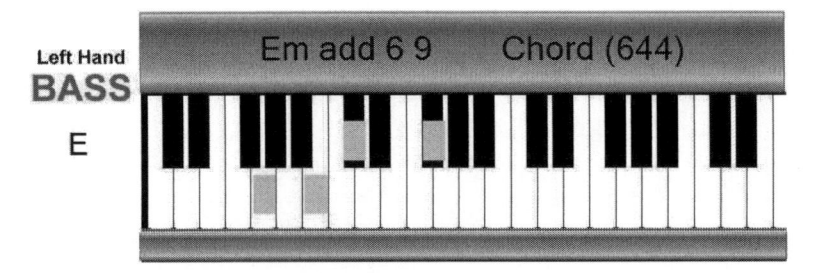

[Keyboard diagram: Left Hand BASS E — Em add 6 9 Chord (644)]

Figure 9-10 Chord 3 (Em add 6, 9) "the"

Remember we told you when you start using voicings on the melody tone, you will be into some really pretty voicing's and advanced movements. Well look at what just happened! You are in the key of (Db) playing this song "Joy to the World" and you just used an (E) chord for harmonization!!! There is no (E) in the key of (Db), but Wow, it does sound good! There is NO other course that is going to teach you to play chords on these notes that are not part of the major scale; we call these out of scale voicings! There are hundreds of them in this course.

9.4.1.2.3   Detailed Analysis - Chord 4

To harmonize directly on the (F) melody note, a [III], we simply open our reference "Adventures in Harmony – Core Reference –Volume – Harmonization on the Melody", and turn to the chapter on Harmonizing on the [III], and select one of the advanced voicing's available.

In the "Adventures in Harmony – Core Reference –Volume – Harmonization on the Melody", in the section on "Melody Harmonization on the III", we selected "The **[#V] 7#9#5**   Chord (604)" for this chord. Again, look at this a little more carefully. Its telling us in order to harmonize on a [III] in the melody (F), we need to play a (**[#V] 7#9#5**)! Remember we learned how to read this notation earlier (**[#V] 7#9#5**). A [#V] in the scale of (Db) is an (A). So it's telling us to play an (**A 7#9#5**). Again, don't let the fact that we looked up a [III] confuse you, again that [III] was a melody note, but we are going to be playing a [#V] in the bass (A). So that's how we got Chord number 4 for the word "Lord" in our contemporary version of "Joy to the World!"

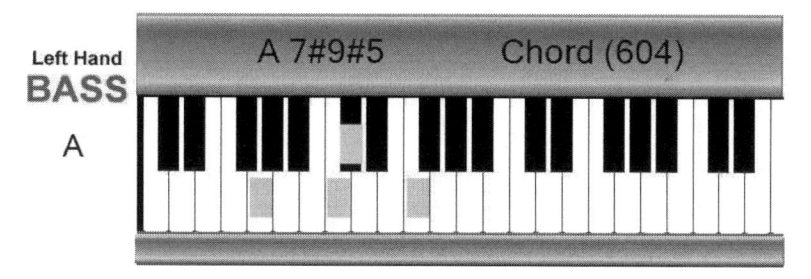

Figure 9-11 Chord 4 (A7 #9#5) "Lord"

Again, look at what just happened! You are in the key of (Db) playing this song "Joy to the World" and we just harmonized using an (A) chord! There is no (A) in the key of (Db), but again wow, it does sound good too! Like we said, there is NO other course that is going to teach you to play these beautiful out of scale voicings!

You see there are many possibilities and choices. The ones in the example for chords 2, 3 and 4 are just our favorites. You are going to have your own favorites.

9.4.1.3   Detailed Analysis - Chords 5-6

For Chords numbers 5 and 6 on the words "is" and "come", we went back to our original Roman numbers to determine the voicings, [V] followed by [I].

9.4.1.3.1   Detailed Analysis - Chords 5

 The word "is" is a [V] Chord, so we simply open our reference "Adventures in Harmony – In Scale Harmonization - Substitution and Passing Chords", and turn to the chapter on Harmonizing on the [V] Chord and choose one of the advanced voicing's available. Again, it really doesn't matter which one you choose. It's 100% up to you depending on what the mood is and what kind of contemporary voicing you want to play. In the "Adventures in Harmony – In Scale Harmonization - Substitution and Passing Chords", we selected "The 9sus (651)" for Chord number 5.

Figure 9-12 Chord 5 (Ab 9sus) "is"

9.4.1.3.2   Detailed Analysis - Chord 6

The word "come" is a [I] Chord, so we simply open our reference "Adventures in Harmony – In Scale Harmonization - Substitution and Passing Chords", and turn to the chapter on Harmonizing on the [I] Chord and choose one of the advanced voicings available. In the "Adventures in Harmony – In Scale Harmonization - Substitution and Passing Chords", we selected "The Major 7 (704)" for Chord 6.

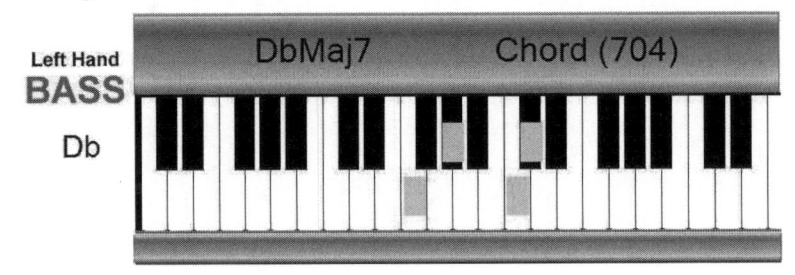

Figure 9-13 Chord 6 (Db Major7) "come"

9.4.1.4   Notes

Remember as long as you follow our number system, it is impossible to choose a wrong chord. The only questions are, "do you think it sounds good? Is it a good enough sound?" If not, simply choose another until you get the sound that you want. In time you will have your favorites! In the next sections we will switch the chords around, and even add passing chords so you can see how interchangeable the Adventures in Harmony Play by Number System is, but first let us tell you about how this course is divided.

9.4.2 Truly the most amazing music lesson you have ever had!

We told you that there is NO other course like this. We told you that we would expose it all. We told you that we would explain EVERY CHORD Transition. We told you that this was not a "show-off" that is going to leave you in the dark. We are going to continue to do this throughout the entire Adventures in Harmony Series and in every product that we sell!! We got lots more for you....

Here are just some of the voicing volumes that are available

1. Harmonizations In-Scale - Substitution and Passing Chords

    This reference contains all of the harmonizations for all of the Roman numbers I-MajVII including the 7th. With this you will be able to harmonize on Roman numbers [I], [II], [III], [IV], [V], [VI], [VII], and [Major VII].

2. Harmonizations Out-Of-Scale - The Tritone and Beyond

    This reference contains all of the harmonizations for all of the accidentals in every scale Roman numbers [bII], [bIII] or [–III], and the [bV] or [#V] including the [VII]. These out of scale harmonizations are usually part of the most beautiful progressions and transitions in contemporary music.

3. Advanced Harmonizations on the Melody

    This reference contains all of the harmonizations in every key for when you harmonizing directly on the melody. For example, if the melody note is a (G), which means you must have a (G) on top of the chord that you are playing with your right hand. This reference will tell you what chord voicing's are available that will allow you to keep that (G) in the melody.

4. Preaching Chords – Special Edition

    This reference contains additional harmonizations in every key for when you harmonizing directly on the melody. With this you will be able to harmonize on Roman numbers [I], [II], [III], [IV], [V], [VI], [VII], and [Major VII], and all the accidentals.

Your course may include different voicing reference volumes, but the procedure for harmonization is the same.

Now let's move on to another contemporary version of "Joy to the world."

9.4.3 Joy to the World - Contemporary Version 2

In this example, we have replaced Chords 1 and 6, the detailed analysis will follow.

Chord number 6 that we play on the word "come" is a [I] Chord. We simply choose one of the voicings chords available for the [I] chord.

For Chord 1, when we harmonize on the melody note a (Db) [I] we find that one of our choices is this really nice [II] chord! This (Eb) chord is a really beautiful chord. Please listen to it moving to Chord 2. You can now hear that the voicing in the Adventures in Harmony Course are truly unique. We expose them all, the secret is out! This will truly the most amazing music lesson you have ever had!

DON'T FORGET TO PLAY THE BASS WITH YOUR LEFT HAND AND OR FOOT!!!

Chord	TONE	Left Hand BASS	Chord
Chord 1 **Joy to the**	II	Eb	Ebm9 Chord (114)
Chord 2 **World**	III	F	Fm7#5 Chord (273)
Chord 3 **The**	bIII	E	Em add 6 9 Chord (644)

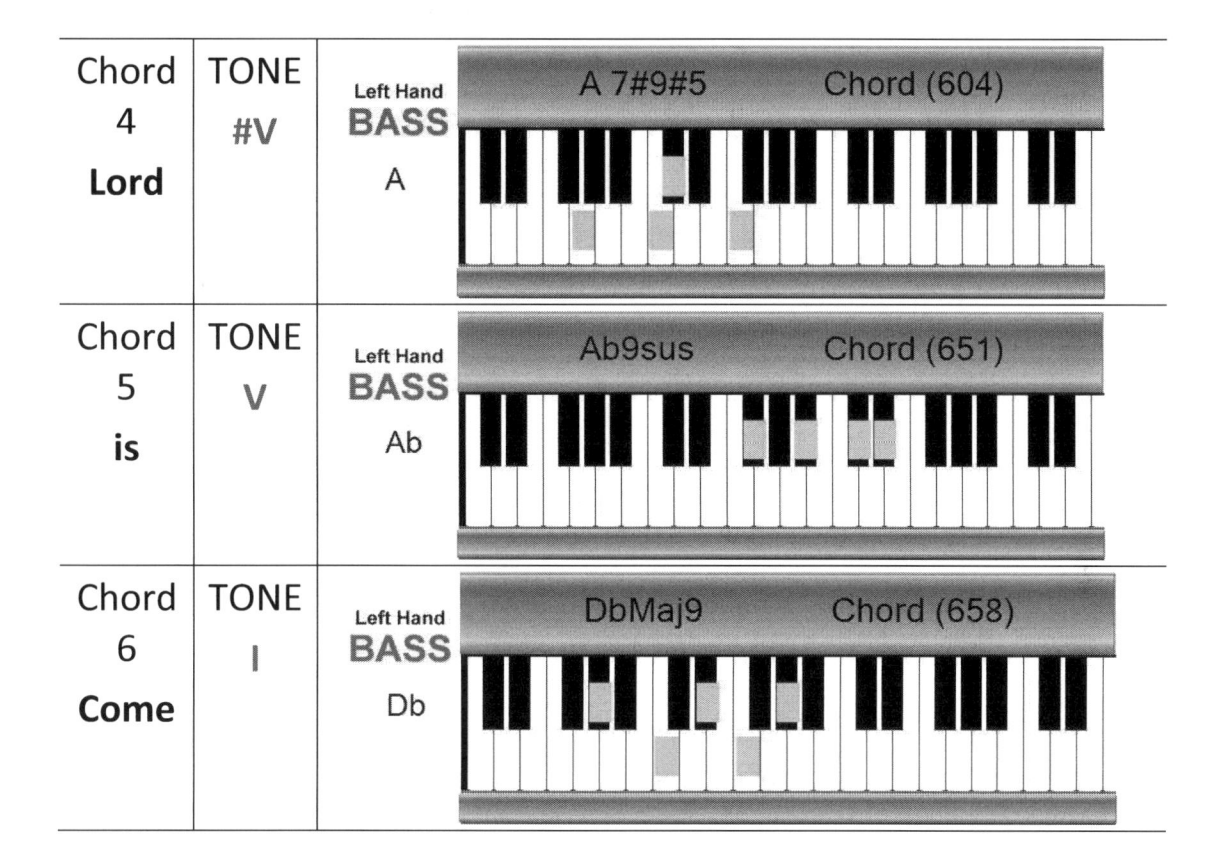

Chord 4 **Lord**	TONE #V	Left Hand BASS A	A 7#9#5 Chord (604)
Chord 5 **is**	TONE V	Left Hand BASS Ab	Ab9sus Chord (651)
Chord 6 **Come**	TONE I	Left Hand BASS Db	DbMaj9 Chord (658)

9.4.3.1   *Detailed Analysis - Chord 1*

Chord number 1 that we play on the words "Joy to the," we have simply harmonized on the melody note, the Db [I] and selected one of the advanced voicings available when doing melody harmonization on the [I].

To harmonize directly on the (Db) melody note, a [I], we simply open our reference "Adventures in Harmony –Harmonization on the Melody", and turn to the chapter on Harmonizing on the [I], and select one of voicings available.

In the "Adventures in Harmony – Harmonization on the Melody", in the section on "Melody Harmonization on the [I]", we selected "The II minor 9 Chord (114)" for this chord. Again, look at this a little more carefully. It's telling us in order to harmonize on a [I] in the melody (Db), we need to play a **[II] minor 9**. Remember we learned how to read this notation earlier (**[II] minor 9**). A [II] in the scale of (Db) is an (Eb). So it's telling us to play an (**Eb minor 9**). Don't let the fact that we looked up a [I] confuse you, again that [I] was a melody note, but we are going to be playing a [II] in the bass (Eb). So that's how we got Chord number 1 for the words "Joy to the" in our contemporary version of "Joy to the World!"

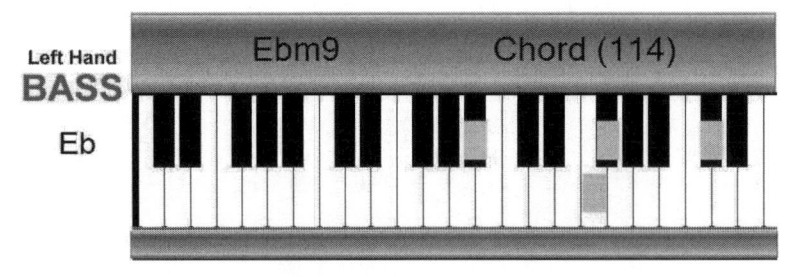

Figure 9-14 Chord 1 (Eb minor 9) "Joy to the"

9.4.3.2 *Detailed Analysis Chord 6*

The word "come" is a [I] Chord, so we simply open our reference "Adventures in Harmony – In Scale Harmonization - Substitution and Passing Chords", and turn to the chapter on Harmonizing on the [I] Chord and choose one of the many advanced voicings available. In the "Adventures in Harmony – In Scale Harmonization - Substitution and Passing Chords", we selected "The Major 9 (658)" for Chord number 6.

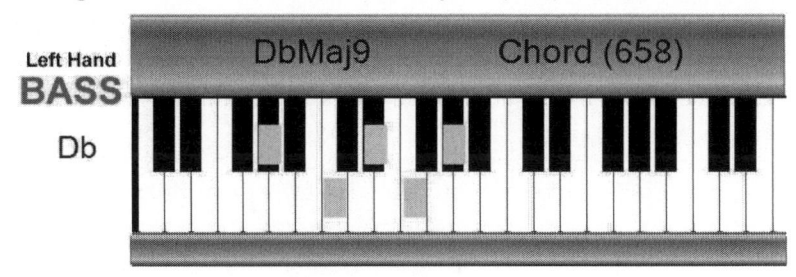

Figure 9-15 Chord 6 (Db Major 9) "come"

9.4.3.3 *Experiment*

Now we are really going to blow your mind. We know the new chord you just played for Chord 6, is one of the chords available when you are harmonizing the [I].Well Chord 1 is also a chord that we played for Harmonizing on the [I]. Did you know, and can you see there is NO PROBLEM switching the chords!!

Play chord number 6, where you played Chord 1, and play Chord 1 at the end where Chord 6 is! They are both good for harmonizing on the [I].

This chord will now be the new chord played for Chord 1,

Adventures in Harmony – Introduction to the System

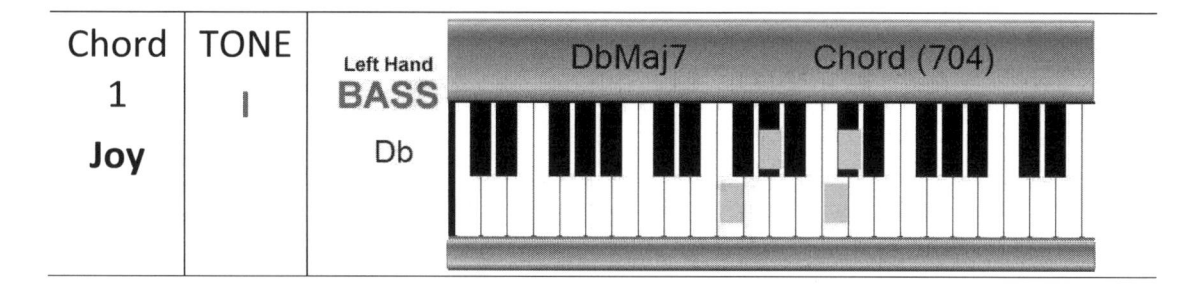

| Chord 1 **Joy** | TONE I | Left Hand BASS Db | DbMaj7 Chord (704) |

and you can now end on the (**Ebm9**) as Chord 6.

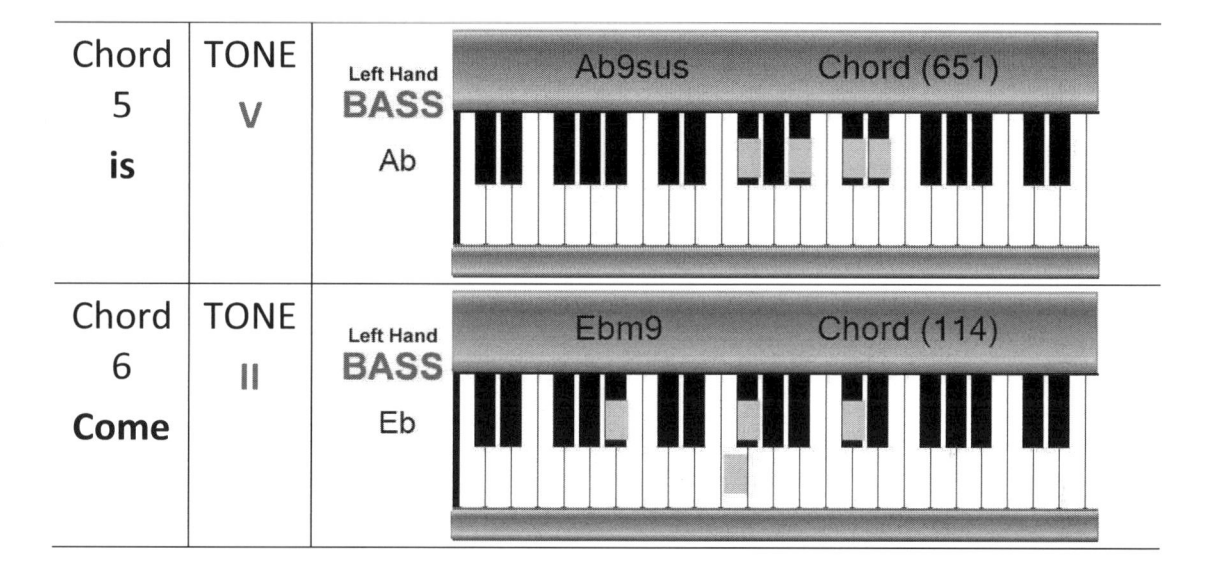

| Chord 5 **is** | TONE V | Left Hand BASS Ab | Ab9sus Chord (651) |

| Chord 6 **Come** | TONE II | Left Hand BASS Eb | Ebm9 Chord (114) |

The only thing you might notice is that when you play the (Eb) chord at the end, it seems like more chords should follow....but that's just a question of your personal taste... you may think it sounds funky, or you may remember for next time that it's not really a good ending chord. But in the jazz world, to end on that chord is fine. Is your mind starting to open up now... do you see the possibilities?

Or if you don't like ending there, then pick another [I] chord to go after it, and use that (Eb) chord as a passing chord.

Chord 5 is	TONE V	Left Hand BASS Ab	Ab9sus Chord (651)
Chord 6	TONE II	Left Hand BASS Eb	Ebm9 Chord (114)
Chord 7	TONE I	Left Hand BASS Db	DbMaj9 Chord (658)

You can even play the (Gb) (IV) chord that you used earlier as a [I], as the chord at the end on the word "Come."

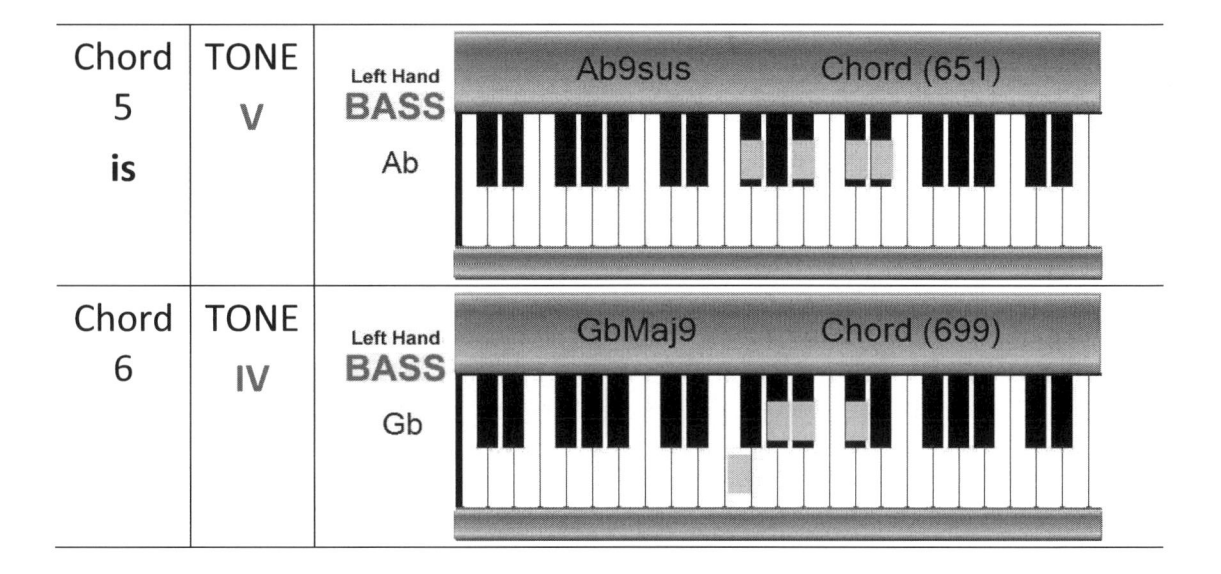

Chord 5 is	TONE V	Left Hand BASS Ab	Ab9sus — Chord (651)
Chord 6	TONE IV	Left Hand BASS Gb	GbMaj9 — Chord (699)

You now know three chords that you can choose from whenever you see a [I] chord!!!!!

Adventures in Harmony – Introduction to the System

The chords in this system are truly like LEGO™ building blocks that you can put together thousands of ways. To aid in your experimentation we also have all of our chords available on 4x6 cards. You may use these cards to arrange chords and try out new progressions while sitting at your instrument. The front of the cards contains a large picture of the chords so that you may easily put your hands right on the chord. The back of the cards contains the chords detailed note-by-note in all 12 keys. The cards are available at our website www.gospel-chords.com.

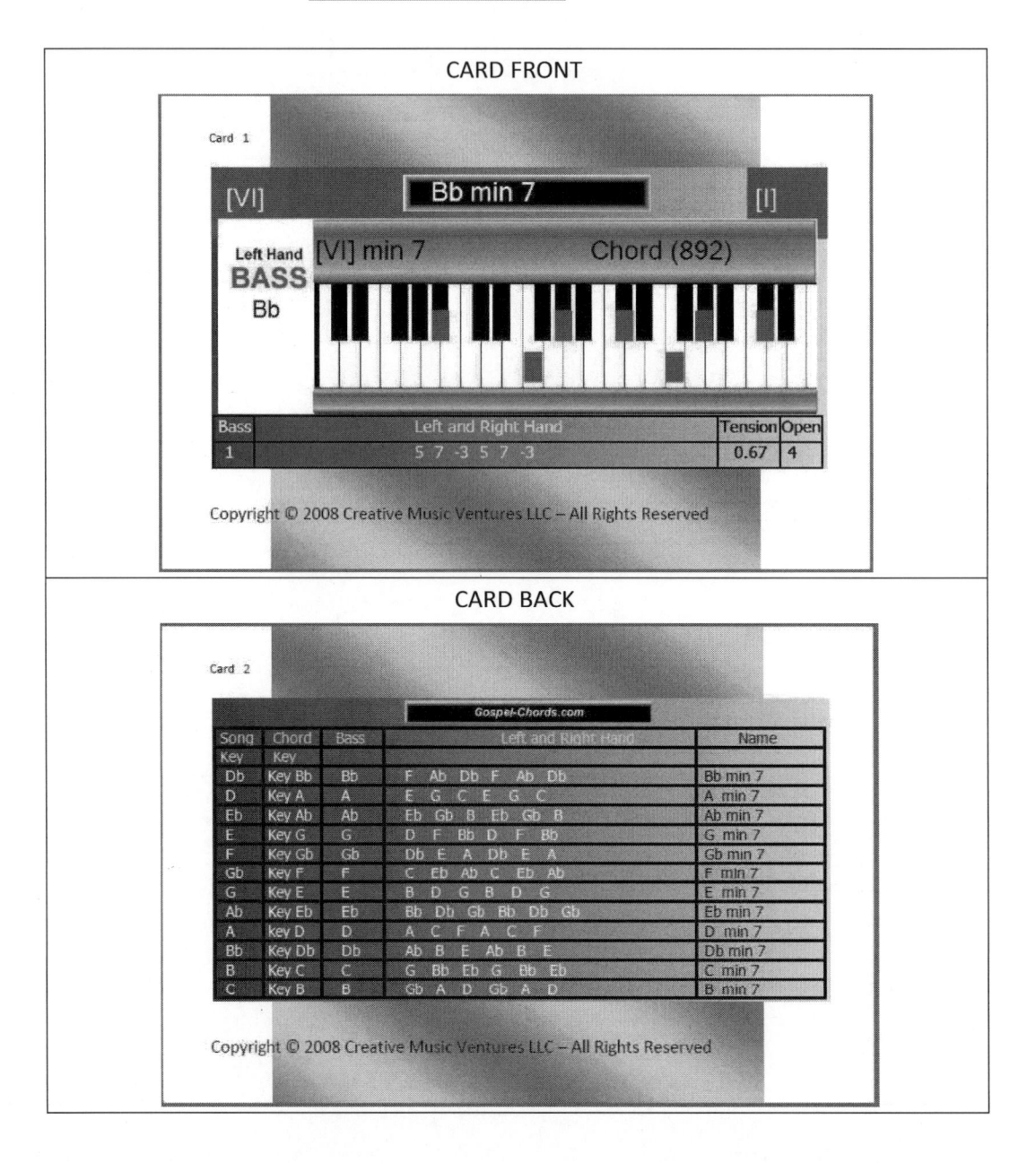

CARD FRONT

Card 1

[VI]   Bb min 7   [I]

Left Hand   [VI] min 7   Chord (892)
BASS
Bb

Bass	Left and Right Hand	Tension	Open
1	5 7 -3 5 7 -3	0.67	4

Copyright © 2008 Creative Music Ventures LLC – All Rights Reserved

CARD BACK

Card 2

Gospel-Chords.com

Song Key	Chord Key	Bass	Left and Right Hand	Name
Db	Key Bb	Bb	F Ab Db F Ab Db	Bb min 7
D	Key A	A	E G C E G C	A min 7
Eb	Key Ab	Ab	Eb Gb B Eb Gb B	Ab min 7
E	Key G	G	D F Bb D F Bb	G min 7
F	Key Gb	Gb	Db E A Db E A	Gb min 7
Gb	Key F	F	C Eb Ab C Eb Ab	F min 7
G	Key E	E	B D G B D G	E min 7
Ab	Key Eb	Eb	Bb Db Gb Bb Db Gb	Eb min 7
A	Key D	D	A C F A C F	D min 7
Bb	Key Db	Db	Ab B E Ab B E	Db min 7
B	Key C	C	G Bb Eb G Bb Eb	C min 7
C	Key B	B	Gb A D Gb A D	B min 7

Copyright © 2008 Creative Music Ventures LLC – All Rights Reserved

9.4.4 Joy to the World - Contemporary Version 3

In this next example, we have inserted a passing chord between the words "is" and "Come", Chords 5 and 7. Chord 6, the (Ab) is now our passing chord. Just listen to how sweet the movement is between Chord 5 to 6 and then to Chord 7. In the next section, we will discuss passing chords in general and analyze this and other possible passing chords.

DON'T FORGET TO PLAY THE BASS WITH YOUR LEFT HAND AND OR FOOT!!!

Chord	TONE	Left Hand BASS	Chord
Chord 1 **Joy to the**	II	Eb	Ebm9 Chord (114)
Chord 2 **World**	III	F	Fm7#5 Chord (273)
Chord 3 **The**	bIII	E	Em add 6 9 Chord (644)
Chord 4 **Lord**	#V	A	A 7#9#5 Chord (604)

Adventures in Harmony – Introduction to the System

Chord 5 is	TONE V	Left Hand BASS Ab	Ab9sus Chord (651)
Chord 6	TONE V	Left Hand BASS Ab	Ab13b9 Chord (660)
Chord 7 Come	TONE I	Left Hand BASS Db	DbMaj9 Chord (658)

Very pretty passing chord (for Chord 6)

9.5 Inserting Passing Chords into a Progression

Using the basic harmonization techniques that we have discussed so far, you may feel that you know how to change a sufficient amount of chords in the harmonization process that you need go no further. However, if you wish to take things a step further, you may wish to insert more chords and transitions. For the purpose of this course, we are going to define chords that you insert between two existing chords, to be known as passing chords.

In general, in listening to passing chords, what you are most likely hearing are changes from consonance to dissonance and back to consonance. The sound of consonance is a pleasing pure sound. The sound of dissonance is a harsh sound, a sound that creates tension, a sound that needs to be resolved, and a sound that really wants to move to a sound of consonance. A more accurate example of this movement is a movement from a sound of minimal dissonance, to one of more dissonance and back to one of minimal dissonance, where the minimal dissonance can be no dissonance. Essentially there is a build up tension and then a release as if you were riding a bicycle up a hill and the coasting down to the finish line.

The passing chords that are inserted are usually the dissonance or sound of tension that are between the sounds of consonance. Therefore it's the movement from consonance, to dissonance and back to consonance, which becomes pleasing to your ear when you are listening to those beautiful contemporary chord transitions.

The sound of consonance is created by chords that have pure tones as long as those tones are not played in closed harmony. A chord has closed harmony when the tones are physically close together on the keyboard. A chord that has pure tones is one that does not have any accidentals. Chords that are made up of only the following tones are usually considered chords that create consonance (1), (2), (3), (5), (6), (7), and the (Maj7). A chord has open harmony when the tones are physically spread wide apart on the keyboard. When the tones start to get physically close together, the chord starts to create dissonance, even though we are using the above tones that are usually considered pure. This dissonance is minimal compared to that which is created when accidentals are added.

The sound of dissonance is created by chords that have accidentals or closed harmony. Chords that contain any of the following tones are usually considered to be dissonant (b2), (-3), (4), (b5), and (#5).

So, if you have a chord where the notes are real close together, like for example when you play four notes in a row (B), (C), (D), and (E), you are creating dissonance or tension just because the notes are close together in closed harmony. Even though all the tones are pure [Maj VII], [I], [II], and [III], and you don't see any alterations like (#5) or (b5), the fact that the chord is closed harmony is enough to create dissonance.

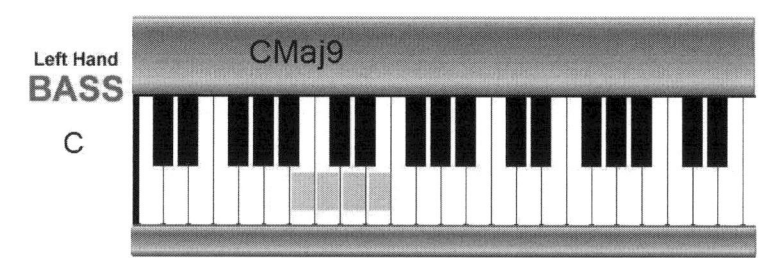

Figure 9-16 C Major 9 (closed harmony)

If we take the same chord, and play it with the notes spread apart in open harmony, we no longer have that sound of tension or dissonance and we have a sound of consonance.

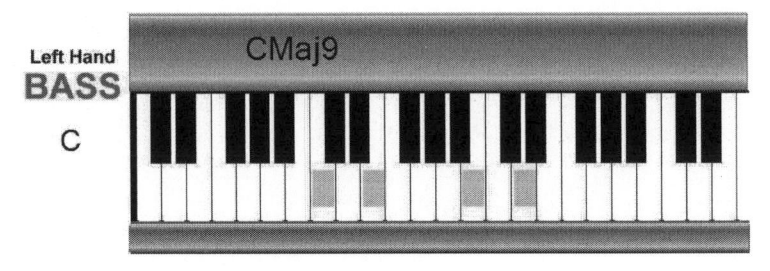

Figure 9-17 C Major 9 (open harmony)

Now if we take the chord above (**C Major 9**), and add alterations and make it a (#5), (**C Major 9#5**), now all of a sudden that chord has tension and dissonance because we added the accidental (#5).

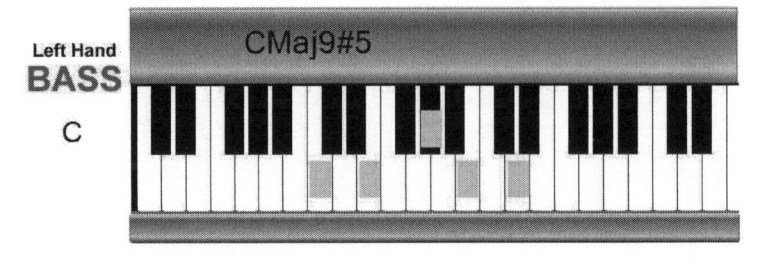

Figure 9-18 C Major 9#5

There is no rule as to whether a particular chord can be used as a passing chord, but you should be able to look at a chord and decide if it might be used as a passing chord. If the chord has closed harmony, or has accidentals, then in my opinion it's a good candidate for use as a passing chord because any of those two items create tension.

The two chords that you are inserting the passing chord between, probably already provide the sound of consonance, therefore when you insert the dissonant passing chord in-between, you will have the natural movement from consonance (less dissonance) to dissonance, and then back to consonance (less dissonance).

Getting back to our last example of "Joy to the World" (Section 9.4.4), in looking at the movement from the words "is" to "come," we see that is a movement from a [V] to a [I]. We inserted an (Ab) [V] as a passing chord between this [V] and [I] to give us a [V]-[V]-[I]. In choosing a passing chord, we could have selected any chord voicing from any tone!! It didn't have to be a [V]. The only criteria we used, was that it created tension. The chord that we selected created tension solely because of its accidentals. The chord was already open harmony, so that didn't create the tension. We simply opened our reference "Adventures in Harmony – In Scale Harmonization - Substitution and Passing Chords", and turned to the chapter on Harmonizing on the [V] Chord and choose one of the available voicings. In the "Adventures in Harmony – In Scale Harmonization - Substitution and Passing Chords", we selected "The 13 b9 (660)" for Chord number 6.

Figure 9-19 Chord 6 (Ab 13b9)

The accidentals the (13th) and (b9) are the notes in this chord that create the tension, The (F) is a (13th) and the (A) is a (b9).

Remember in the Adventures in Harmony Play by number system, there is no restriction on the tone number that can be inserted as the passing tone. In this particular instance, we inserted another [V] between a [V] and a [I]. The tone that we select doesn't even have to be physically between the [V] and the [I]. We could have selected a [VI]!

9.5.1 Joy to the World - Contemporary Version 3.1

Like we told you before.... There is no other course that will give you these beautiful voicing's! And no other course allows you to just plug them in at will. Like we said, there are NO progressions to memorize. Simply follow our system and you will be creating your own beautiful progressions!

In the previous example where we inserted another [V] in between the [V] and [I], we could have inserted any other voicing from any of the other Roman numbers!!!

Don't believe us then watch this!!!! Instead of inserting another [V], we could have inserted a [III] (F) Chord.

Chord 5 is	TONE V	Left Hand BASS Ab	Ab9sus Chord (651)
Chord 6	TONE III	Left Hand BASS F	F7#9#5 Chord (249) Passing chord
Chord 7 Come	TONE I	Left Hand BASS Db	DbMaj9 Chord (658)

9.5.1.1 Analysis of choosing passing chord 6

We simply opened our reference "Adventures in Harmony – In Scale Harmonization - Substitution and Passing Chords", and turned to the chapter on Harmonizing on the [III] Chord and selected one of the available voicings. In the "Adventures in Harmony – In Scale Harmonization - Substitution and Passing Chords", we selected "The 7#9#5 (249)" for Chord number 6.

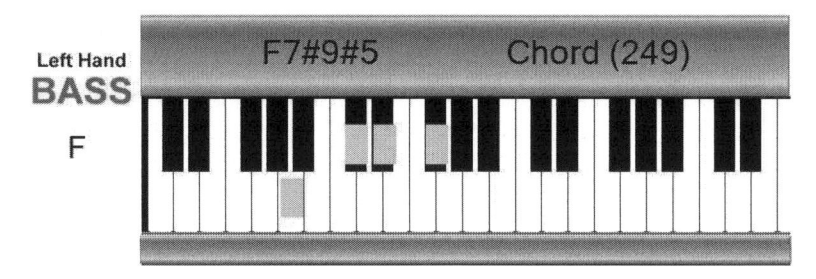

Figure 9-20 Chord 6 (F7 #9#5)

9.5.2 Joy to the World - Contemporary Version 3.2

Let's get real wild and use a [bIII] chord! That's right that's an (E) Chord! And remember there is no (E) in the key of (Db)! Now we are going to be sounding really sweet!! Anytime you add a chord that is out of scale, the transitions are extra pretty. We used the reference "Adventures in Harmony – Out of Scale Harmonization - The Tritone and Beyond," to select Chord 6 that will be a new passing chord between the [V] and the [I].

Chord	TONE	Left Hand BASS	Chord
Chord 5 is	V	Ab	Ab9sus Chord (651)
Chord 6	bIII	E	Em add 6 9 Chord (645) Passing chord

Chord 7 Come	TONE I	
		Left Hand BASS Db — DbMaj9 Chord (658)

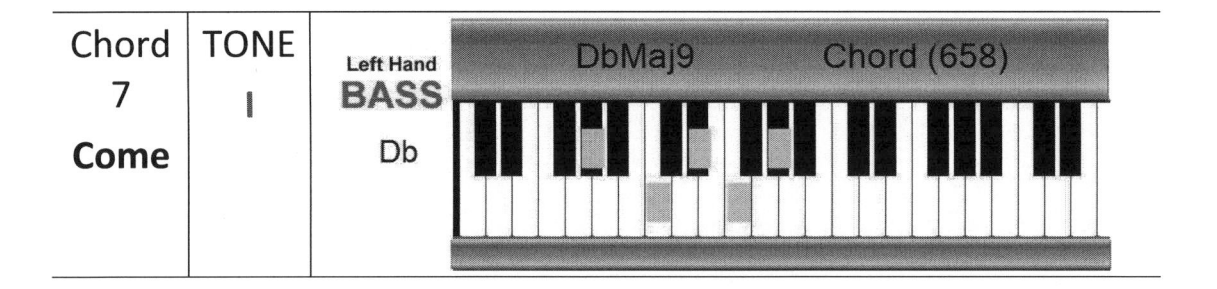

9.5.2.1 Analysis of choosing passing chord 6

We simply opened our reference "Adventures in Harmony – Core Reference –Volume – Out of Scale Harmonization - The Tritone and Beyond,"", and turned to the chapter on Harmonizing on the [bIII] Chord and selected one of the available voicings. We selected "The minor add 6,9 (645) " for Chord number 6.

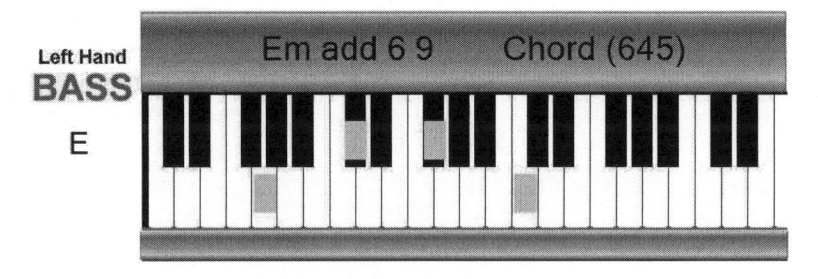

Figure 9-21 Chord 6 (E minor add 6, 9)

9.5.3 Joy to the World - Contemporary Version 4

In this example we added two passing chords before the last chord. We used the (Ab) that we used before, and selected to add a [III] Chord. There is no limit to the number of passing chords that you can insert as long as you follow the system. Therefore our [V] – [V] – [I] just became a [V] – [V] – [III] – [I] (Ab, Ab, F, Db) on Chords 5-8.

Adventures in Harmony – Introduction to the System

DON'T FORGET TO PLAY THE BASS WITH YOUR LEFT HAND AND OR FOOT!!!

		Left Hand BASS	Chord
Chord 1 **Joy to the**	TONE II	Eb	Ebm9 — Chord (114)
Chord 2 **World**	TONE III	F	Fm7#5 — Chord (273)
Chord 3 **The**	TONE bIII	E	Em add 6 9 — Chord (644)
Chord 4 **Lord**	TONE #V	A	A 7#9#5 — Chord (604)
Chord 5 **is**	TONE V	Ab	Ab9sus — Chord (651)

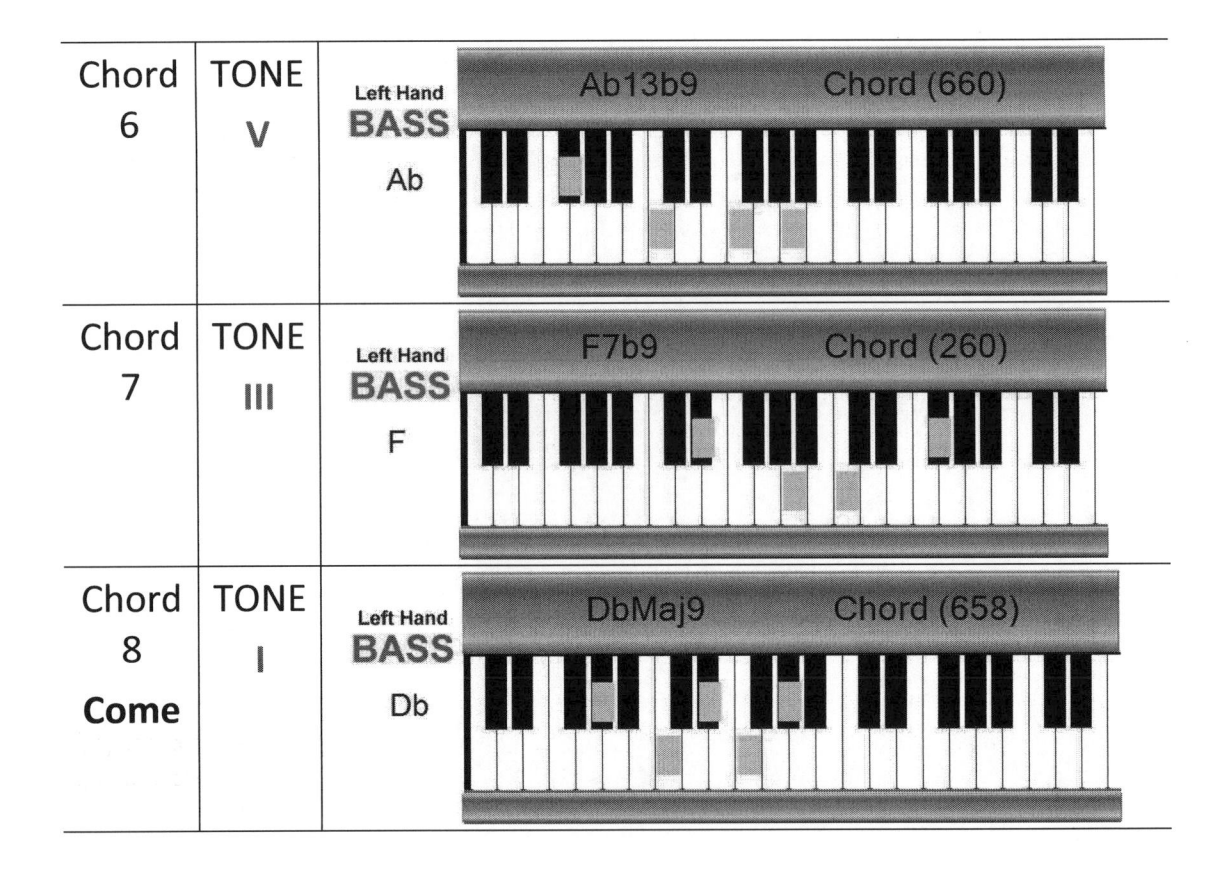

Chord 6	TONE V	Left Hand BASS Ab	Ab13b9 Chord (660)
Chord 7	TONE III	Left Hand BASS F	F7b9 Chord (260)
Chord 8 **Come**	TONE I	Left Hand BASS Db	DbMaj9 Chord (658)

9.5.3.1   Analysis of choosing passing chord 7

We simply opened our reference "Adventures in Harmony – In Scale Harmonization - Substitution and Passing Chords", and turned to the chapter on Harmonizing on the [III] Chord and selected one of the available voicings. In the "Adventures in Harmony – In Scale Harmonization - Substitution and Passing Chords", we selected "The 7 b9 (260)" for Chord number 7.

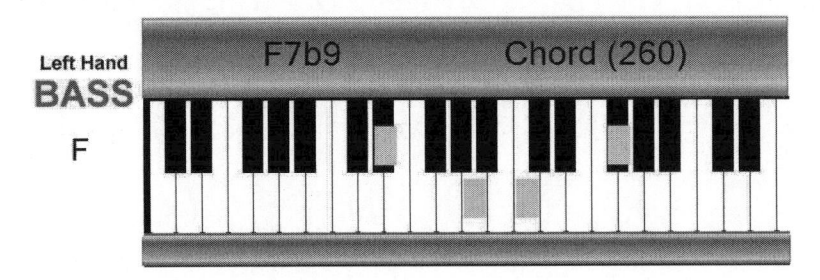

Left Hand BASS F — F7b9   Chord (260)

Figure 9-22 Chord 7 (F 7b9)

9.5.3.2 *Experiment*

Hey, isn't Chord 2 that we used on the word "World" a [III] Chord? It sure is, and there is no reason why we can't use it as a passing chord between the [V] and the [I], between the words "is" and "come."

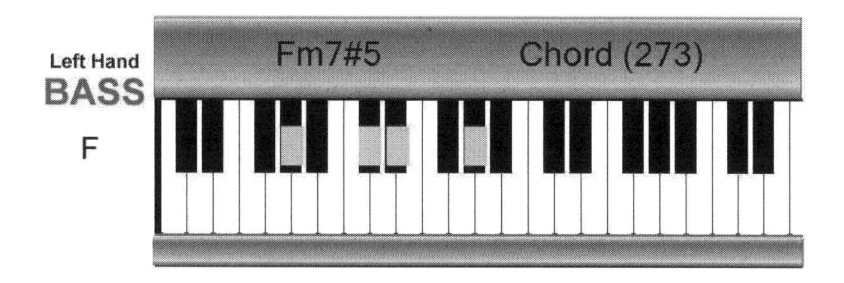

[Keyboard diagram: Left Hand BASS F — Fm7#5 Chord (273)]

It surely meets the criteria of looking like a passing chord; it has accidentals, the (#5).

This chord is in our reference "Adventures in Harmony – In Scale Harmonization - Substitution and Passing Chords", in the chapter on Harmonizing on the [III] Chord. It is a "The minor 7#5 (273)." In fact there is no reason why we can't play both of these [III] chords as passing chords. We can even switch the order that we play these passing chords for additional flavor. We can play the (**F minor7#5**) followed by the (**F 7b9**), or the (**F 7b9**) followed by the (**F minor7#5**).

9.5.4 Joy to the World - Contemporary Version 5

In this example, we inserted a [bIII] chord, (E) as passing chord (Chord 8) before the last chord.

Our [V] – [V] – [bIII] – [I] progression, just became a [V] – [V] – [III] – **[bIII]** – [I] (Ab, Ab, F, **E**, Db).

And for Chord 1, we switched to that [IV] chord (Gb) that we used earlier for chord 1.

And for Chord 9 on the word "Come" we already know that is a [I] Chord. We simply selected another one of the contemporary voicings for the [I] Chord!

And YES YOU CAN PLAY CHORD 9 in place of CHORD 1 since they are both [I] Chords!

Adventures in Harmony – Introduction to the System

DON'T FORGET TO PLAY THE BASS WITH YOUR LEFT HAND AND OR FOOT!!!

Chord	TONE	Left Hand BASS	Chord
Chord 1 **Joy to the**	IV	Gb	GbMaj9 Chord (699)
Chord 2 **World**	III	F	Fm7#5 Chord (273)
Chord 3 **The**	bIII	E	Em add 6 9 Chord (644)
Chord 4 **Lord**	#V	A	A 7#9#5 Chord (604)
Chord 5 **is**	V	Ab	Ab9sus Chord (651)

All Rights Reserved - @ Copyright 2009 Creative Musuc Ventures LLC www.gospel-chords.com 9.02.10 Page 76

Chord	TONE			
Chord 6	V	Left Hand BASS Ab	Ab13b9 Chord (660)	
Chord 7	III	Left Hand BASS F	F7b9 Chord (260)	
Chord 8	bIII	Left Hand BASS E	Em add 6 9 Chord (645)	
Chord 9 **Come**	I	Left Hand BASS Db	Db 6 add 9 Chord (57) WOW!	

9.5.4.1   Analysis of choosing Chord 9

The word "come" is a [I] Chord, so we simply open our reference "Adventures in Harmony – In Scale Harmonization - Substitution and Passing Chords", and turn to the chapter on Harmonizing on the [I] Chord and choose one of the available voicings. In the "Adventures in Harmony – In Scale Harmonization - Substitution and Passing Chords", we selected "The 6, 9 (57)" for Chord number 9.

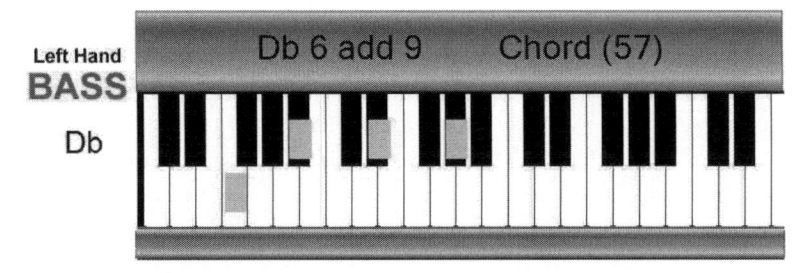

Figure 9-23 Chord 9 (Db 6, 9)

And remember, yes you can play this chord in place of Chord 1 since they are both [I] Chords!!!

9.5.4.2 Analysis of passing Chord 8

Chord 8 is a [bIII] Chord (E), so we simply opened our reference "Adventures in Harmony – In Scale Harmonization - Substitution and Passing Chords", and turned to the chapter on Harmonizing on the [bIII] Chord and choose one of the advanced voicings available. We selected "The m add 6,9 (645) " for Chord 8.

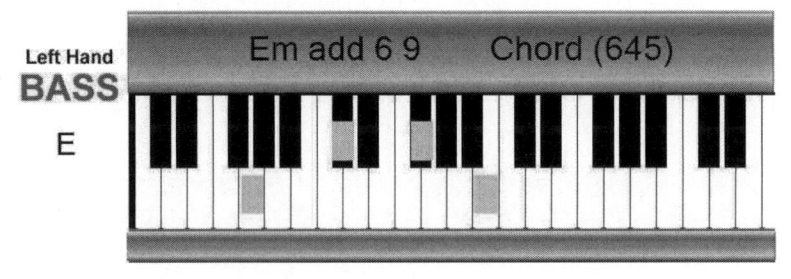

Figure 9-24 Chord 8 (Em add 6,9)

9.5.5 Joy to the World - Contemporary Version 6

In this version we have replaced Chord 2 and added a new chord after Chord 1. We saw previously that Chord 2 was a [III] chord (F) for the word "World." So there is no reason why we can't select another [III] chord from the choice of contemporary voicings available for the [III] …… And that's exactly what we did!!

Hopefully you are now seeing how powerful our system is!!!! Our chords are truly like kids LEGO™ building blocks. This truly becomes an adventure in harmony when you can start to experiment with these chords on our cards and easily arrange them in different sequences.

Adventures in Harmony – Introduction to the System

DON'T FORGET TO PLAY THE BASS WITH YOUR LEFT HAND AND OR FOOT!!!

	TONE	Left Hand BASS	Chord
Chord 1 **Joy to**	II	Eb	Ebm9 Chord (114)
Chord 2 **the**	bIII	E	E 6,9 b5 Chord (599)
Chord 3 **World**	III	F	Fm7 Chord (701)
Chord 4 **The**	bIII	E	Em add 6 9 Chord (644)
Chord 5 **Lord**	#V	A	A 7#9#5 Chord (604)

Adventures in Harmony – Introduction to the System

Chord 6 **is**	TONE V	Left Hand BASS Ab	Ab9sus — Chord (651)
Chord 7	TONE V	Left Hand BASS Ab	Ab13b9 — Chord (660)
Chord 8	TONE III	Left Hand BASS F	F7b9 — Chord (260)
Chord 9	TONE bIII	Left Hand BASS E	Em add 6 9 — Chord (645)
Chord 10 **Come**	TONE I	Left Hand BASS Db	Db 6 add 9 — Chord (57) WOW!

9.5.5.1 Analysis of Passing Chord 3

Chord 3 is a [III] Chord (F), so we simply opened our reference "Adventures in Harmony – In Scale Harmonization - Substitution and Passing Chords", and turned to the chapter on Harmonizing on the [III] Chord and selected one of the available voicings. We selected "The minor 7 (701)" for Chord 3.

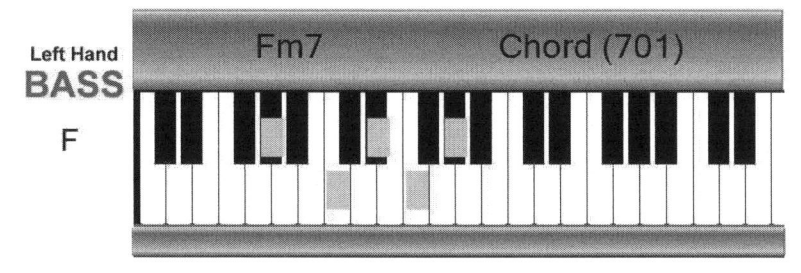

Figure 9-25 Chord 2 (F minor 7)

9.5.5.2 Analysis of Passing Chord 2

Chord 3 is a [bIII] Chord (E), so we simply opened our reference "Adventures in Harmony – Out of Scale Harmonization – The Tritone and Beyond", and turned to the chapter on Harmonizing on the [bIII] Chord and selected one of the available voicings. We selected "The 6,9 b5 (599)" for Chord 2. Remember there is no (E) in the key of (Db), therefore we must use the reference for harmonizing tones that are not in the major scale.

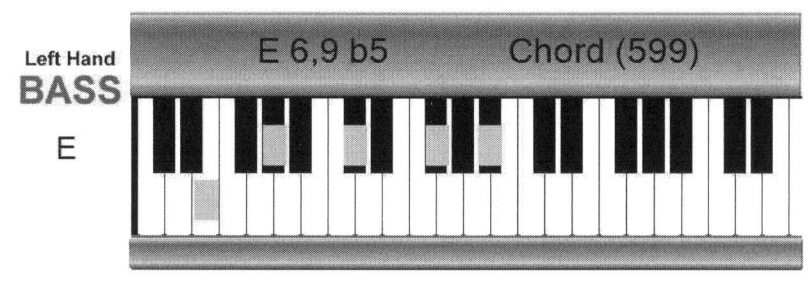

9.5.6 Joy to the World - Contemporary Version 7

In this example, we simply inserted a passing chord, a [II] chord (Eb) between the words "Joy" and "World." This chord we are going to play on the words "to the."

Now, what better way to get to the [III] Chord (F) on the word "World", from the [I] Chord then to stop on the [II] Chord ([IV] –[II] – [III] is a nice smooth movement). Remember the (Gb) [IV] Chord is just a substitute for the [I]!

So we essentially have a [IV] - [II] - [III] movement, where a [IV] was substituted for the [I].

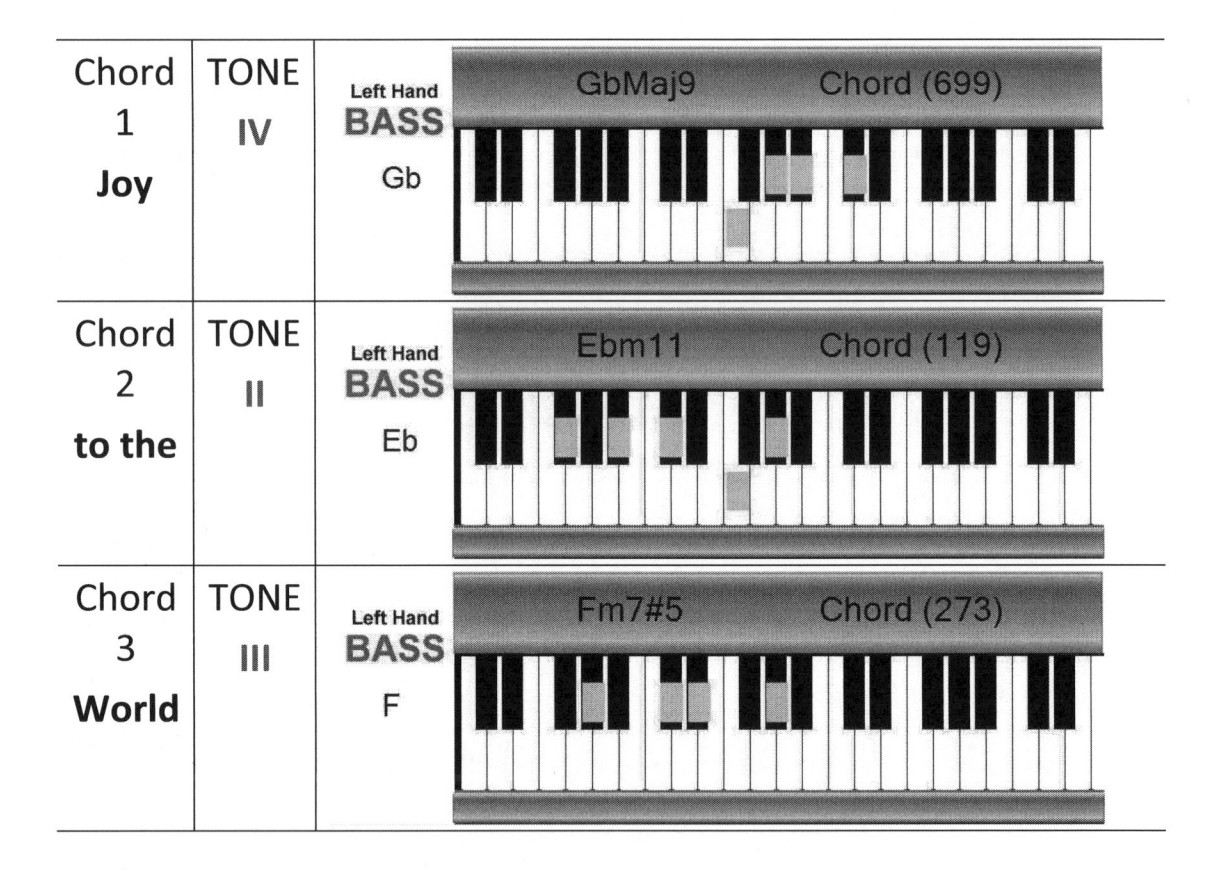

Chord 1 Joy	TONE IV	Left Hand BASS Gb	GbMaj9 Chord (699)
Chord 2 to the	TONE II	Left Hand BASS Eb	Ebm11 Chord (119)
Chord 3 World	TONE III	Left Hand BASS F	Fm7#5 Chord (273)

9.5.6.1 Analysis of Passing Chord 2

Chord 2 is a [II] Chord (Eb), so we simply opened our reference "Adventures in Harmony – In Scale Harmonization - Substitution and Passing Chords", and turned to the chapter on Harmonizing on the [II] Chord and selected one of the available voicings. We selected "The minor 11 (119)" for Chord 2.

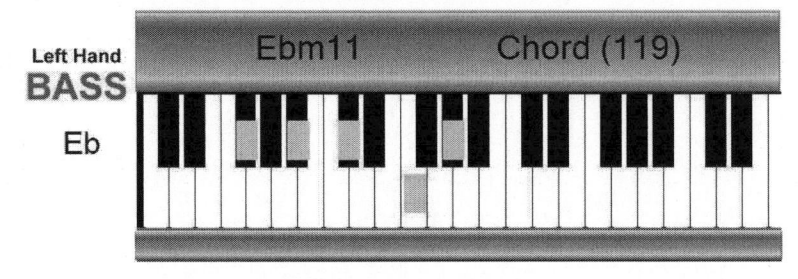

Figure 9-26 Chord 2 (F minor11)

9.5.7 Joy to the World - Contemporary Version 8

Remember that new [III] chord (F) we played for the [III] in (Section 9.5.5).

Now why don't we play that one along with the original one, and now play two chords on the word "World."

Chord	TONE	Left Hand BASS	Chord
Chord 1 **Joy**	IV	Gb	GbMaj9 Chord (699)
Chord 2 **to the**	II	Eb	Ebm11 Chord (119)
Chord 3 **Wor-**	III	F	Fm7#5 Chord (273)
Chord 4 **-ld**	III	F	Fm7 Chord (701)

And now for the [I] Chord (the last chord) that we need to play on the word "Come," lets choose a different [I] Chord. Try out this [I] Chord.

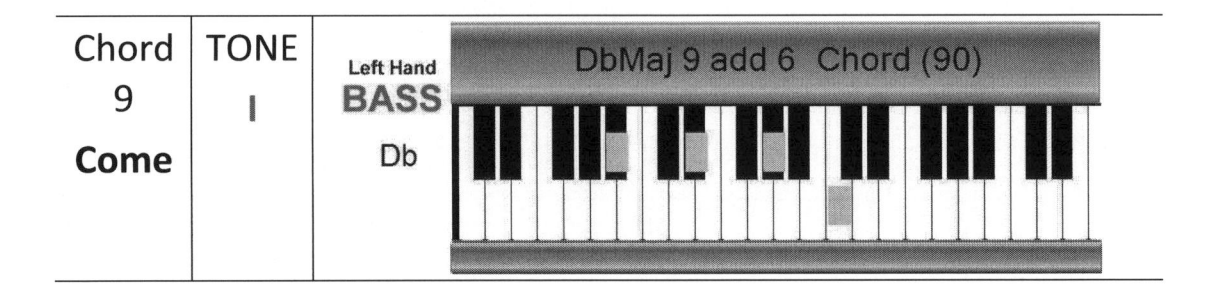

Chord 9 Come	TONE I	Left Hand BASS Db	DbMaj 9 add 6 Chord (90)

We simply opened our reference "Adventures in Harmony – In Scale Harmonization - Substitution and Passing Chords", and turned to the chapter on Harmonizing on the [I] Chord and selected one of the available voicings. We selected "The Major 9 add 6 (90)" for this new ending chord. This is a very pretty chord.

9.6 Case Study Summary - Has the light bulb turned on yet?

We hope you can see how powerful our Adventures in Harmony Play by Number System is. Do you understand the power in information that you just learned? In case you still don't see where this is going, lets us attempt to steer you in the right direction.

Whenever you see ANY piece of music and you happen to be in the key of Db, and anybody asks you to play a chord for the [I] chord (Db) …….**you are free to PLAY ANY ONE OF THESE CHORDS!!!**

Chord Choice 1	TONE IV	Left Hand BASS Gb	GbMaj9 Chord (699)

Chord Choice 2	TONE I	Left Hand BASS Db	DbMaj 9 add 6 Chord (90)
Chord Choice 3	TONE II	Left Hand BASS Eb	Ebm9 Chord (114)
Chord Choice 4	TONE I	Left Hand BASS Db	DbMaj9 Chord (658)

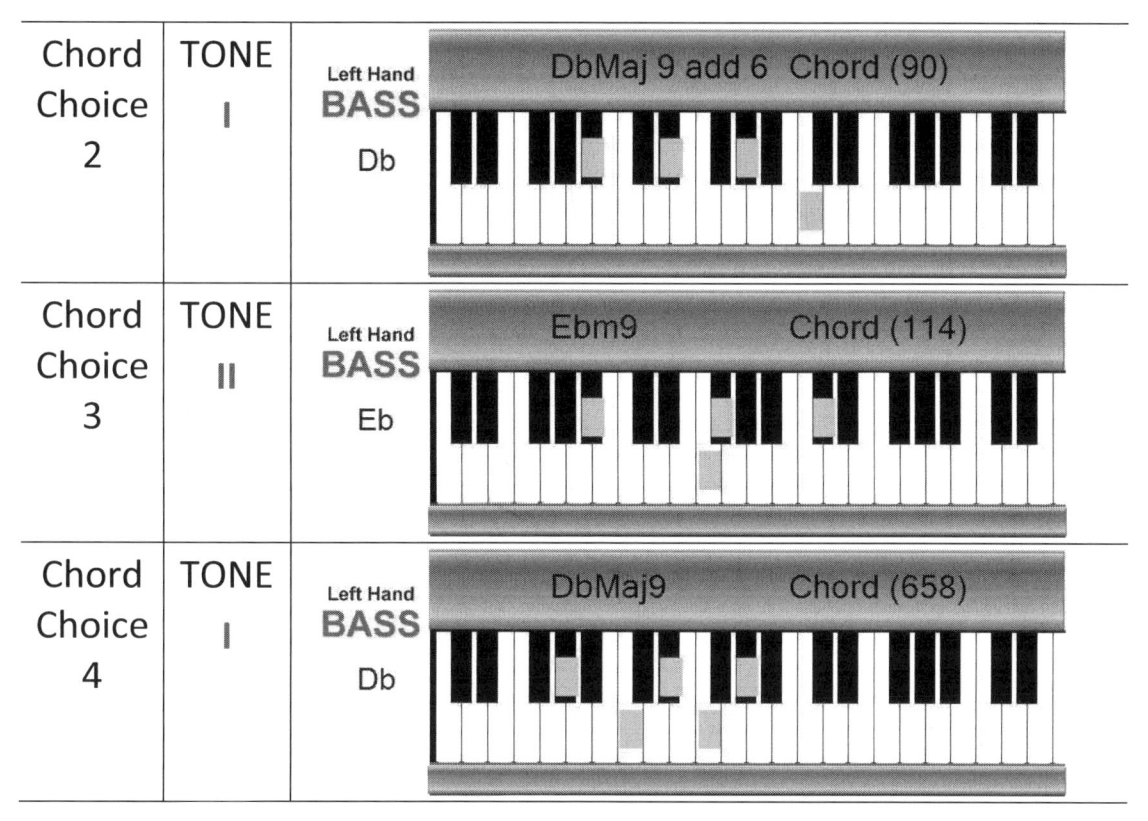

Figure 9-27 Contemporary Voicing Choices for the I Chord

Consider these contemporary voicings as part of your personal toolbox or library for whenever you see a (Db) or [I] Chord. These are just 4 examples; there are many other advanced voicings for the [I] chord!

Remember we also learned some contemporary voicing's for the [III] Chord (F) in the key of (Db).

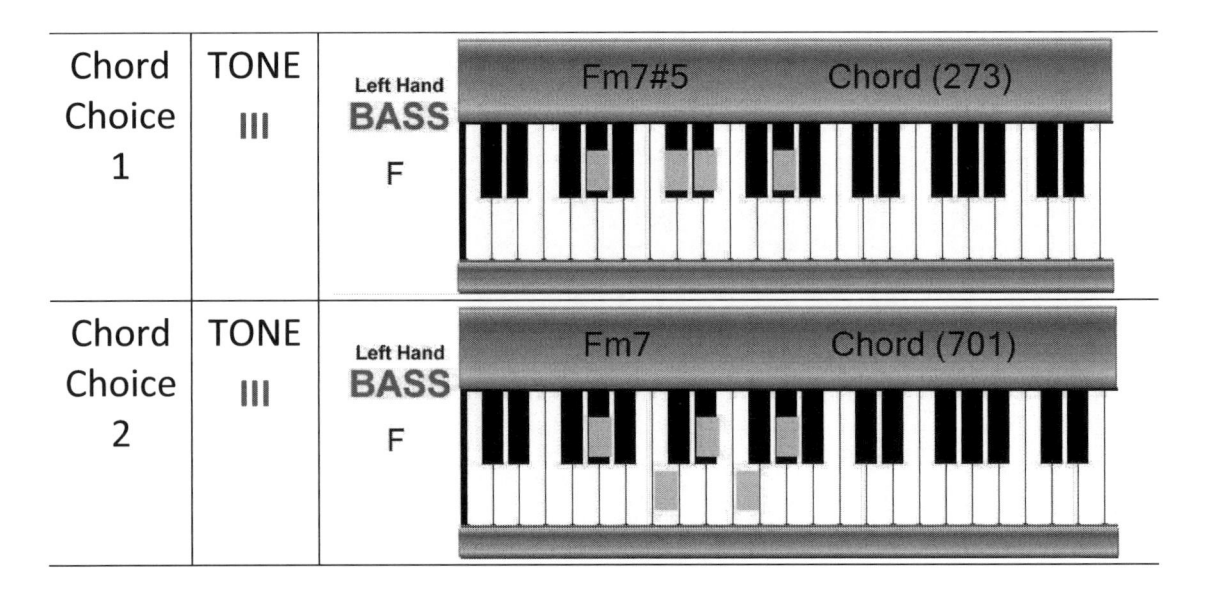

Chord Choice 1	TONE III	Left Hand BASS F	Fm7#5 Chord (273)
Chord Choice 2	TONE III	Left Hand BASS F	Fm7 Chord (701)

Figure 9-28

And again, whenever you see ANY piece of music and you happen to be in the key of (Db), just as you saw in all the previous examples, and anybody asks you to play a chord for the [III] chord (F), or you see a (F) chord written on some music ……..**you are free to PLAY ANY ONE OF THESE CHORDS** (Figure 9-28).

In the Adventures in Harmony course you will have hundreds of beautiful voicings to choose from for every tone of the scale!

This course has over 1200 advanced contemporary voicing's. What you have seen here only scratches the surface of what's available in our complete series;

You see this is the most amazing music lesson you have ever had!!!!

But your adventure is only just beginning.

10 Hark the Herald Angels Sing – Case Study

This is an example of the harmonization process used on a real piece of music. We will use the first line of the Christmas song "Hark the Herald Angels Sing" in this example. The following is an example of how this song might be written in its original plain version.

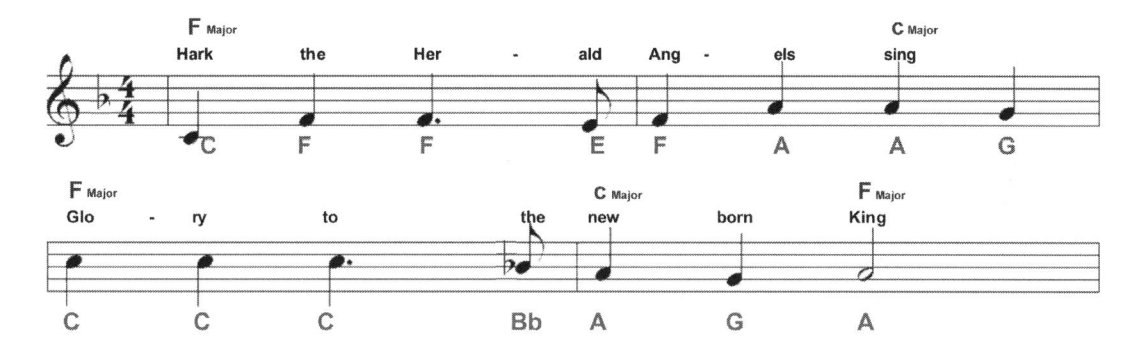

[Musical notation: First line with F Major and C Major chords, lyrics "Hark the Her-ald Ang-els sing" with notes C F F E F A A G; second line with F Major, C Major, F Major chords, lyrics "Glo-ry to the new born King" with notes C C C Bb A G A]

The result after our harmonization process will be the following beautiful version

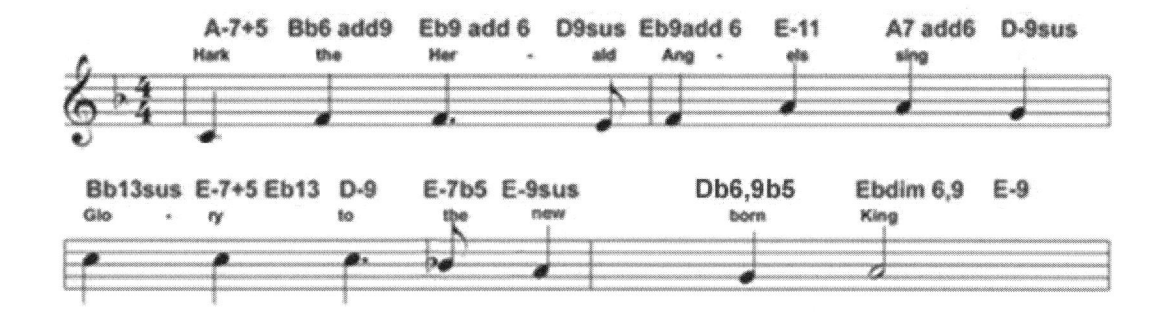

[Musical notation: First line with chords A-7+5, Bb6add9, Eb9 add 6, D9sus, Eb9add 6, E-11, A7 add6, D-9sus, lyrics "Hark the Her-ald Ang-els sing"; second line with chords Bb13sus, E-7+5, Eb13, D-9, E-7b5, E-9sus, Db6,9b5, Ebdim 6,9, E-9, lyrics "Glo-ry to the new born King"]

No matter how complicated the original piece of music is in terms of number of staffs, and all the notes on the different staffs, that music should be reduced down to a simple single staff single note melody line. All other notes on the page should be ignored. This results in just a simple melody line as we see above.

Our goal is to number each of the notes in the song with its tone number. Before we can label each note with a tone number, we must first determine the key signature. The tone number for a given note is relative to the key signature. If we looked at the same note in different key signatures, we would see that in each key the tone number is different for the same note. Therefore we must first determine the key signature before we can number the notes. The pictures of the chords in the Adventures in Harmony Reference Volumes are pictures of the chords if the song is written in the key of (Db). If the song is in another key, we must use the numbers to determine what keys to play.

1. Determine Key Signature

Determining the key signature that the piece of music is written can be done by looking at the key signature designation at the beginning of the piece of music and matching the image of the key signature with a table of known key signatures. The song above has the key signature image as shown below

This key signature image signature corresponds to the key of (F).

The song "Hark the Herald Angels Sing" is written in the key of (F). This was determined my matching the key signature symbol with the chart below.

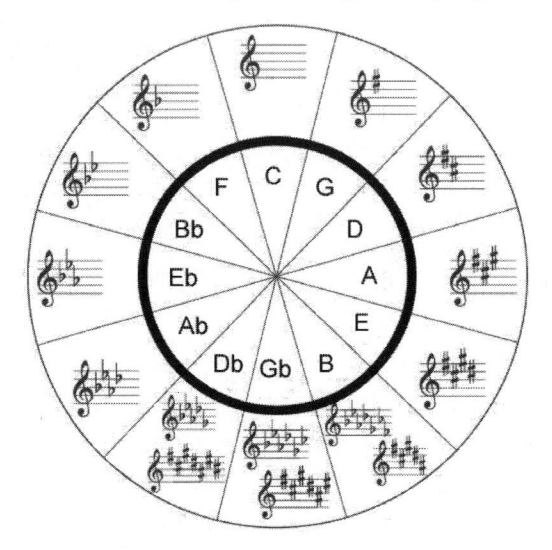

Adventures in Harmony – Introduction to the System

You may use the chart above to determine the key signature for any piece of music. Simply match the key signature symbol that you find at the beginning of your music with the chart above.

Now that we know the key signature, we will use the numbers from the corresponding scale (F) to label each melody note. Now that we know the note names and the key signature, we can label each note with its tone number by looking at the scale for that key signature. Therefore we will use the (F) scale to determine the Tone Numbers for the notes in our song.

F Chromatic Scale												
Note Name	F	Gb	G	Ab	A	Bb	B	C	Db	D	Eb	E
Tone	1	b2	2	-3	3	4	b5	5	+5	6	b7	M7

The final result is below, with each one of the notes in our song numbered with its corresponding tone number.

Hark the Her - ald Ang - els sing
5   1   1   M7   1   3   3   2

Glo - ry to the new born King
5   5   5   4   3   2   3

When an experienced musician looks at a piece of music, it is common for the musician in their mind to actually see the music numbered as it is above. This would be the starting point from the musician's perspective in harmonizing a piece of music with this new process.

Adventures in Harmony – Introduction to the System

Your next step will be to harmonize each one of the 15 notes in this song with a separate chord

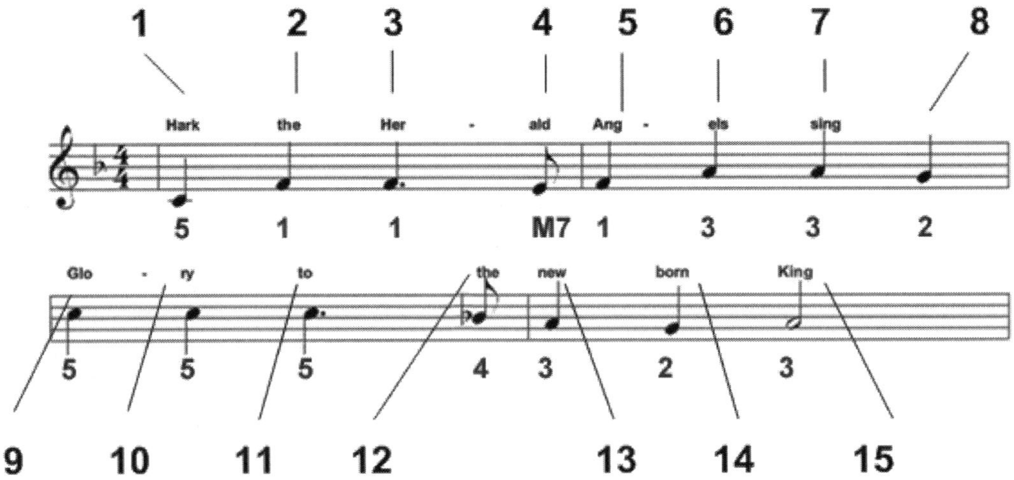

[Musical notation showing "Hark the Herald Angels sing" with notes numbered 1-8 above and chord numbers 5, 1, 1, M7 1, 3, 3, 2 below]

[Musical notation showing "Glory to the new born King" with chord numbers 5, 5, 5, 4, 3, 2, 3 above and numbers 9, 10, 11, 12, 13, 14, 15 below]

There will be an extra step in the harmonization process for this song because the song is not in the key of (Db). We will need to use the numbers in the reference volumes to determine what keys to play. The pictures will do us no good, because the pictures correspond to a song that is written in the key of (Db). Use the table at the bottom of the page in the reference volumes to get the notes for the chord in a different key.

TIP: If you use the pictures that are in the reference volumes, you will have not done anything wrong. By using the pictures, you have simply automatically transposed your song to the key of (Db). As long as you represent your song by using the number system, you can immediately play the song in the key of (Db) by using the chord pictures in the reference volumes.

The following page is the resulting harmonization that we have come up for the song "Hark the Herald Angels Sing." There are an infinite number of possibilities with the Adventures in Harmony Course.

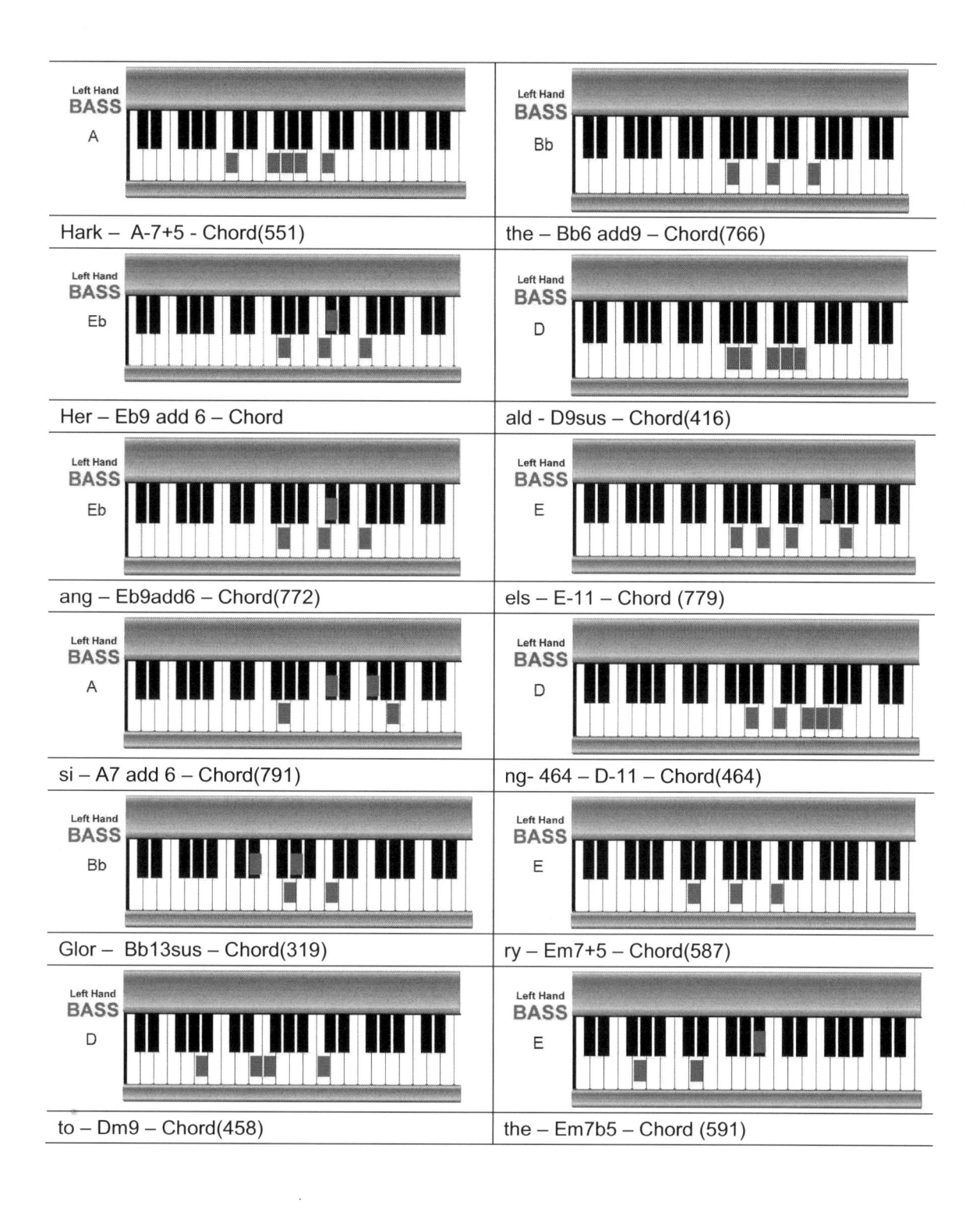

Hark – A-7+5 - Chord(551)	the – Bb6 add9 – Chord(766)
Her – Eb9 add 6 – Chord	ald - D9sus – Chord(416)
ang – Eb9add6 – Chord(772)	els – E-11 – Chord (779)
si – A7 add 6 – Chord(791)	ng- 464 – D-11 – Chord(464)
Glor – Bb13sus – Chord(319)	ry – Em7+5 – Chord(587)
to – Dm9 – Chord(458)	the – Em7b5 – Chord (591)

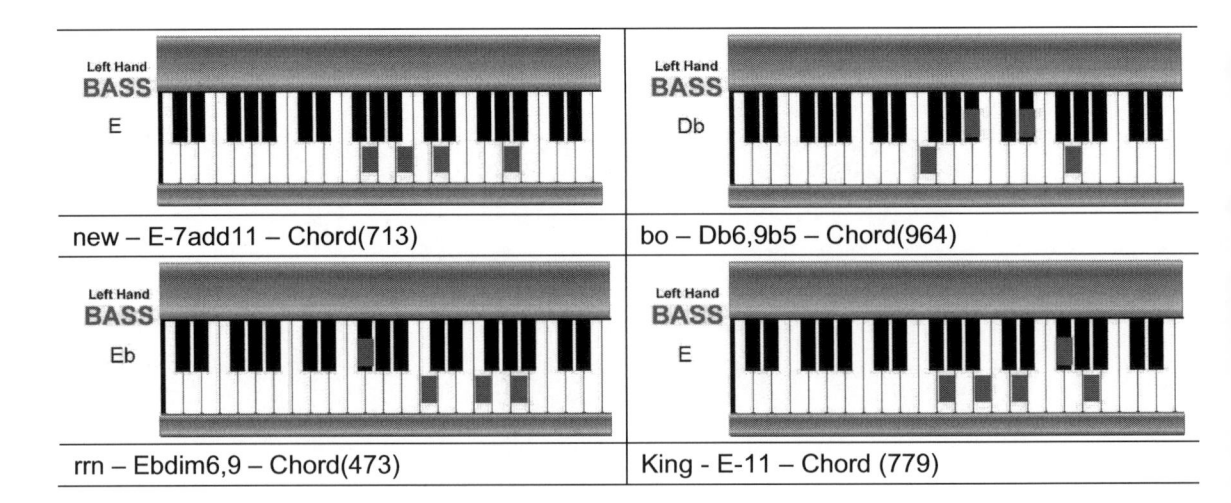

Adventures in Harmony – Introduction to the System

Left Hand BASS — E	Left Hand BASS — Db
new – E-7add11 – Chord(713)	bo – Db6,9b5 – Chord(964)
Left Hand BASS — Eb	Left Hand BASS — E
rrn – Ebdim6,9 – Chord(473)	King - E-11 – Chord (779)

Following is a detailed analysis of how we harmonized the 15 notes of the song "Hark the Herald Angels Sing".

Adventures in Harmony – Introduction to the System

1) Harmonize the first note (1) of the song. (Chord 551)

The first note (1) in the song is a (C). This note (C) is tone number (V) in the key of (F). This melody note of (C) can be harmonized with any chord that has a (C) as the topmost melody note.

This would be any chord in Chapter on the (V) in the Adventures in Harmony Volume "Harmonizing on the Melody." The musician is free to pick any one of those chords to harmonize on the (C), all of these chords have a (C) on top as the melody note.

Chord 551 is a (III) minor 7#5. The (III) is telling us to make a chord based on tone (III) of the key we are in. Tone (III) in the key of (F) is an (A). Therefore this is going to be some kind of (A) chord, a chord based on the A scale.

Chord 551 tells us to use tones 1, -3, #5, 7, 8 and -10 to construct this chord.

We are going to use those tones in the key of (A) because this is a (III) chord, remember (A) is the third (III) in the (F) scale. Tones 1, -3, #5, 7, 8 and -10 in the key of (A) are notes A, C, F, G, A and C. Remember a (-3) is where you lower the (3) by ½ step. The (3) is a (Db), so the (-3) is a (C). Remember a (#5) is where you raise the (5) by ½ step. The (5) is an (E), so the (#5) is an (F).

A Scale														
Note	A	B	Db	D	E	Gb	Ab	A	B	Db	D	E	Gb	Ab	A
Number	1	2	3	4	5	6	M7	8	9	10	11	12	13	M14	15

Numbering for Key of A

Using those tones we get the following chord, an A minor 7#5.

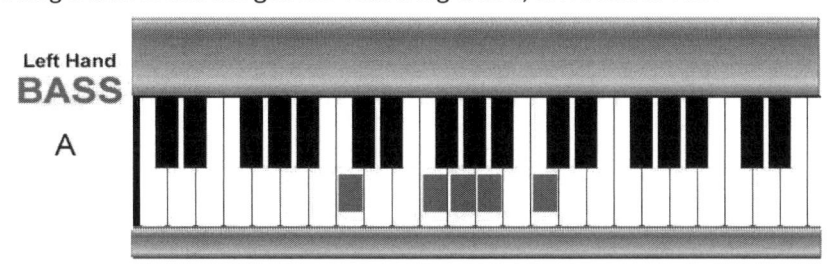

2) Harmonize the second note (2) of the song. (Chord 766)

The second note (2) in the song is an (F). This note (F) is tone number (I) in the key of (F). This melody note of (F) can be harmonized with any chord that has a (F) as the topmost melody note.

This would be any chord in Chapter on the (I) in the Adventures in Harmony Volume "Harmonizing on the Melody." The musician is free to pick any one of those chords to harmonize on the (F), all of these chords have a (F) on top as the melody note.

Chord 766 is a (IV) 6 add 9. The (IV) is telling us to make a chord based on tone (IV) of the key we are in. Tone (IV) in the key of (F) is a (Bb). Therefore this is going to be some kind of (Bb) chord, a chord based on the Bb scale.

Chord 766 tells us to use tones 1, -3, #5, 7, 8 and -10 to construct this chord.

We are going to use those tones in the key of (Bb) because this is a (IV) chord, remember (Bb) is the forth (IV) in the (F) scale. Tones 1, 6, 9 and 12 in the key of (Bb) are notes Bb, G, C, and F.

Bb Scale															
Note	Bb	C	D	Eb	F	G	A	Bb	C	D	Eb	F	G	A	Bb
Number	1	2	3	4	5	6	M7	8	9	10	11	12	13	M14	15

Numbering for Key of Bb

Using those tones we get the following chord, a Bb6 add 9.

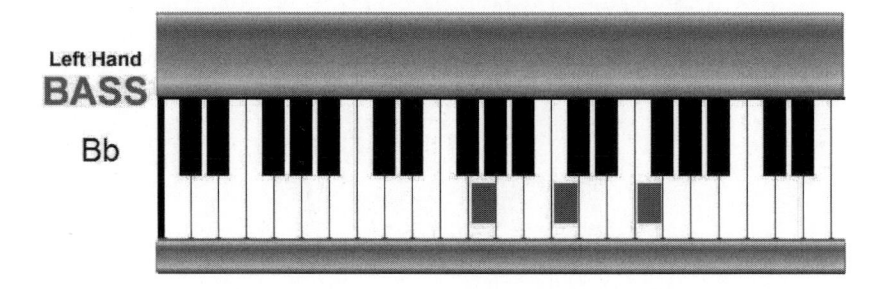

3) Harmonize the third note (3) of the song. (Chord 772)

The third note (3) in the song is an (F). This note (F) is tone number (I) in the key of (F). This melody note of (F) can be harmonized with any chord that has a (F) as the topmost melody note.

This would be any chord in Chapter on the (I) in the Adventures in Harmony Volume "Harmonizing on the Melody." The musician is free to pick any one of those chords to harmonize on the (F), all of these chords have a (F) on top as the melody note.

Chord 772 is a (VII) 9 add 6 (b5 added below for more color). The (VII) is telling us to make a chord based on tone (VII) of the key we are in. Tone (VII) in the key of (F) is an (Eb). Therefore this is going to be some kind of (Eb) chord, a chord based on the Eb scale.

Chord 772 tells us to use tones 1, b5, 3, 6, 7 and 9 to construct this chord.

We are going to use those tones in the key of (Eb) because this is a (VII) chord, remember (Eb) is the seventh (Maj VII) in the (F) scale. Tones 1, b5, 3, 6, 7 and 9 in the key of (Eb) are notes Eb, G, A, C, Db and F. Remember a (b5) is where you lower the (5) by ½ step. The (5) is a (Bb), so the (b5) is an (A).

						Eb Scale								
Note	Eb	F	G	Ab	Bb	C	D	Eb	F	G	Ab	Bb	C	D	Eb
Number	1	2	3	4	5	6	M7	8	9	10	11	12	13	M14	15

Numbering for Key of Eb

Using those tones we get the following chord, an Eb9b5 add 6.

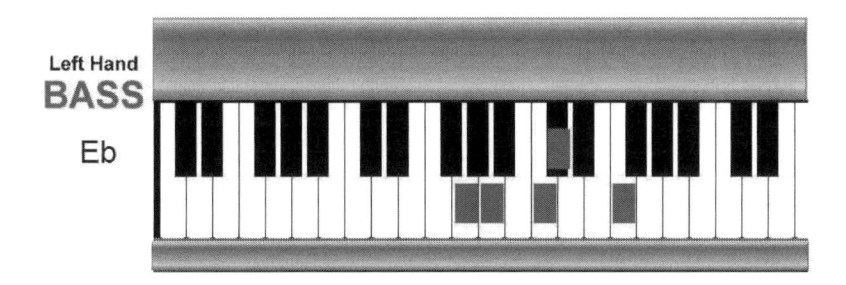

4) Harmonize the forth note (4) of the song. Chord (416)

The forth note (4) in the song is an (E). This note (E) is tone number (M7) in the key of (F). This melody note of (F) can be harmonized with any chord that has an (E) as the topmost melody note.

This would be any chord in Chapter on the (M7) in the Adventures in Harmony Volume "Harmonizing on the Melody." The musician is free to pick any one of those chords to harmonize on the (E), all of these chords have a (E) on top as the melody note.

Chord 416 is a (VI) 9 sus. The (VI) is telling us to make a chord based on tone (VI) of the key we are in. Tone (VI) in the key of (F) is a (D). Therefore this is going to be some kind of (D) chord, a chord based on the D scale.

Chord 416 tells us to use tones 1, 4, 5, 7, 8 and 9 to construct this chord.

We are going to use those tones in the key of (D) because this is a (VI) chord, remember (D) is the sixth (VI) in the (F) scale. Tones 1, 4, 5, 7, 8 and 9 in the key of (D) are notes D, G, A, C, D and E. Remember a (7) is where you lower the (M7) by ½ step. The (M7) is a (Db), so the (7) is a (C).

D Scale (Enharmonic)														
Note	D	E	Gb	G	A	B	Db	D	E	Gb	G	A	B	Db	D
Number	1	2	3	4	5	6	M7	8	9	10	11	12	13	M14	15

Numbering for Key of D

Using those tones we get the following chord, a D9sus.

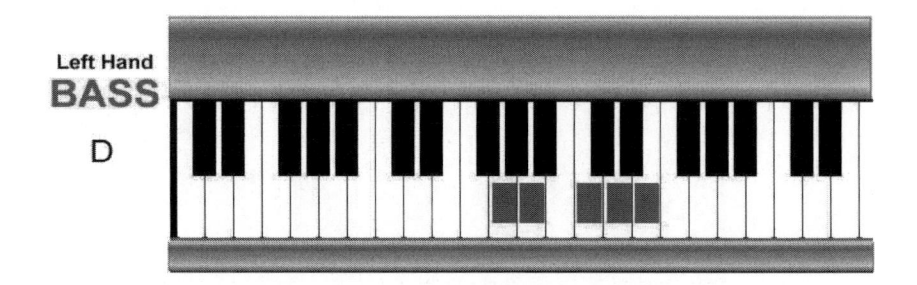

5) Harmonize the fifth note (5) of the song. Chord (772)

The fifth note (5) in the song is an (F). This note (F) is tone number (I) in the key of (F). This melody note of (F) can be harmonized with any chord that has an (F) as the topmost melody note.

This would be any chord in Chapter on the (I) in the Adventures in Harmony Volume "Harmonizing on the Melody." The musician is free to pick any one of those chords to harmonize on the (F), all of these chords have a (F) on top as the melody note.

Chord 772 is a (VII) 9 add 6 (b5 added for color). The (VII) is telling us to make a chord based on tone (VII) of the key we are in. Tone (VII) in the key of (F) is an (Eb). Therefore this is going to be some kind of (Eb) chord, a chord based on the Eb scale.

Chord 772 tells us to use tones 1, 3, b5, 6, 7 and 9 to construct this chord.

We are going to use those tones in the key of (Eb) because this is a (VII) chord, remember (Eb) is the seventh (Maj VII) in the (F) scale. Tones 1, 3, b5, 6, 7 and 9 in the key of (Eb) are notes Eb, G, A, C, Db and F. Remember a (b5) is where you lower the (5) by ½ step. The (5) is a (Bb), so the (b5) is an (A). Remember a (7) is where you lower the (M7) by ½ step. The (M7) is an (D), so the (7) is a (Db).

						Eb Scale								
Note	Eb	F	G	Ab	Bb	C	D	Eb	F	G	Ab	Bb	C	D	Eb
Number	1	2	3	4	5	6	M7	8	9	10	11	12	13	M14	15

Numbering for Key of Eb

Using those tones we get the following chord, an Eb9b5 add 6.

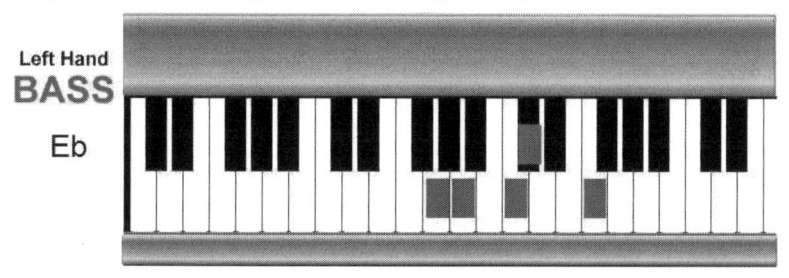

6) Harmonize the sixth note (6) of the song. (Chord 779)

The sixth note (6) in the song is an (A). This note (A) is tone number (III) in the key of (F). This melody note of (A) can be harmonized with any chord that has an (A) as the topmost melody note.

This would be any chord in Chapter on the (III) in the Adventures in Harmony Volume "Harmonizing on the Melody." The musician is free to pick any one of those chords to harmonize on the (A), all of these chords have a (A) on top as the melody note.

Chord 779 is a (Maj VII) m11. The (Maj VII) is telling us to make a chord based on tone (Maj VII) of the key we are in. Tone (Maj VII) in the key of (F) is an (E). Therefore this is going to be some kind of (E) chord, a chord based on the E scale.

Chord 779 tells us to use tones 1, -3, 5, 7, 9 and 11 to construct this chord.

We are going to use those tones in the key of (E) because this is a (Maj VII) chord, remember (E) is the Major seventh (Maj VII) in the (F) scale. Tones 1, -3, 5, 7, 9 and 11 in the key of (E) are notes E, G, B, D, Gb and A. Remember a (-3) is where you lower the (3) by ½ step. The (3) is an (Ab), so the (-3) is a (G). Remember a (7) is where you lower the (M7) by ½ step. The (M7) is an (Eb), so the (7) is a (D).

						E Scale (Enharmonic)							
Note	E	Gb	Ab	A	B	Db	Eb	E	Gb	Ab	A	B	Db	Eb	E
Number	1	2	3	4	5	6	M7	8	9	10	11	12	13	M14	15

Numbering for Key of E

Using those tones we get the following chord, an E – 11.

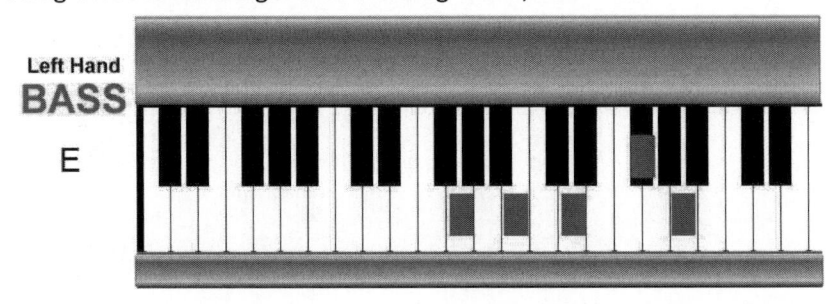

7) Harmonize the seventh note (7) of the song. (Chord 791)

The seventh note (7) in the song is an (A). This note (A) is tone number (3) in the key of (F). This melody note of (A) can be harmonized with any chord that has an (A) as the topmost melody note.

This would be any chord in Chapter on the (III) in the Adventures in Harmony Volume "Harmonizing on the Melody." The musician is free to pick any one of those chords to harmonize on the (A), all of these chords have a (A) on top as the melody note.

Chord 791 is a (III) 7 add 6. The (III) is telling us to make a chord based on tone (III) of the key we are in. Tone (III) in the key of (F) is an (A). Therefore this is going to be some kind of (A) chord, a chord based on the A scale.

Chord 791 tells us to use tones 1, 7, 3, 6 and 8 to construct this chord.

We are going to use those tones in the key of (A) because this is a (III) chord, remember (A) is the third (III) in the (F) scale. Tones 1, 7, 3, 6 and 8 in the key of (A) are notes A, G, Db, Gb, and A. Remember a (7) is where you lower the (M7) by ½ step. The (M7) is an (Ab), so the (7) is a (G).

A Scale (Enharmonic)														
Note	A	B	Db	D	E	Gb	Ab	A	B	Db	D	E	Gb	Ab	A
Number	1	2	3	4	5	6	M7	8	9	10	11	12	13	M14	15

Numbering for Key of A

Using those tones we get the following chord, an A7 add 6.

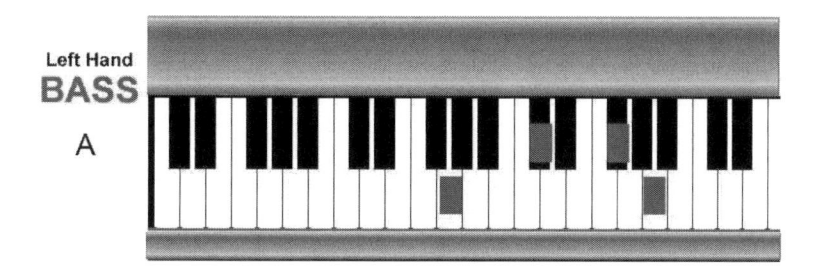

8) Harmonize the eighth note (8) of the song. (Chord 464)

The eighth note (8) in the song is a (G). This note (G) is tone number (2) in the key of (F). This melody note of (G) can be harmonized with any chord that has a (G) as the topmost melody note.

This would be any chord in Chapter on the (II) in the Adventures in Harmony Volume "Harmonizing on the Melody." The musician is free to pick any one of those chords to harmonize on the (G), all of these chords have a (G) on top as the melody note.

Chord 464 is a (VI) m11. The (VI) is telling us to make a chord based on tone (VI) of the key we are in. Tone (VI) in the key of (F) is a (D). Therefore this is going to be some kind of (D) chord, a chord based on the D scale.

Chord 464 tells us to use tones 1, 5, 7, 9, -3 and 11 to construct this chord.

We are going to use those tones in the key of (D) because this is a (VI) chord, remember (D) is the sixth (VI) in the (F) scale. Tones 1, 5, 7, 9, -3 and 11 in the key of (D) are notes D, A, C, E, F and G. Remember a (-3) is where you lower the (3) by ½ step. The (3) is a (Gb), so the (-3) is an (F). Remember a (7) is where you lower the (M7) by ½ step. The (M7) is a (Db), so the (7) is a (C).

D Scale (Enharmonic)														
Note	D	E	Gb	G	A	B	Db	D	E	Gb	G	A	B	Db	D
Number	1	2	3	4	5	6	M7	8	9	10	11	12	13	M14	15

Numbering for Key of D

Using those tones we get the following chord, a D minor 11.

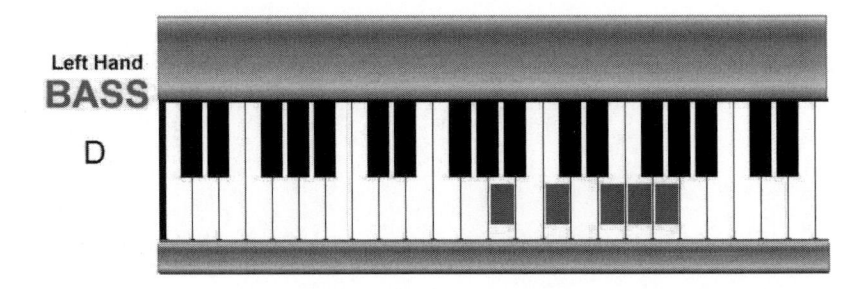

9) Harmonize the ninth note (9) of the song. (Chord 319)

The ninth note (9) in the song is a (C). This note (C) is tone number (5) in the key of (F). This melody note of (C) can be harmonized with any chord that has a (C) as the topmost melody note.

This would be any chord in Chapter on the (V) in the Adventures in Harmony Volume "Harmonizing on the Melody." The musician is free to pick any one of those chords to harmonize on the (C), all of these chords have a (C) on top as the melody note.

Chord 319 is a (IV) 13sus. The (IV) is telling us to make a chord based on tone (IV) of the key we are in. Tone (IV) in the key of (F) is a (Bb). Therefore this is going to be some kind of (Bb) chord, a chord based on the Bb scale.

Chord 319 tells us to use tones 1, 4, 6, 7 and 9 to construct this chord.

We are going to use those tones in the key of (Bb) because this is a (IV) chord, remember (Bb) is the forth (IV) in the (F) scale. Tones 1, 4, 6, 7 and 9 in the key of (Bb) are notes Bb, Eb, G, Ab, and C. Remember a (7) is where you lower the (M7) by ½ step. The (M7) is an (A), so the (7) is an (Ab).

	Bb Scale													
Note	Bb	C	D	Eb	F	G	A	Bb	C	D	Eb	F	G	A	Bb
Number	1	2	3	4	5	6	M7	8	9	10	11	12	13	M14	15

Numbering for Key of Bb

Using those tones we get the following chord, a Bb13sus.

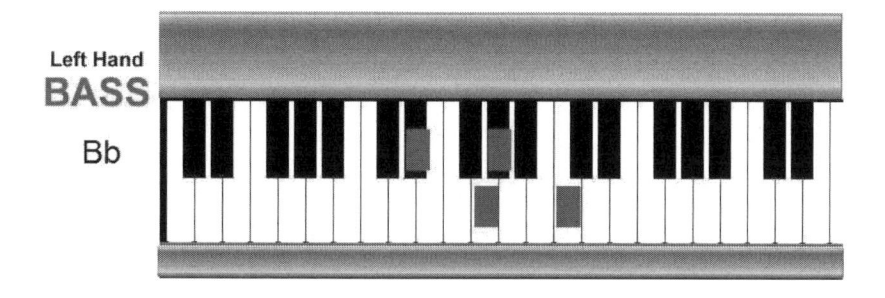

Adventures in Harmony – Introduction to the System

10) Harmonize the tenth note (10) of the song. (Chord 587).

The tenth note (10) in the song is a (C). This note (C) is tone number (5) in the key of (F). This melody note of (C) can be harmonized with any chord that has a (C) as the topmost melody note.

This would be any chord in Chapter on the (V) in the Adventures in Harmony Volume "Harmonizing on the Melody." The musician is free to pick any one of those chords to harmonize on the (C), all of these chords have a (C) on top as the melody note.

Chord 587 is a (Maj VII) m7#5. The (Maj VII) is telling us to make a chord based on tone (Maj VII) of the key we are in. Tone (Maj VII) in the key of (F) is an (E). Therefore this is going to be some kind of (E) chord, a chord based on the E scale.

Chord 587 tells us to use tones 1, 7, 3 and #5 to construct this chord.

We are going to use those tones in the key of (E) because this is a (Maj VII) chord, remember (E) is the Major seventh (Maj VII) in the (F) scale. Tones 1, 7, -3 and #5 in the key of (E) are notes E, D, G, and C. Remember a (#5) is where you raise the (5) by ½ step. The (5) is a (B), so the (#5) is a (C). Remember a (7) is where you lower the (M7) by ½ step. The (M7) is an (Eb), so the (7) is an (E).

E Scale (Enharmonic)														
Note	E	Gb	Ab	A	B	Db	Eb	E	Gb	Ab	A	B	Db	Eb	E
Number	1	2	3	4	5	6	M7	8	9	10	11	12	13	M14	15

Numbering for Key of E

Using those tones we get the following chord, an Em7#5.

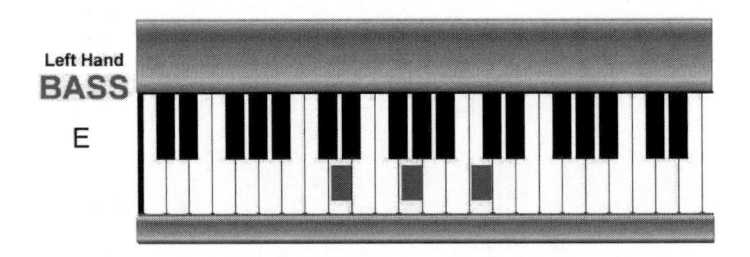

11) Harmonize the eleventh note (11) of the song. (Chord 458)

The eleventh note (11) in the song is a (C). This note (C) is tone number (5) in the key of (F). This melody note of (C) can be harmonized with any chord that has a (C) as the topmost melody note.

This would be any chord in Chapter on the (V) in the Adventures in Harmony Volume "Harmonizing on the Melody." The musician is free to pick any one of those chords to harmonize on the (C), all of these chords have a (C) on top as the melody note.

Chord 458 is a (VI) minor 9. The (VI) is telling us to make a chord based on tone (VI) of the key we are in. Tone (VI) in the key of (F) is an (D). Therefore this is going to be some kind of (D) chord, a chord based on the D scale.

Chord 458 tells us to use tones 1, 5, 9, -3 and 7 to construct this chord.

We are going to use those tones in the key of (D) because this is a (VI) chord, remember (D) is the sixth (VI) in the (F) scale. Tones 1, 5, 9, -3 and 7 in the key of (D) are notes D, A, E, F, and C. Remember a (-3) is where you lower the (3) by ½ step. The (3) is a (Gb), so the (-3) is an (F). Remember a (7) is where you lower the (M7) by ½ step. The (M7) is a (Db), so the (7) is a (C).

D Scale (Enharmonic)														
Note	D	E	Gb	G	A	B	Db	D	E	Gb	G	A	B	Db	D
Number	1	2	3	4	5	6	M7	8	9	10	11	12	13	M14	15

Numbering for Key of D

Using those tones we get the following chord, a Dm9.

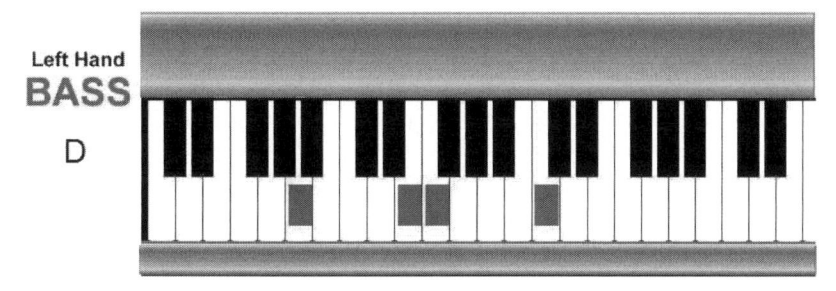

Left Hand
BASS
D

12) Harmonize the twelfth note (12) of the song. (Chord 591)

The twelfth note (12) in the song is a (Bb). This note (Bb) is tone number (4) in the key of (F). This melody note of (Bb) can be harmonized with any chord that has a (Bb) as the topmost melody note.

This would be any chord in Chapter on the (IV) in the Adventures in Harmony Volume "Harmonizing on the Melody." The musician is free to pick any one of those chords to harmonize on the (Bb), all of these chords have a (Bb) on top as the melody note.

Chord 591 is a (Maj VII) minor 7b5. The (Maj VII) is telling us to make a chord based on tone (Maj VII) of the key we are in. Tone (Maj VII) in the key of (F) is an (E). Therefore this is going to be some kind of (E) chord, a chord based on the E scale.

Chord 591 tells us to use tones 1, -3, 7 and b5 to construct this chord.

We are going to use those tones in the key of (E) because this is a (Maj VII) chord, remember (E) is the Major seventh (Maj VII) in the (F) scale. Tones 1, -3, 7 and b5 in the key of (E) are notes E, G, D, and Bb. Remember a (-3) is where you lower the (3) by ½ step. The (3) is an (Ab), so the (-3) is a (G). Remember a (b5) is where you lower the (5) by ½ step. The (5) is a (B), so the (b5) is a (Bb).

E Scale (Enharmonic)															
Note	E	Gb	Ab	A	B	Db	Eb	E	Gb	Ab	A	B	Db	Eb	E
Number	1	2	3	4	5	6	7	8	9	10	11	12	13	14	15

Numbering for Key of E

Using those tones we get the following chord, an E-7b5.

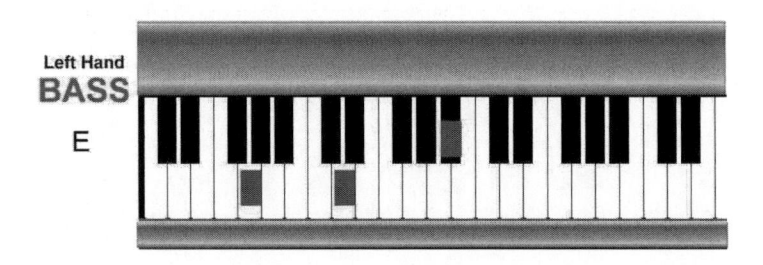

13) Harmonize the thirteenth note (13) of the song. (Chord 713)

The thirteenth note (13) in the song is an (A). This note (A) is tone number (3) in the key of (F). This melody note of (A) can be harmonized with any chord that has an (A) as the topmost melody note.

This would be any chord in Chapter on the (III) in the Adventures in Harmony Volume "Harmonizing on the Melody." The musician is free to pick any one of those chords to harmonize on the (A), all of these chords have a (A) on top as the melody note.

Chord 713 is a (Maj VII) -7 add 11. The (Maj VII)) is telling us to make a chord based on tone (Maj VII)) of the key we are in. Tone (Maj VII)) in the key of (F) is an (E). Therefore this is going to be some kind of (E) chord, a chord based on the E scale.

Chord 713 tells us to use tones 1, -3, 5, 7 and 11 to construct this chord.

We are going to use those tones in the key of (E) because this is a (Maj VII) chord, remember (E) is the Major seventh (Maj VII) in the (F) scale. Tones 1, -3, 5, 7 and 11 in the key of (E) are notes E, G, B, D, and A. Remember a (-3) is where you lower the (3) by ½ step. The (3) is an (Ab), so the (-3) is a (G). Remember a (7) is where you lower the (M7) by ½ step. The (M7) is an (Eb), so the (7) is a (D).

E Scale (Enharmonic)															
Note	E	Gb	Ab	A	B	Db	Eb	E	Gb	Ab	A	B	Db	Eb	E
Number	1	2	3	4	5	6	M7	8	9	10	11	12	13	M14	15

Numbering for Key of E

Using those tones we get the following chord, an E-7 add 11.

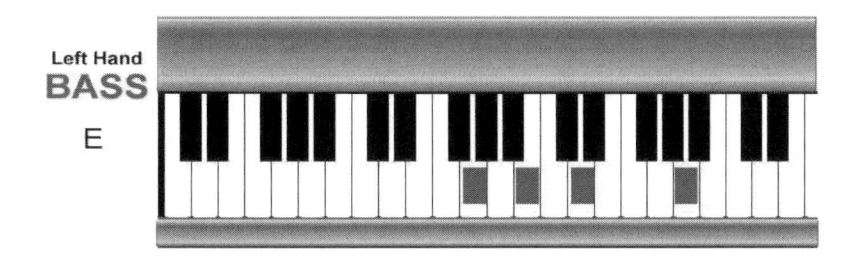

14) Harmonize the fourteenth note (14) of the song. (Chord 804)

The fourteenth note (14) in the song is a (G). This note (G) is tone number (II) in the key of (F). This melody note of (G) can be harmonized with any chord that has a (G) as the topmost melody note.

This would be any chord in Chapter on the (II) in the Adventures in Harmony Volume "Harmonizing on the Melody." The musician is free to pick any one of those chords to harmonize on the (G), all of these chords have a (G) on top as the melody note.

Chord 804 is a (#V) 6,9b5. The (#V) is telling us to make a chord based on tone (#V) of the key we are in. Tone (#V) in the key of (F) is a (Db). Therefore this is going to be some kind of (Db) chord, a chord based on the Db scale.

Chord 804 tells us to use tones 1, 3, 6, 9 and b5 to construct this chord.

We are going to use those tones in the key of (Db) because this is a (#V) chord, remember (Db) is the sharp fifth (#V) in the (F) scale. Tones 1, 3, 6, 9 and b5 in the key of (Db) are notes Db, F, Bb, Db and G. Remember a (b5) is where you lower the (5) by ½ step. The (5) is an (Ab), so the (b5) is a (G).

Db Scale															
Note	Db	Eb	F	Gb	Ab	Bb	C	Db	Eb	F	Gb	Ab	Bb	C	Db
Number	1	2	3	4	5	6	M7	8	9	10	11	12	13	M14	15

Numbering for Key of Db

Using those tones we get the following chord, a Db6,9b5.

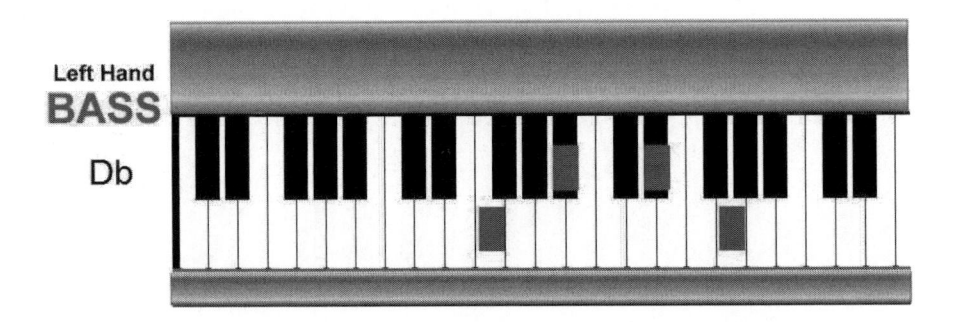

Left Hand
BASS
Db

15) Harmonize the fifteenth note (15) of the song. (Chord 473)

The fifteenth note (15) in the song is an (A). This note (A) is tone number (3) in the key of (F). This melody note of (A) can be harmonized with any chord that has an (A) as the topmost melody note.

This would be any chord in Chapter on the (III) in the Adventures in Harmony Volume "Harmonizing on the Melody." The musician is free to pick any one of those chords to harmonize on the (A), all of these chords have a (A) on top as the melody note.

Chord 473 is a (VII) dim 6,9. The (VII) is telling us to make a chord based on tone (VII) of the key we are in. Tone (VII) in the key of (F) is an (Eb). Therefore this is going to be some kind of (Eb) chord, a chord based on the Eb scale.

Chord 473 tells us to use tones 1, -3, 6, 9 and b5 to construct this chord.

We are going to use those tones in the key of (Eb) because this is a (VII) chord, remember (Eb) is the seventh (VII) in the (F) scale. Tones 1, -3, 6, 9 and b5 in the key of (Eb) are notes Eb, Gb, C, F, and A. Remember a (-3) is where you lower the (3) by ½ step. The (3) is a (G), so the (-3) is a (Gb). Remember a (b5) is where you lower the (5) by ½ step. The (5) is a (Bb), so the (b5) is an (A).

		Eb Scale												
Note	Eb	F	G	Ab	Bb	C	D	Eb	F	G	Ab	Bb	C	D	Eb
Number	1	2	3	4	5	6	M7	8	9	10	11	12	13	M14	15

Numbering for Key of Eb

Using those tones we get the following chord, an Eb dim 6,9.

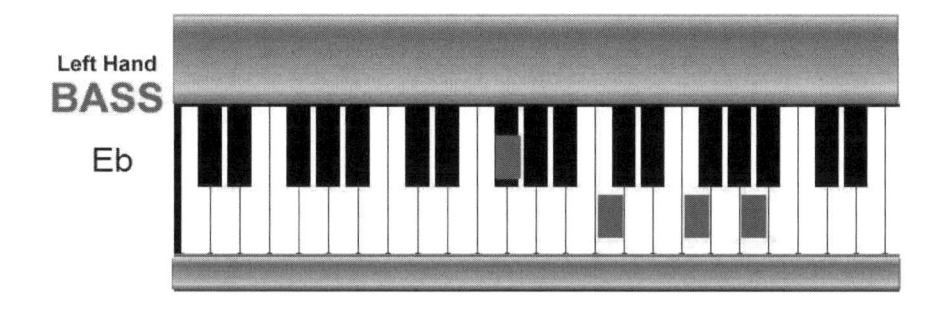

Adventures in Harmony – Introduction to the System

16) Harmonize the fifteenth note (15) of the song. (Chord 779)

We are playing a second chord on this fifteenth note. The fifteenth note (15) in the song is an (A). This note (A) is tone number (3) in the key of (F). This melody note of (A) can be harmonized with any chord that has an (A) as the topmost melody note.

This would be any chord in Chapter on the (III) in the Adventures in Harmony Volume "Harmonizing on the Melody." The musician is free to pick any one of those chords to harmonize on the (A), all of these chords have a (A) on top as the melody note.

Chord 779 is a (Maj VII) minor 11. The (Maj VII) is telling us to make a chord based on tone (Maj VII) of the key we are in. Tone (Maj VII) in the key of (F) is an (E). Therefore this is going to be some kind of (E) chord, a chord based on the E scale.

Chord 779 tells us to use tones 1, -3, 5, 7, 9 and 11 to construct this chord.

We are going to use those tones in the key of (E) because this is a (Maj VII) chord, remember (E) is the Major seventh (Maj VII) in the (F) scale. Tones 1, -3, 5, 7, 9 and 11 in the key of (E) are notes E, G, B, D, Gb and A. Remember a (-3) is where you lower the (3) by ½ step. The (3) is an (Ab), so the (-3) is a (G). Remember a (7) is where you lower the (M7) by ½ step. The (M7) is an (Eb), so the (7) is a (D).

E Scale (Enharmonic)														
Note	E	Gb	Ab	A	B	Db	Eb	E	Gb	Ab	A	B	Db	Eb	E
Number	1	2	3	4	5	6	M7	8	9	10	11	12	13	M14	15

Numbering for Key of E

Using those tones we get the following chord, an E-11.

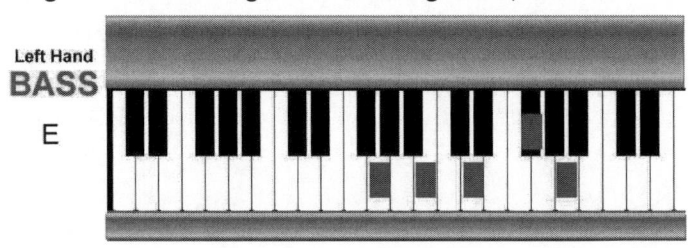

Left Hand
BASS
E

11 Approach to Course

There are many chord voicing reference volumes for this course. You may choose from any one of the available reference volumes to perform your harmonization.

What is important is that you have a good selection to choose from for each one of the tones. You should learn at least three or four voicing's for each tone. Therefore if you learned four voicing's per day, at the end a week on the eighth day, you will have learned enough voicing's to harmonize almost any song instantly. As you become more and more comfortable, you can go back and learn additional voicing's for each tone and build your personal library at your own pace.

You will notice that for each tone, each chord may have more than one voicing just pick one of them, then go to another tone and pick one of those voicings.

For the first pass, we suggest that you pick at least one major chord and one minor chord for each tone.

In picking out the voicings for each tone, we suggest that you actually play and listen to each one and pick the ones that you like.

These chords and voicing can then become part of your "signature and style" and will surely set you apart you from everybody else.

At the end of the week, if you did the mental Roman number analysis on a song or you say a progression such as I, Maj VII, III, VI, II, you should be able to play that immediately with many variations!

12 The Secrets to the Numbers

At this point you may be asking yourself, "How are you going to learn all the notes for all of the numbers of all of the scales?" You may be thinking it will take you forever to answer such questions as "What is the 9th of (Ab)", "What is the 11th of (D)?" or "What is the 8th of (Eb)?"

We are going to show you some tricks that will allow you to answer most of these questions in less than one second, even if you do not know your scales!!!

12.1 The 1 (I)

There should be no absolutely no discussion here. To figure out the (1) of any key, is the name of the key itself. The (1) of (Ab) is (Ab). The (1) of (E) is (E). Also, the (1) is the same as the (8), which is also the same as the (15). Therefore, the (8th) of (C) is (C), the (15th) of (F) is (F). We can draw a table and see all the numbers that are equivalent, by just looking at any column. All the numbers in any column are equivalent (Table 12-1).

Note Number						
1	2	3	4	5	6	7
8	9	10	11	12	13	14
15	16	17	18	19	20	21

Table 12-1

Or, if you have any number greater than seven, just keep subtracting seven from it until the number is less than seven. For example, the (21) is the same as the (7), because 21 – 7 = 14 and 14 is still greater than (7), so subtract another (7). 14 – 7 = (7), and since we can't subtract anymore, we see know that the (21) has been reduced down to a (7), therefore the (21) is the same as the (7).

Now, if you need to play the (1) or the (8) of any key, you should be able to put your hand on it immediately!

12.2 The 2 (II)

To figure out what the (2) is of any scale, all you need to do is play the note that is one whole step above the scale you are trying to find the (2) of. So if you are sitting at the keyboard, and you need to play the (2) of (C), all you are doing is playing the note that is right next to (C), or one whole step above (C), which would be the (D). So if you are sitting at the keyboard, and you need to play the (2) of (A), all you do is play the note that is right next to (A), or one whole step above (A), which would be the (B). Figure 12-1 shows the 9ths of (C), (Gb) and (A). Remember the 9th and the 2nd refer to the same note (Table 12-1).

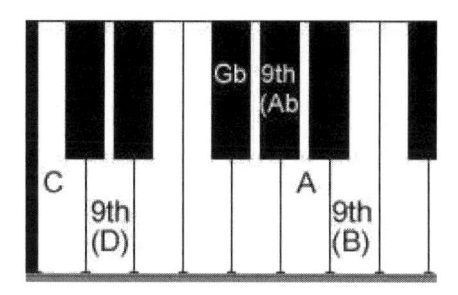

Adventures in Harmony – Introduction to the System

Figure 12-1

Now, if you need to play the (2) or the (9th) of any key, you should be able to put your hand on it immediately!

12.3 The 4 and 5 (IV and V)

12.3.1 The Circle of Fifths and Fourths

You may have heard of the circle of fifths and fourths in the past, if not, that's ok. But we need you to memorize the ordering of the letters around the circle both clockwise and counterclockwise. You may have seen the circle written like this:

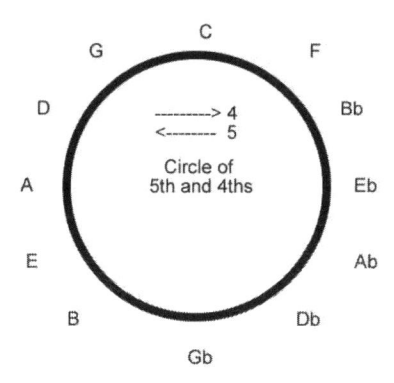

Well forget about looking at the circle of fifths and forth's like that, because we are going to tell you how to memorize it in less than 30 seconds! Look at it like this.

Bb Eb Ab Db   Gb
B E A D   G C F

Adventures in Harmony – Introduction to the System

Look at it as two rows of notes.

The first row of notes spells out the word "BEAD" followed by the letter "G."

The second row of notes spells out the word "BEAD" followed by the letters "G C F."

And remember the first rows of notes are flats when spelling out the word "BEADG," and the second row are not.

We all know how to spell the word "BEAD."

Essentially all you are memorizing is the word "BEAD" followed by G and then "BEAD" followed by GCF, and that the first "BEAD G", are all flats.

So now if you were asked what note is after (Eb) you can immediately say (Ab), because we know how to spell "BEAD" and A is after E in the word "BEAD," you just have to remember to say "flat." If you are asked what note is after (B) you can immediately say (E). The only tricky part is that you have to remember that after (F) you go back to (Bb), and that after (Gb) you go to (B).

You can now say or play the 4th or 5th in any key in less than 1 second!

Do you realize that you have just learned the 4ths and 5ths of every scale? If you read the sequence of letters that you just learned right to left "Bb Eb Ab Db Gb, B E A D G C F", you are going in fourths, if you read it left to right, which is backwards, you are going in fifths.

Example:

What letter is after (Bb)? The answer is (Eb). (Eb) is the 4th of (Bb), (Eb) is the 4th note in the Bb scale

What letter is after (E)? The answer is (A). (A) is the 4th of (E), (A) is the 4th note in the E scale

You now know the 4th of every scale just by moving one letter to the right, in the sequence you just learned. You also know the 5th of every scale just by moving one letter to the left in the sequence you just learned.

The 5th of (E) is (B), because (B) comes before the letter (E) in the word "BEAD."

The 4th of (A) is (D), because (D) comes after the letter (A) in the word "BEAD."

The 4th of (Bb) is (Eb), because (Eb) comes after the letter (Bb) in the word "Bb Eb Ab Db (BEAD)."

Remember the 4th and the 11th are the same, just as the 5th and the 12th are the same.

12.4 The 7 (VII)

To figure out what the (7th) is of any scale, all you need to do is play the note that is one whole step below the scale you are trying to find the (7th) of. So if you are sitting at they keyboard, and you need to play the (7th) of (C), simply play the note that is one whole step right below (C), which would be the (Bb). If you need to play the (7th) of (G), simply play the note that is one whole step below (G), which would be the (F). Figure 12-2 shows the 7ths of (Eb), (G) and (C).

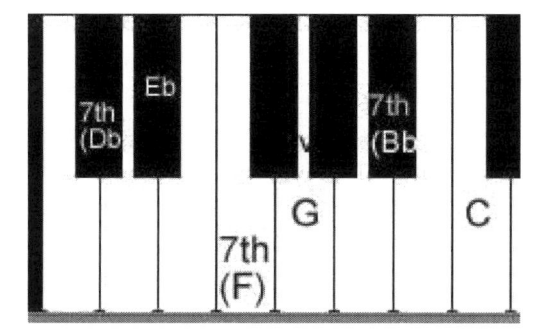

Figure 12-2

Now, if you need to play the (7th) of any key, you should be able to put your hand on it immediately! Remember the 7th is the same as the 14th.

12.5 The Major 7 (VII)

To figure out what the (Maj7th) is of any scale, all you need to do is play the note that is ½ step below the scale you are trying to find the (Maj7th) of. So if you are sitting at the keyboard, and you need to play the (Maj7th) of (C), all you are doing is playing the note that is ½ step below (C), which would be the (B). If you need to play the (Maj7th) of (G), simply play the note that is ½ step below (G), which would be the (Gb). Figure 12-3 shows the Maj7ths of (C) and (G).

Adventures in Harmony – Introduction to the System

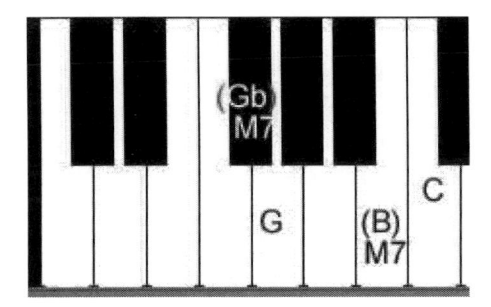

Figure 12-3

Now, if you need to play the (Maj7th) of any key, you should be able to put your hand on it immediately! Remember the Maj 7th is the same as the Maj 14th.

12.6 The 3 (III)

To figure out what the (III) is of any key, simply figure out the 4th, which you already know how to do immediately, and play the note that is ½ step below the 4th. For example, the (III) of (E) is (Ab), because we already know the (4) of (E) is (A) from the word "BEAD", (A) comes after (E), so ½ step below the (A) is (Ab). Remember the (3) is the same as the (10). Another way to figure out what the (III) is the (III) is always 2 whole steps above the (I). The (III) of (Ab) is (C), since (C) is 2 whole steps above (Ab).

12.7 The 6 (VI)

To figure out what the (6) is of any key, simply figure out the 5th, which you already know how to do immediately, and play the note that is one whole step above the 5th. For example, the (6) of (E) is (Db), because we already know the (5) of (E) is (B) from the word "BEAD", (B) comes before (E), so one whole step above the (B) is (Db). Remember the (6) is the same as the (13).

Now that you know the Adventures in Harmony Play by Number System and the shortcuts to finding the notes in the number system, you are ready to explore the other core references Volumes.

These volumes contain all of the Advanced Voicings. The Adventures in Harmony Play by Number System is used to describe all the chords in these volumes.

13 Interval Sizing

Each one of the tones of the major scale has a distance or size associated with it. That name of the tone indicates the physical distance that the tone is from the root.

For example if we consider the 5th of (C). This is the 5th note in the key of (C) which would be the (G). The name "5th" also refers to the distance that the note is from the root of the scale. Remember the root of the scale is the [I]. So the distance between the (C) and the (G) is a fifth.

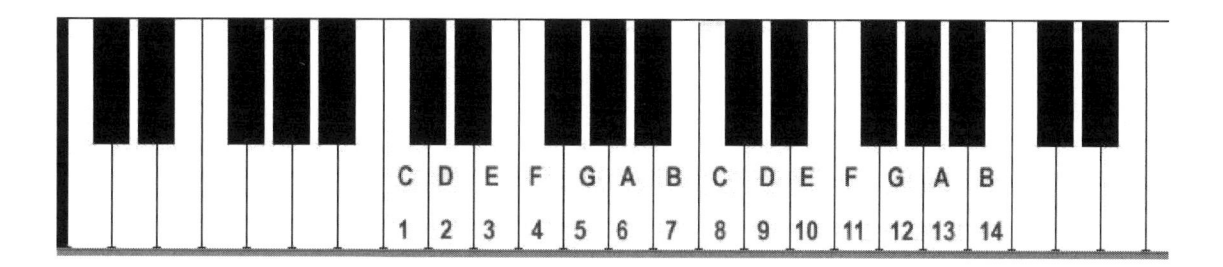

And just how big is a fifth, a fifth is 3 ½ whole steps. So anywhere on the keyboard where the first note and the second note are separated by 3 ½ whole steps, you have a fifth.

Just as an example, the following pairs of notes are fifths

(C) and (G), (D) and (A), (F) and (C), (Gb) and (Db).

This means that the second note is the 5th note in the scale that's indicated by the first note.

As we indicated, each tone of the scale has a distance associated with it and here are the distances associated with each tone:

Tone	Distance
1st	0 Steps
2nd	1 Step
3rd	2 Steps
4th	2.5 Steps
5th	3.5 Steps
6th	4.5 Steps
Maj7th	5.5 Steps
8th	6 Steps

Adventures in Harmony – Introduction to the System

There is a real easy way to memorize how big each one of intervals for 4 through 7. Simply subtract 2 from the tone number and say ½. For example if you wanted to know how big a 5th is, simply subtract 2, 5 – 2 is 3 and then say the word "1/2." So the interval of a 5th is 3 ½ steps. How big is a 6th, 6 - 2 is 4 and the say the word "1/2", so an sixth is 4 ½ steps. Knowing this trick is very handy in doing visual analysis of chords or even creating chords in the number system. For example, if you had to play the 4th of (D) you would know that it's simply 2 ½ steps up from (D).

Adventures in Harmony – Introduction to the System

14 The Duality of Chords

This is going to be one of the most important concepts that you are going to learn in this course. Every chord that you play from now on has two purposes. The first purpose you're already familiar with, and that is to harmonize a particular tone of the scale.

The second purpose is to suspend the melody of some tone of the scale. What is meant by this is that the chord that you are playing can always be used to harmonize its suspension in the melody.

The suspension is defined as the topmost note of any chord. For example, look at the following chord that you have seen earlier. We used this chord to harmonize on the (III) in the key of Db when we looked at "Joy to the World."

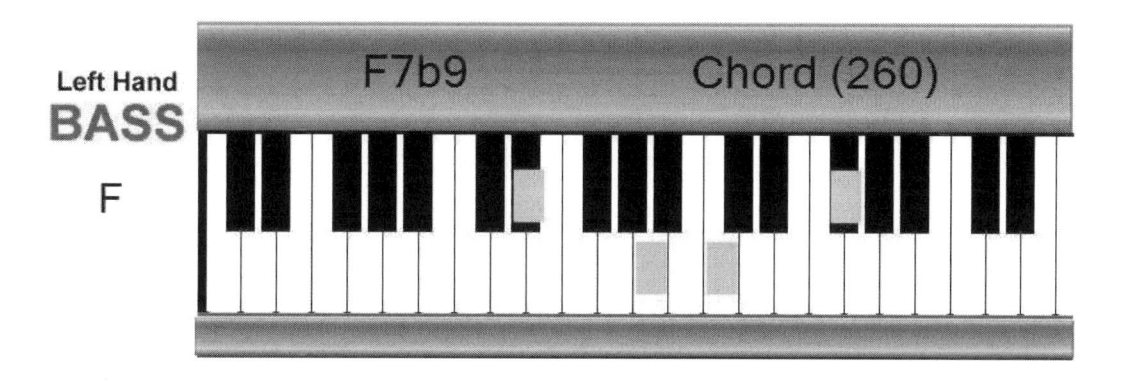

Left Hand BASS F — F7b9 Chord (260)

The suspension in this chord is the (Gb), because the (Gb) is the topmost note in the chord. Therefore other function of this chord is to harmonize a song anytime there is a (Gb) in the melody while we are in the key of (Db)!

So now at this point you have a new option available to you, whenever you look at ANY piece of music in the key of (Db) and there is a (Gb) in the melody, this is a possible chord that you can play.

All you really need now is seven of these chords where each one has a different suspension.

So in the key of (Db) all you need is a chord that has a (Db), (Eb), (F), (Gb), (Ab), (Bb), and (C) as a suspension, once you know a chord that has each one of those suspensions, you will be able to look at ANY piece of music and only look at the melody note and have a contemporary voicing to play.

Adventures in Harmony – Introduction to the System

I'm going to say this again because this concept is so important. Once you know seven more of these chords, each one with a different suspension corresponding to a tone in the major scale, you will be able to take a single one note melody and play full chords immediately for that melody! And if you are reading a piece of music, you only have to look at the melody note because you will have a chord for every suspension!

The only issue that may arise in using this technique is that the particular chord and its suspension that you are playing may not be the sound that you are looking for. Therefore this technique becomes really powerful when you have more than one chord available for each suspension. As you go through this course and learn more chords, you will find that you will have many options available to you. If you want to explore this in detail and have all the suspensions and chords available to you in a reference, then you need to look at Volume III in our course "Adventures in Harmony – Harmonization on the Melody"

So from now on whenever you look at any chord, make a mental note of the suspension.

Please sit down and take a moment and think about what I just told you in this section. This concept is really a lot bigger than you think. If you took this concept a step further and had 12 chords instead of 7, this means you knowing a chord with a suspension for every single tone; this means that you can play any song that is written in any key immediately with full chords.

Let me take a moment to make an even more powerful statement that I just want you to think about for the rest of this course as you go through and play the chords. I am not going to explain this statement, but as you go through the course and get more experience with the system, you are going to realize that for a keyboard player, the key signature means absolutely nothing with regard to chords and harmonization.

This further implies that there is never a need to transpose a song to a new key. **Simply play the chord that has the proper suspension in the melody!** You are going to see this as you learn more chords for each tone of the scale.

If someone asks you what key are you in, eventually you will be able to say with confidence, "I am in whatever key you think I am in" You can make this statement because you are not restricting your chords to any specific tones. If you don't understand this now, believe me you will later.

Adventures in Harmony – Introduction to the System

If you go back and look at "Joy to the World" you see that you already know quite a few chords for each suspension. Let's take a look at those chords and the suspensions on those chords.

Here are all the chords that you played that had a (Db), the [I] as the suspension. Therefore whenever you have a song in the key of (Db) and a (Db) is in the melody, you have the following chord choices to harmonize on that (Db) suspension:

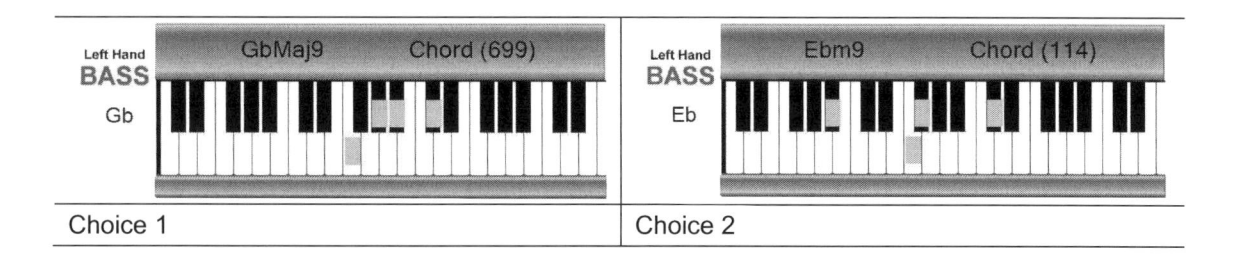

Left Hand BASS: Gb — GbMaj9 Chord (699)	Left Hand BASS: Eb — Ebm9 Chord (114)
Choice 1	Choice 2

Here are all the chords that you played that had a (Eb), the [II] as the suspension. Therefore whenever you have a song in the key of (Db) and an (Eb) is in the melody, you have the following chord choices to harmonize on that (Eb) suspension:

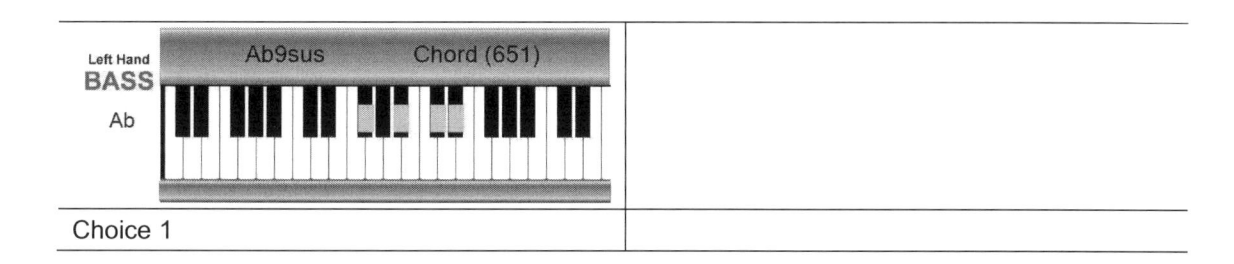

Left Hand BASS: Ab — Ab9sus Chord (651)	
Choice 1	

Here are all the chords that you played that had an (F), the [III] as the suspension. Therefore whenever you have a song in the key of (Db) and an (F) is in the melody, you have the following chord choices to harmonize on that (F) suspension:

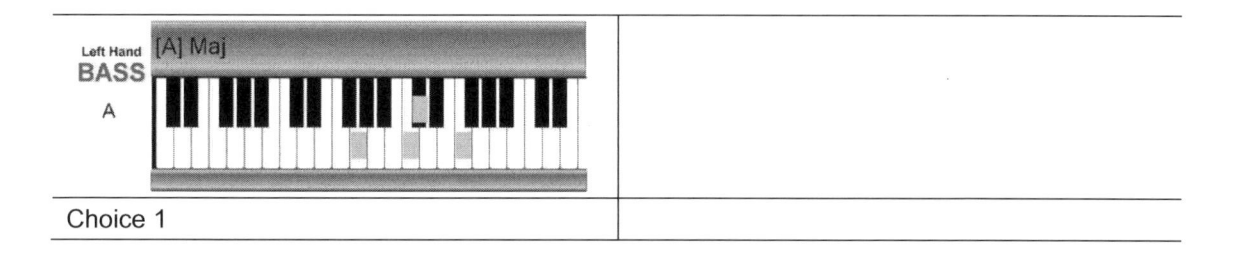

Left Hand BASS: A — [A] Maj	
Choice 1	

Adventures in Harmony – Introduction to the System

Here are all the chords that you played that had a (Gb), the [IV] as the suspension. Therefore whenever you have a song in the key of (Db) and a (Gb) is in the melody, you have the following chord choices to harmonize on that (Gb) suspension:

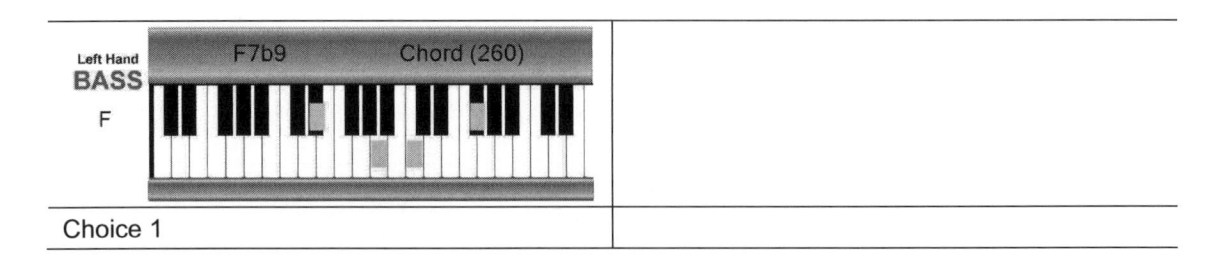

Left Hand BASS: F — F7b9 — Chord (260)
Choice 1

Here are all the chords that you played that had an (Ab), the [V] as the suspension. Therefore whenever you have a song in the key of (Db) and an (Ab) is in the melody, you have the following chord choices to harmonize on that (Ab) suspension:

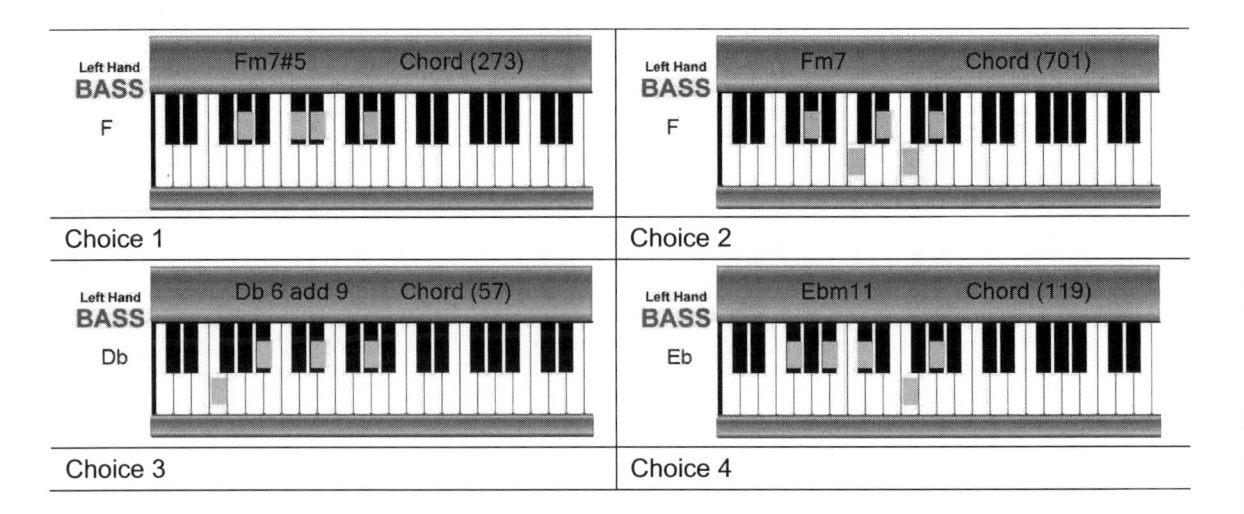

Left Hand BASS: F — Fm7#5 — Chord (273)
Choice 1

Left Hand BASS: F — Fm7 — Chord (701)
Choice 2

Left Hand BASS: Db — Db 6 add 9 — Chord (57)
Choice 3

Left Hand BASS: Eb — Ebm11 — Chord (119)
Choice 4

Here are all the chords that you played that had a (Bb), the [VI] as the suspension. Therefore whenever you have a song in the key of (Db) and a (Bb) is in the melody, you have the following chord choices to harmonize on that (Bb) suspension:

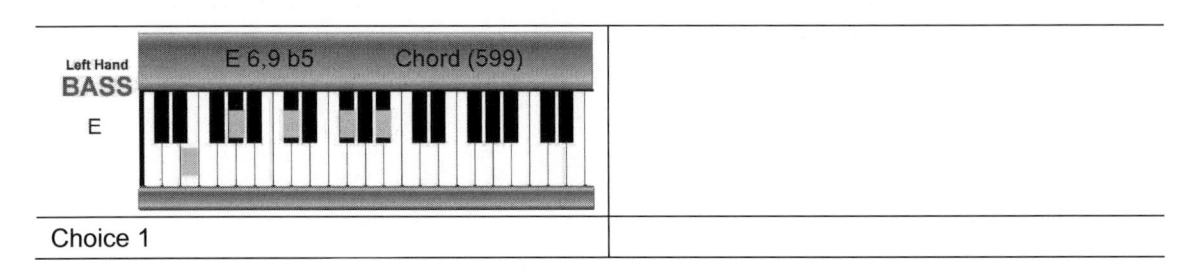

Left Hand BASS: E — E 6,9 b5 — Chord (599)
Choice 1

Adventures in Harmony – Introduction to the System

Here are all the chords that you played that had a (Db), the [Maj VII] as the suspension. Therefore whenever you have a song in the key of (Db) and a (C) is in the melody, you have the following chord choices to harmonize on that (C) suspension:

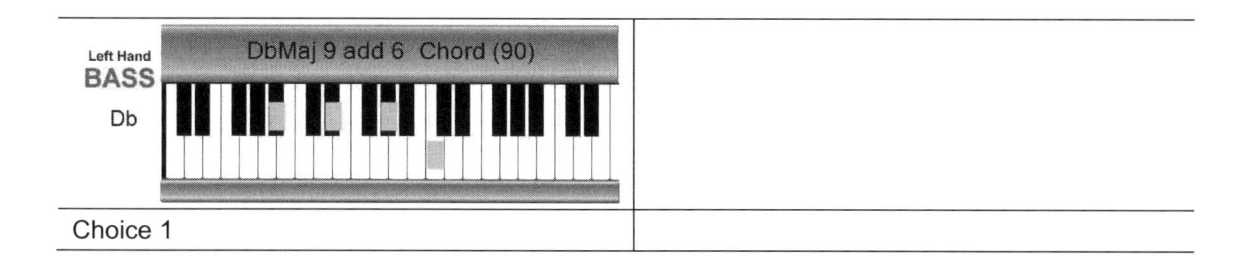

DbMaj 9 add 6 Chord (90) — Left Hand BASS Db	
Choice 1	

As you learn more chords, you will have more choices to harmonize on the melody suspension notes. Now let's take a look at how important this concept is in an actual song in case you still don't see it. Let's look at that song from the Wizard of Oz, "Over the Rainbow" and let's look at the first phrase in that song which is "Somewhere over the rainbow."

14.1 Duality of Chords – "Over the Rainbow"

In number notation, the first phrase of this song is as follows:

1	8	7	5	6	7	8
Some	Where	Ov-	-ver	the	rain	bow
Db	**Db**	**C**	**Ab**	**Bb**	**C**	**Db**

From the few chords that we now know, we can now harmonize this phrase "Somewhere over the rainbow", by simply looking at the melody note above and playing the chord that we know that has that note as the suspension.

Below is the harmonization for the first phrase of "Over the Rainbow" using suspensions that you already are have used earlier in the course.

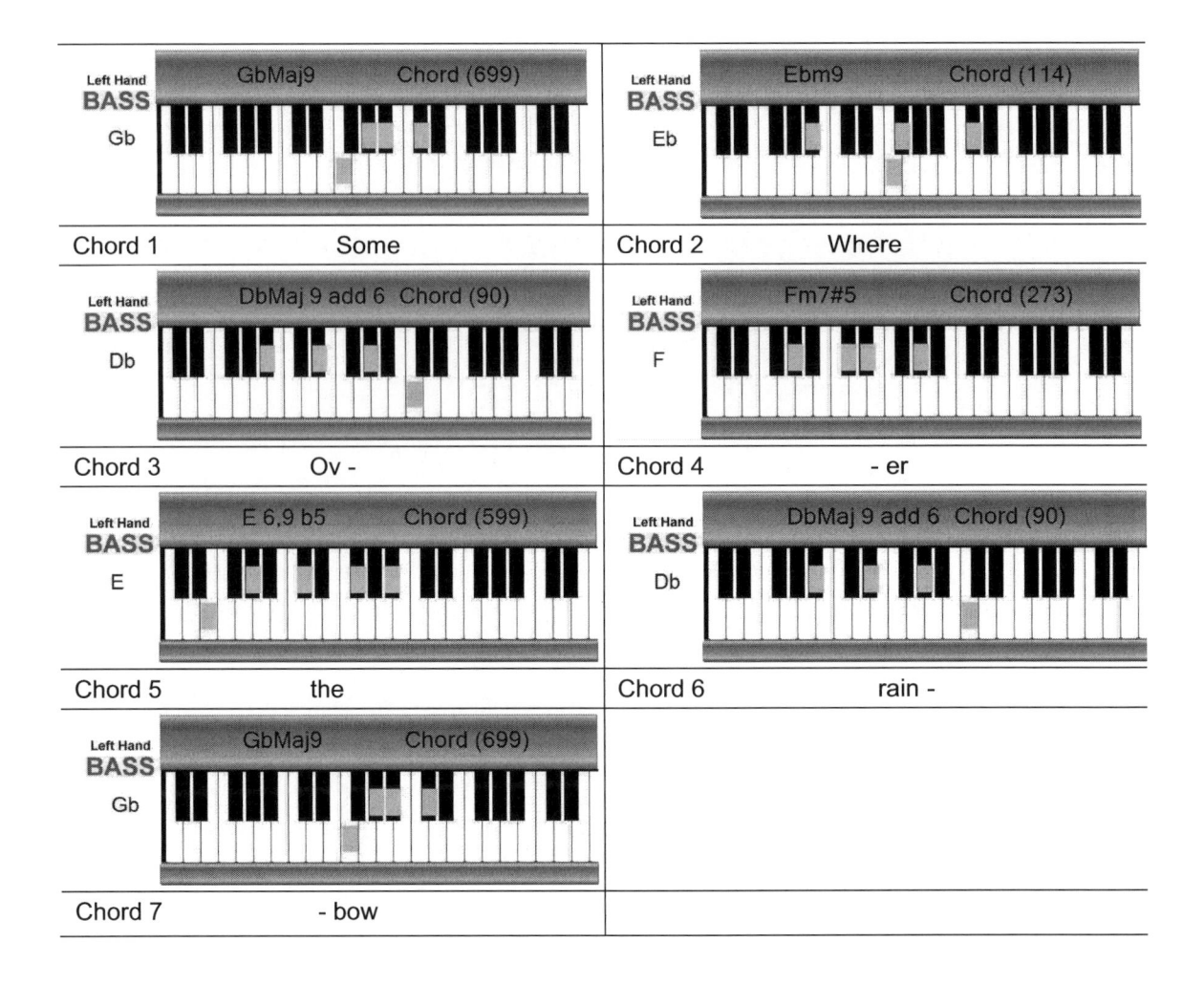

Adventures in Harmony – Introduction to the System

Left Hand BASS Gb	GbMaj9 Chord (699)	Left Hand BASS Eb	Ebm9 Chord (114)
Chord 1	Some	Chord 2	Where
Left Hand BASS Db	DbMaj 9 add 6 Chord (90)	Left Hand BASS F	Fm7#5 Chord (273)
Chord 3	Ov -	Chord 4	- er
Left Hand BASS E	E 6,9 b5 Chord (599)	Left Hand BASS Db	DbMaj 9 add 6 Chord (90)
Chord 5	the	Chord 6	rain -
Left Hand BASS Gb	GbMaj9 Chord (699)		
Chord 7	- bow		

See how simple it was for us to get that full blown harmonization from simply looking at the single melody note!!!! This example only used 4 tones of the (Db) scale as suspensions; we only had suspensions (Db), (Ab), (Bb) and (C).

Think about this, suppose you knew the other chords that had the other 3 tones of the (Db) scale as suspensions (Eb, F, Gb). This means you would know a chord corresponding to every note of the (Db) Major scale, where that note was a suspension.

This means you would be able to harmonize just about any song instantly, because the melody would be the suspension, and you would know the chord for that suspension!!

Adventures in Harmony – Introduction to the System

The only thing you would need to do is add more variety and choices and not always choose the same chord for a particular suspension. You will be able to do that in time as you learn more chords.

If you really want to be original you can go a step further and use the technique and these chords in any key. For example, use the chords that you know for a particular suspension regardless of the key signature that the song is in. i.e. Whenever you see a (Db) in the melody, play the chord that you know that has the (Db) as the suspension, whenever you see a (G) in the melody, play the chord that you know that has the (G) as the suspension, etc.

15 An Introduction to Picture Passing Chords

The next category of passing chords is perhaps the most interesting. We are going to call these chords picture chords. These are chords that are perhaps the easiest to play because you can virtually play them instantly with no practice, and you can use these chords, as passing chords at will. These chords have another interesting property; this is that they are key agnostic. Their harmonics are such that they can be played on any tone of the scale. They are called picture chords because you play them based on their shape and the shape of your hand when playing them. Just from looking at a picture of the chord, you can play it immediately in any key!

Many very famous musicians use these types of chords. They may have no idea what the chord is, but know they can use it anywhere, and that it will sound good, and that they can put their hand on it instantly in any key simply based on its shape!

The dynamics and power and flexibility that these classes of passing chords give you are unbelievable. Lets visualize an actual scenario before we see it in practice.

You are sitting at your keyboard playing a chord, and at that moment you feel that you need to add more chords or another chord as a passing chord to get to your next chord. At that very moment, you can say to yourself, "... hey, I think I want to add an (Ab) chord right now as a passing chord…. Yes, I want (Ab) in the bass." And at that point you would instantly be able to play the right notes in the right hand to go with that bass!!! You could have actually picked any note in the bass, and at that very moment, play the correct chord in the right hand!

That's just another example of how the Adventures in Harmony Play by Number System allows you to instantly make those beautiful passing chord transitions!

When we show you an actual example of using this little known secret of Picture Chords, you will see that we really do mean instantly play.

We will show you these Picture Chords using the same format that we have shown all the rest of the chords in the Adventures in Harmony System. We will then share with you some tips and or tricks that will allow you find this chord immediately.

15.1 The 7b5#5 Picture Chord

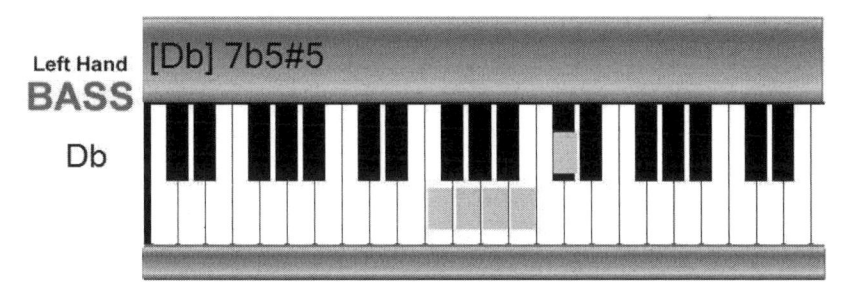

Figure 15-1 – The 7b5#5

Play the following notes of any key to create this chord

Right Hand	Left Hand				
1	3	b5	#5	7	8

15.1.1 When can I use this chord?

This chord has a closed voicing so make sure you resolve it.

The harmonics of this chord allow it be played on any tone of the scale.

It may be used as a passing chord between any two chords.

HEY YOU CAN USE THIS CHORD AS A PASSING CHORD IN THE "JOY TO THE WORLD EXAMPLE" IN THE V- I movement

If we were creating this chord using the Adventures in Harmony Play by Number System as we have done for all chords up to this point, we would see that the notes in this chord in the key of Db are as follows:

(F) is the 3rd of Db

(G) is the b5 of Db

(A) is the #5 of Db

(B) is the 7th of Db   Note: Remember when we refer to the 7th of a scale it's always the b7.

(Db) is the 8th of Db

15.1.2 Creating the 7b5

This chord is created by playing the (3), (b5), (#5), (7), and (8). Figure 7.1.1

But this chord is one of the chords that you can create faster by using the picture system where you mentally know what the chord looks like in your head based upon its shape and how your fingers are positioned.

I have a nickname for this chord; I call it "5" in a row, bass on top." I call it this because on the keyboard you are really playing 5 notes in a row and the note on the top is the note that you are going to play in the bass with your left hand or foot.

Playing 5 notes in a row, each separated by a whole-step, easily makes this chord. Another way of saying this is with your right hand, play a note on top with your pinky finger, then working your way down on the keyboard, skip a note, then play the next note, then skip the next note, then play the next note, skip another note, play the next note, skip one more note, then play the last note with your thumb. You are playing 5 notes in a row skipping every other note. Now how much easier can it be...? It's pretty simple....you should be able to easily make that chord starting at any note on the keyboard After you have done it once or twice, you can probably make any of those chords in less than 1 second. And that's more than enough time for you not to even worry about this chord until it's time for you to play it!!

The note that is on top is the note that is played in the bass with your left hand of foot.

The fastest way to create this chord while you are playing is to first decide what the bass note is. In the example below, the bass note is a (C). Then with your right hand, play that note with your pinky. Then just play four more notes below that note, each a whole step apart. The figure below indicates how you would play a (**C7b5#5**).

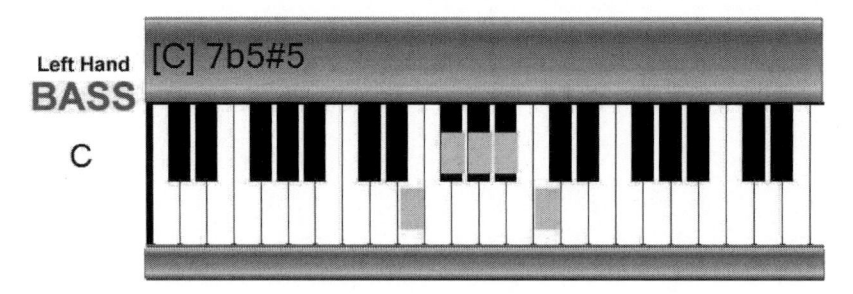

Figure 15-2- The C7b5#5

Adventures in Harmony – Introduction to the System

You can easily play a **7b5#5** chord for any key by following the same steps. If you wanted to create an (**F7b5#5**), place your pinky of your right hand on (F) and then simply play four more notes below the (F), each a whole step apart.

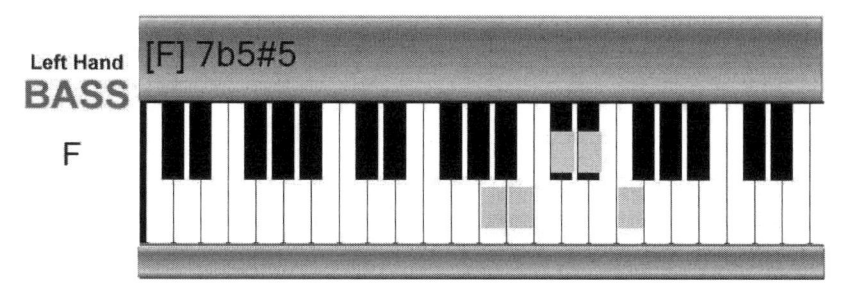

Figure 15-3 – The F7b5#5

We just showed you the (**F7b5#5**) and the (**C7b5#5**) and how easy it was to create them. You should be able to create the other ten **7b5#5** chords just as easily.

Try this as an exercise in creating the other "5 in a row chords."

1. Remove your hands from the keyboard
2. Now decide what the bass note is going to be for the chord.
3. Now look at that bass note on the keyboard (Don't move your hands yet)
4. Remember that is the note that you are going to play with your pinky.
5. Remember also that is the note that you will be playing in the bass with your left hand or foot
6. Now also look at see what are the other 4 notes that you need to play with your right hand
7. Remember these 4 notes are going to be a whole step apart.
8. At this point you should have a good picture in your mind of what notes you are going to play.
9. Now play the chord!!!!

15.1.3 Using the 7b5#5

At this point you have just learned 12 passing chords! You should be able to play any of them almost instantly.

You have just learned the **C7b5#5**, **F7b5#5**, **Bb7b5#5**, **Eb7b5#5**, **Ab7b5#5**, **Db7b5#5**, **Gb7b5#5**, **B7b5#5**, **E7b5#5**, **A7b5#5**, **D7b5#5**, and **7b5#5**.

We are now going to see this chord in action and use it as a passing chord. In this example we are going to use the **7b5#5** as a passing chord between a [V] to [I] movement.

This chord works well as a one of many passing chords that you can insert between a [V] to [I] movement.

Hmm... yes any of these chords can be used as passing chord between the words "is and come" in our previous "Joy to the World" harmonizations.

A [V] to [I] movement means we are moving from a chord built on the 5th tone of the scale to a chord built on the 1st tone of the scale.

In the key of (C) moving from a (G) Chord to a (C) Chord would be a [V] to [I] movement.

C Scale							
Tone	C	D	E	F	G	A	B
Number	1	2	3	4	5	6	7

Figure 15-4

Other examples of V to I movements would be moving from (Ab) to (Db), (A) to (D), (Bb) to (Eb), (B) to (E), (C) to (F), (Db) to (Ab), (D) to (G), (Eb) to (Ab), (E) to (A), (F) to (Bb), and (Gb) to (B).

In this example we are going to use a [V] to [I] movement in the key of (Db). We will be moving from an (Ab) Chord to a (Db) Chord.

Db Scale							
Tone	Db	Eb	F	Gb	Ab	Bb	C
Number	1	2	3	4	5	6	7

Figure 15-5

Adventures in Harmony – Introduction to the System

This is the same [V] to [I] movement that we saw earlier in our "Joy to the World" harmonization.

For the purpose of this example we are just going to tell you what [V] Chord and what [I] chord to play, how they are created or what their names are, are not important for this example. So we will be moving from an (Ab) Chord to a (Db) Chord. Our intent is to just illustrate the flexibility of this **7b5#5**, otherwise known as the "5 in a row" passing chord.

Practice moving between the two chords below and don't forget to play the bass note with your left hand or foot. These two chords, (**Ab9sus**) and (**DbMaj9**) are other chords covered in detail, elsewhere in the series.

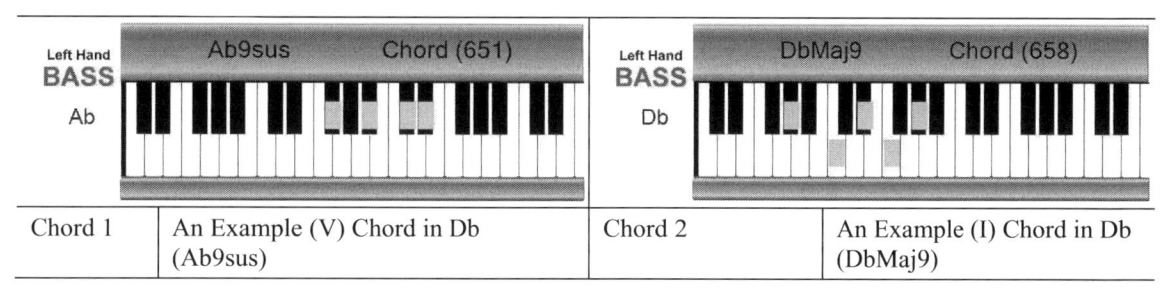

Chord 1	An Example (V) Chord in Db (Ab9sus)	Chord 2	An Example (I) Chord in Db (DbMaj9)

Figure 15-6

Now we can have some fun. You are now going to insert one of the "5 in a row chords" as a passing chord between these two chords. You actually now have 12 passing chords to choose from!!!

1. Play the A^{b}9sus as shown above (Chord 1)
2. Choose one of the "5 in a row chords" that you just learned.
    - You are free to choose the **C7b5#5, F7b5#5, Bb7b5#5, Eb7b5#5, Ab7b5#5, Db7b5#5, Gb7b5#5, B7b5#5, E7b5#5, A7b5#5, D7b5#5,** or **G7b5#5.**
    - Remember try the (**C7b5#5**) and (**F7b5#5**) that are shown in Figure 15-2 and Figure 15-3.
3. Then play the (**DbMaj9**) as shown above (Chord 2)

You will hear that each one of these changes is beautiful and each has their own character. And remember, we have really only shown you one passing chord! Just imagine what you could do if you have lots of them to choose from! Don't worry we got them in this course.

Adventures in Harmony – Introduction to the System

Did you notice you were free to choose a passing chord that had a bass note that was not part of the (Db) Scale!

The **7b5#5** is only one of many picture passing chords that we will cover is this course.

15.1.4 Example 1 - Ab9sus to E7b5#5 to DbMaj9

For example, play and listen to the change where we choose (E) as the passing chord in

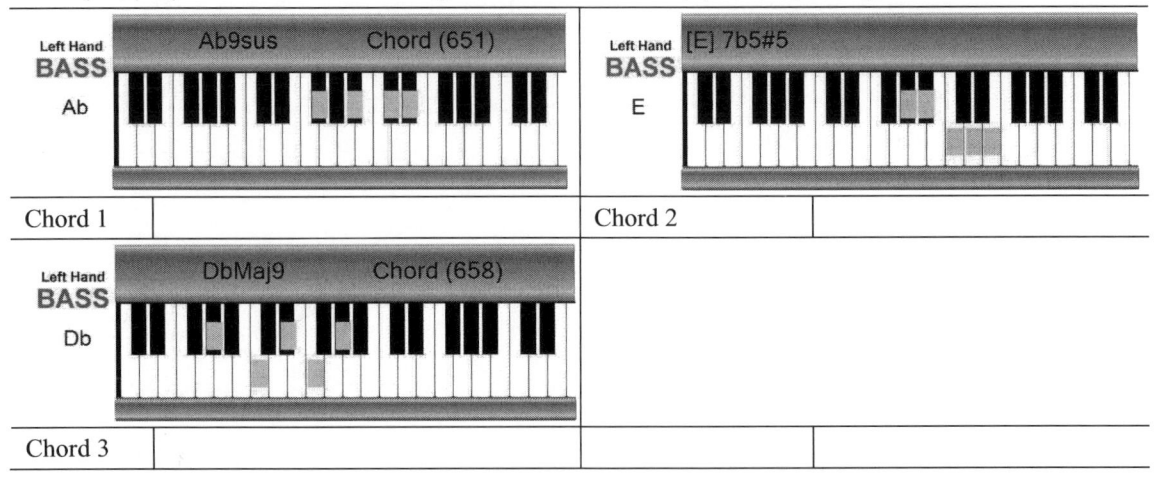

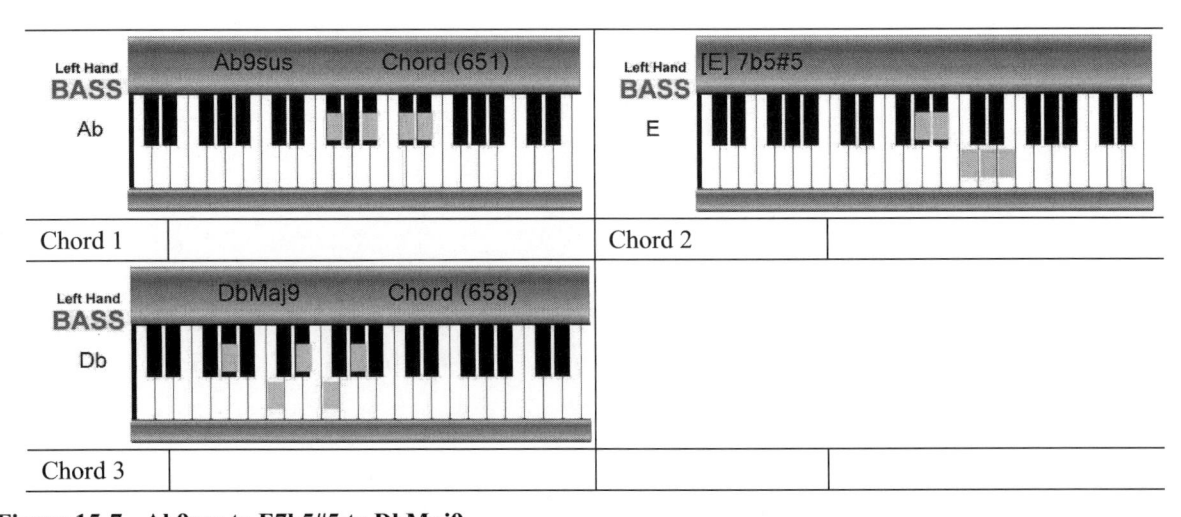

Figure 15-7.

Figure 15-7 - Ab9sus to E7b5#5 to DbMaj9

Are you salivating yet! Listen to how beautiful these changes are.

15.1.5 Example 2 - Ab9sus to F7b5#5 to DbMaj9

Adventures in Harmony – Introduction to the System

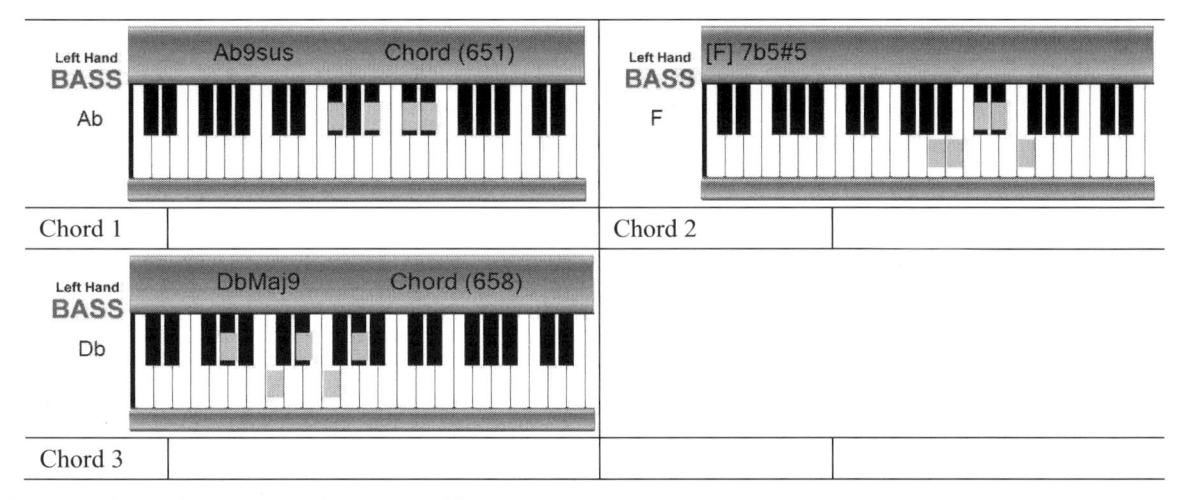

Left Hand BASS Ab — Ab9sus Chord (651)	**Left Hand BASS** F — [F] 7b5#5
Chord 1	Chord 2
Left Hand BASS Db — DbMaj9 Chord (658)	
Chord 3	

Figure 15-8 - Ab9sus to F7b5#5 to DbMaj9

As long as you use the Adventures in Harmony Play By Number System and use the chords that are part of the course, YOU CAN CHOOSE ANY BASS NOTE at anytime to make your changes. There are no restrictions in our system and it's impossible to play a wrong chord as long as you follow the system. See how easy it is to put any one of those changes in at will and on demand as you play. We told no lie! You really can make that decision as you play.

Just to make things a little more interesting here is one more passing chord to play between the [V] and [I].

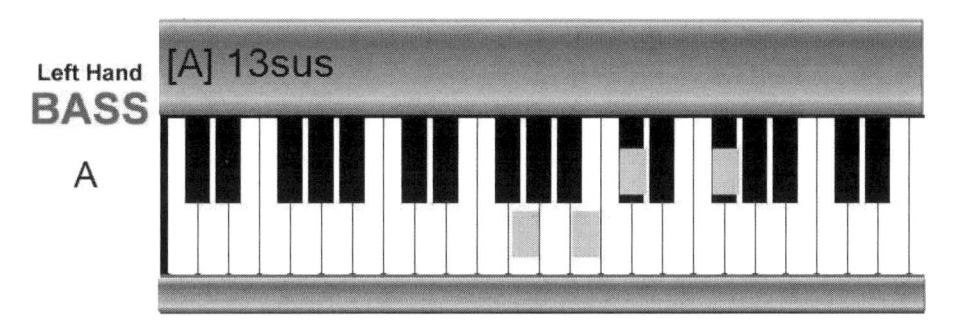

Left Hand BASS A — [A] 13sus

Figure 15-9

We want you to use this exact passing chord as another choice in making the [V] to [I] movement that you just played. Now you can insert two passing chords or maybe even just one… it's up to you ….. and it doesn't matter which order you play them!

After you play the (**Ab9sus**), you can play one of the "5 in a row chords", or this (**A13sus**) chord in Figure 15-9. Or you can do it backward and play the (**Ab9sus**) then play the A chord

Adventures in Harmony – Introduction to the System

in, then one of the "5 in a row chords", the (**DbMaj9**). As you learn more chords the possibilities and combinations are endless!!

1. Play the Ab9sus as shown (Don't forget to play the bass)

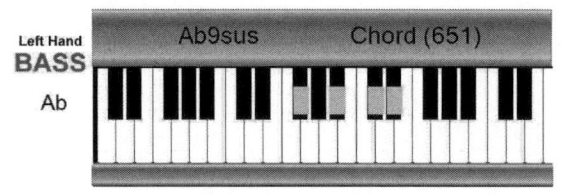

   [Keyboard diagram: Left Hand BASS Ab, Ab9sus Chord (651)]

2. At this point you can go to Step 3a or Step 4a depending on which of the 2 passing chords you want to play first!!!

3.
   a. Now play one of the "5 in a row chords" that you just learned (12 choices).
   b. Now play the (A13sus) chord in Figure 15-9 (Don't forget to play the bass).
   c. Go to step 5

4.
   a. Play the A chord in Figure 15-9. (Don't forget to play the bass).
   b. Now play one of the "5 in a row chords" that you just learned (12 choices).

5. Then finally play the DbMaj9 as shown

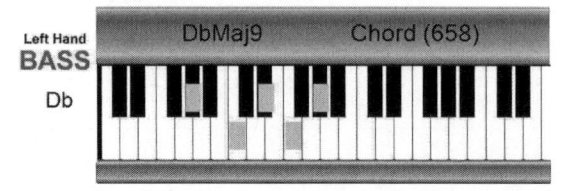

   [Keyboard diagram: Left Hand BASS Db, DbMaj9 Chord (658)]

You can now see that the possibilities and combinations are endless and that this truly is easier than you think!!

Adventures in Harmony – Introduction to the System

15.1.6 Example 3 - Ab9sus to F7b5#5 to A13 to DbMaj9

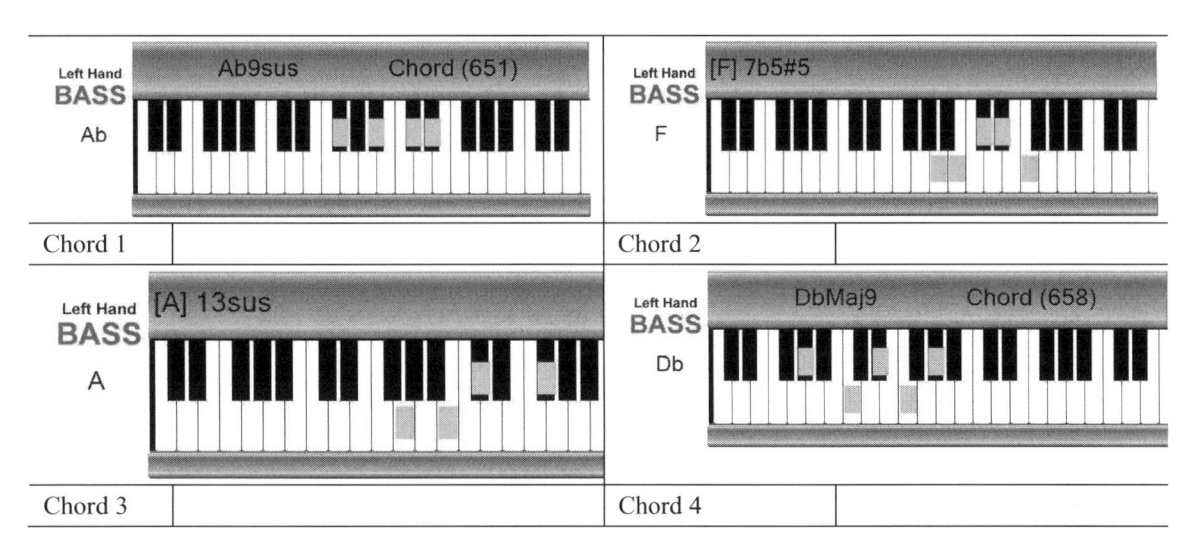

Chord 1: Ab9sus — Bass Ab, Chord (651)	Chord 2: [F] 7b5#5 — Bass F
Chord 3: [A] 13sus — Bass A	Chord 4: DbMaj9 — Bass Db, Chord (658)

Figure 15-10 - Ab9sus to F13 to A7b5#5 to DbMaj9

15.1.7 Example 4 - Ab9sus to A13 to E7b5#5 to DbMaj9 – Reverse the passing chords

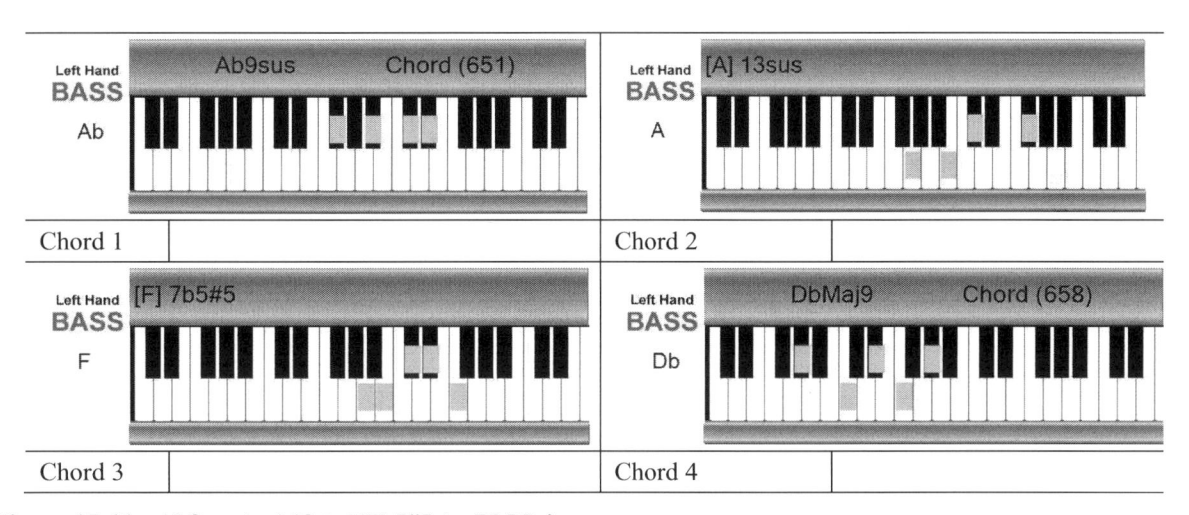

Chord 1: Ab9sus — Bass Ab, Chord (651)	Chord 2: [A] 13sus — Bass A
Chord 3: [F] 7b5#5 — Bass F	Chord 4: DbMaj9 — Bass Db, Chord (658)

Figure 15-11 - Ab9sus to A13 to E7b5#5 to DbMaj

15.2 A Picture chord on the suspension

In the previous section we saw examples of a picture chord where you picked the bass note on demand when you were playing. Let's flip that concept around and look the case where you create the chord based on the melody note. An application of this is where you are already playing a chord and you just want another chord to play without changing the melody note. It may be the case where you think you are holding a chord too long and just want to add flavor by playing a different chord without affecting the melody. You simply want to change the chord but keep the note on top the same. This new chord that you create will simply be used as another passing chord.

Here is an example of a **m7#5 (Gm7#5)**

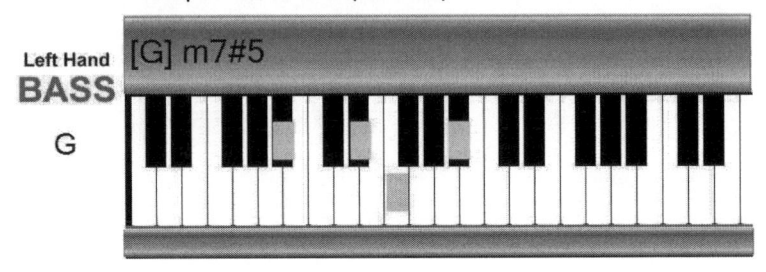

15.2.1.1   Creating the m7#5

Using the play by number system this chord is created by playing the (-3), (#5), (7), and (#9).

Right Hand	Left Hand			
1	-3	#5	7	#9
G Bass	Bb	Eb	F	Bb

So to play the (**Gm7#5**) we simply play the (-3), (#5), (7) and (#9) of the (G) scale.

What we are now going to do is use this chord as a passing chord where the melody note becomes the [#9].

This is the effect that we are trying to achieve; you are playing a chord on the keyboard. This can be any chord. That chord that you are playing has a note that is on top. I am asking you to change to a new chord that is a **m7#5**, but I don't want the note that you are currently playing on top to change. That means that if you are playing a chord, and that chord has a (Bb) on top. I want you to keep that (Bb) on top and switch to a **m7#5**. To do this, and keep

Adventures in Harmony – Introduction to the System

the (Bb) as the top note, means that the (Bb) now becomes a [#9]. Look at the following sample movement where the (Bb) remains on top.

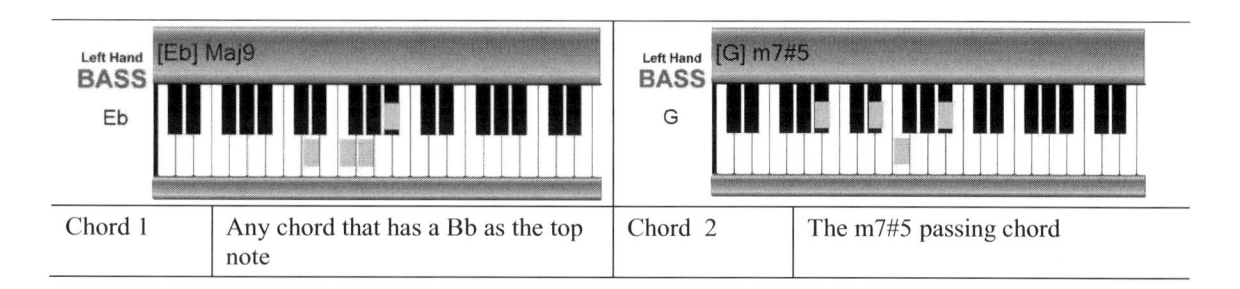

Chord 1	Any chord that has a Bb as the top note	Chord 2	The m7#5 passing chord

To make this movement and create the **m7#5** as the passing chord, you have to ask yourself another question in order to create this chord using the play by number system. If the (Bb) is the (#9) then what is the [I]. You need to know the [I] is so that you can create the chord. Once you know the [I] then you can easily create the **m7#5**, by playing the (-3), (#5), (7) and (#9).

To make a long story short, this is a lot of work but you can still figure this out in under 1 second once you know the secret that I will tell you later.

There still is a faster and better way to do this; I am going to tell you how to make this change instantly from any chord on the keyboard.

Play any chord on the keyboard. The note that is on top of the chord that you are playing is not going to change, and we are going to make a movement to a **m7#5** from the chord that you are playing. Remember it does not matter what chord you are playing to start with. This movement sounds good no matter what.

For this example we will start with the following chord:

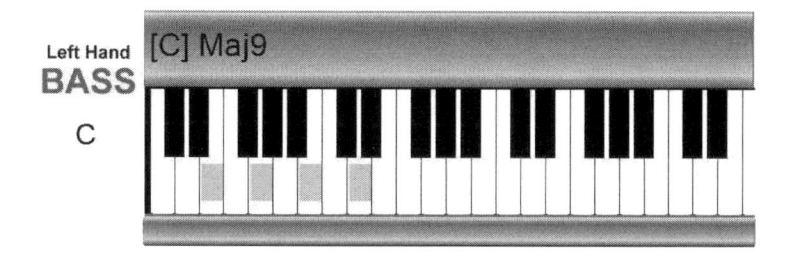

Adventures in Harmony – Introduction to the System

To play the next chord (which will be a **m7#5**), do the following:

1. Look at the note that is on top of the chord that you are playing. That is the only note that will remain. In our example this note would be the (D).
2. Now play that same note, the note that is on top, one octave lower. In our example, this note would be the (D). You are now playing two (D)'s one octave apart.
3. The next note in the chord is the 4th of that note. In our example, this note would be a (G), the 4th of (D) is (G).
4. Now from that note (G), in your mind, visualize three notes in a row a whole step apart. That would be (G), (A) and (B). Play the (G) and (A) but not that last note (B) because that is the base note.

The result in following the above steps is the following chord:

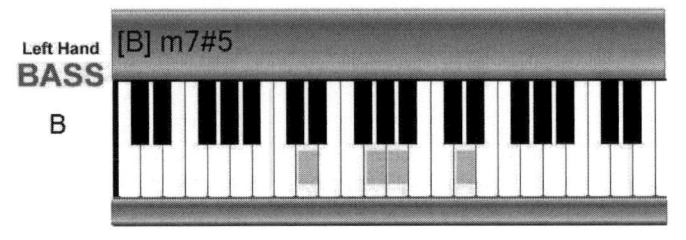

[B] m7#5 — Left Hand BASS — B

This will be the passing chord that you would play and the movement would be as follows:

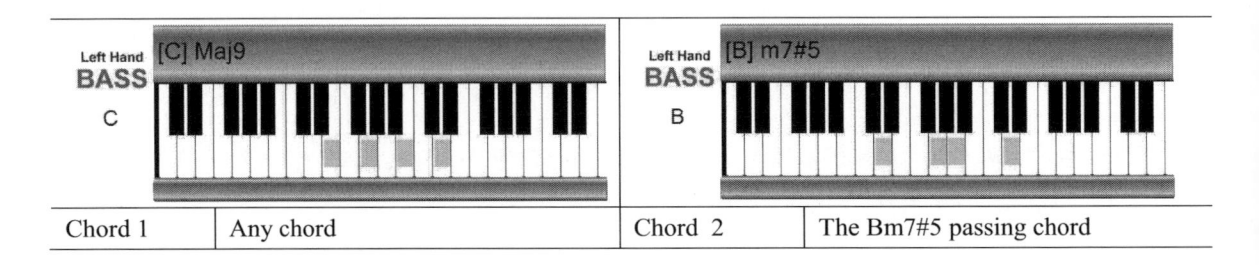

Chord 1	Any chord	Chord 2	The Bm7#5 passing chord

(Chord 1: [C] Maj9, C bass. Chord 2: [B] m7#5, B bass.)

This movement works with any chord. This is just one example of a possible movement that you can make using this single picture chord **m7#5**. Study this example carefully on how to make the movement.

You should be able to make this movement from any chord in less than one second. You should be able to move from a chord with any suspension to the corresponding **m7+5** effortlessly.

If you are still having a problem playing this chord, let's look very carefully at how a **m7#5** is made. This is what we call a visual analysis.

15.3 Chord Visual Analysis

A visual analysis is something you should be doing on each chord that you play. By studying how the chord looks and the relationship among the notes will give you the ability to immediately play a chord without going through a process of transposition to figure out what the correct chord is for the key you are in. Some chords lend themselves to easy visual analysis and others do not. You should stick with the easy ones and include them in your bag of tricks.

This is how musicians are able to put their hands on passing chords immediately. It's because they know what the chord looks like and how it is shaped. They may not even know what the chord is. All they know is that this is a possible chord that can be played and that it will sound good!!

When doing a visual analysis on a chord, you need to do two analyses. The first analysis is with respect to the suspension and the other analysis with respect to the bass.

Remember the concept of chord duality, in doing these two analyses you will be able to play the chord when you have either of these pieces of information.

1. You will be able to play the correct chord when all you know is the melody note.

    i.e. "What is the correct chord to play when I have this (Ab) note in the melody."

2. You will be able to play the correct chord by picking the bass note

    i.e. "I want to play a passing chord, and I want the bass note to be an (Eb), what is the correct chord"

Let's look again at the **m7#5** chord.

15.3.1 Analysis on the suspension note

When we do an analysis on the suspension note (the note on the top), we are trying to figure out how to create this entire chord voicing when all we know is the top note.

The general question is that we want to know how to create a **m7#5** from whatever chord we are on the keyboard, and we want the note on top of the chord that we are playing, to be the suspension of the **m7#5**.

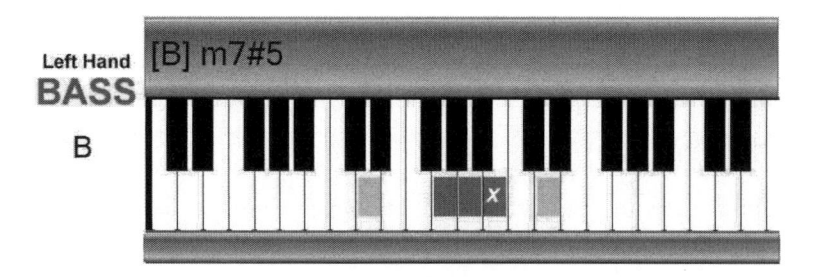

Adventures in Harmony – Introduction to the System

[B] m7#5

Left Hand BASS
B

To do this analysis, we look at the entire chord on the keyboard. We even include the bass note as part of the chord when we do this analysis. In the above example you see we have included the (B) which is the bass note.

1. You will be able to play the correct chord when all you know is the melody note.

    i.e. "What is the correct chord to play when I have this (Ab) note in the melody."

2. You will be able to play the correct chord by picking the bass note

    i.e. "I want to play a passing chord, and I want the bass note to be an (Eb), what is the correct chord"

You now ask yourself the question while looking at the chord, "How could I create this chord if the only note I knew was the note on top?"

1. In looking at this chord the first thing I notice is the general shape.
    a. It has a note on each end and three notes in the middle
2. I also notice that the notes on the end are the same.
3. I also notice that the three notes in the middle are in a row.
    a. The three notes in the middle are one whole step apart.

With this little bit of information you can almost create this chord starting at any note on the keyboard and using that note as the suspension.

1. You know you need to double up on that top note whatever that note is. Just play that same note an octave lower.
2. At this point you simply need to play three notes in the middle. You already know that those three notes are a whole step apart, but what you don't know is, where to position those three notes in a row in between the notes on the end.

Adventures in Harmony – Introduction to the System

This is not a hard problem to solve with just a little bit more analysis. Let's look at the chord again and see if we can figure out where that group of three notes in a row starts in relationship to that lower note (D).

What's the relationship between a (D) and a (G)? Well you can say that (G) is the 4th of (D). That's a good rule, you can say that the three notes in a row starts at the 4th of the notes that are an octave apart. Or you can also say that the three notes in a row start at three whole steps above the notes that are an octave apart. Three whole steps above (D) is (G), both of these rules will allow us to arrive at the same place.

1. The next thing that you are doing is simply playing three notes a whole step apart starting on that 4th which in this example is that (G).
2. But wait, you are really not playing all three notes in a row; you are actually leaving out that last note which is the (B) in this example. That last note that you are leaving out is the bass note. Play that note with your left hand and or foot pedal.

Now that we have gone through this analysis, we should be able to play a **m7#5** using any note on the keyboard as the suspension. Believe me you can do this is less than one second once you understand the movement.

At this point you now know twelve **m7#5** passing chords that you can play instantly. This is a chord that you can move to from playing any other chord on the keyboard.

 Think about the variety that this alone is going to add to your playing. In using this technique, think about this, you really don't know what chord you are going to play until after you create the chord. You don't know if it's going to be a (**Cm7#5**) or an (**Abm7#5**), etc. All you know is the suspension, it's not until you are done creating the chord that you actually know the bass. And this is the variety that you are looking for, you may even consider this a way of surprising yourself as you play.

However there may be times when you want to play a specific passing chord. For example, say your current chord is some kind of (Eb) chord and the next chord is some kind of (G) chord and you want to walk on up to the (G) from the(Eb) by playing an (F) chord in the middle as a passing chord. These walkups are quite common is gospel, but to do them you need to be able to control the chord.

At this point, you would not be able to create a (**Fm7#5**) because we are not dealing with the suspension. If we were dealing with a suspension and creating the chord, the bass note would be a surprise to us and that's not what we want here. In this instance we want to control what the bass is. We want the bass to be a specific note, (F) in this example. To be able to do this, we need to have done the analysis on the chord with respect to the bass note, so that we could create it by only knowing the bass note.

15.3.2 Analysis on the bass note

When we do an analysis on the bass note, we are trying to figure out how to create this entire chord voicing when all we know is the bass note.

The general question is that we want to know how to create a **m7#5** for any given bass note.

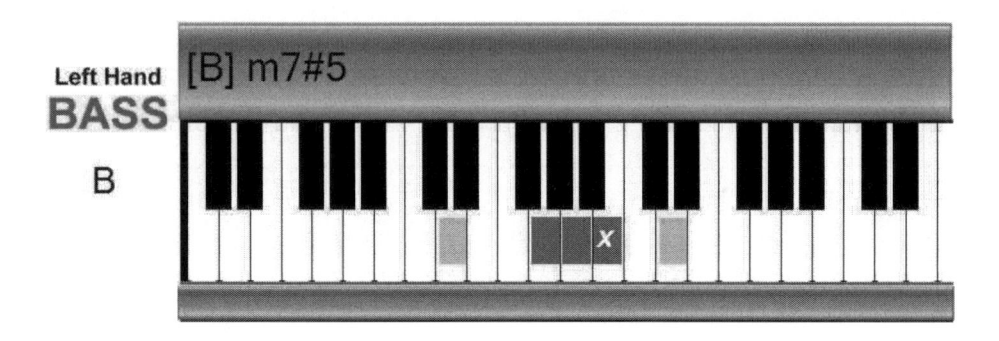

To do this analysis, we again look at the entire chord on the keyboard. We even include the bass note as part of the chord when we do this analysis. In the above example you see we have included the (B) which is the bass note.

1. This simplest way to look at this is if we know what the bass note is, how we figure out what the suspension is. This is because we already know how to create the chord based on the suspension.

2. In looking at the chord above and the base note which is (B) in the example above. How would we know what note is the suspension. We can say that the suspension is 1 ½ steps above the bass! Or we can even say that the suspension is the (-3). 1 ½ steps above (B) is (D), or the (-3) of (B) is (D).

3. Now that we know the note that is the suspension, we can simply double that note an octave apart and use the rules above that we used when we only know the suspension.

Remember our specific situation, we had some sort of (Eb) chord followed by some sort of (G) chord, and we wanted to insert the (**Fm7#5**) as the passing chord so we could walk the bass from (Eb) to (F) and then to (G). So in this situation we know we want specific **m7#5**, we want the one in the key of (F).

So if we wanted to create an (**Fm7#5**), we right away know the suspension is an (Ab), because (Ab) is 1 ½ steps above (F). We can also say the suspension is (Ab), because (Ab) is the (-3) of (F).

Adventures in Harmony – Introduction to the System

We can now easily create this chord since we know the suspension is (Ab) and it will result in an (F) in the bass. Remember the (F) is not played, it is the bass note. The (F) is simply indicated so that you can visualize the three notes in a row in the middle.

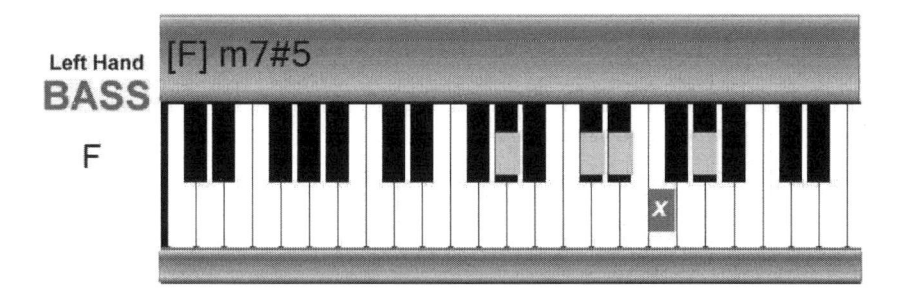

Let's look at a real example we originally had an (Eb) chord followed by a (G) chord.

And we wanted to force the bass to be an (F), so the passing chord will be an **Fm7#5**.

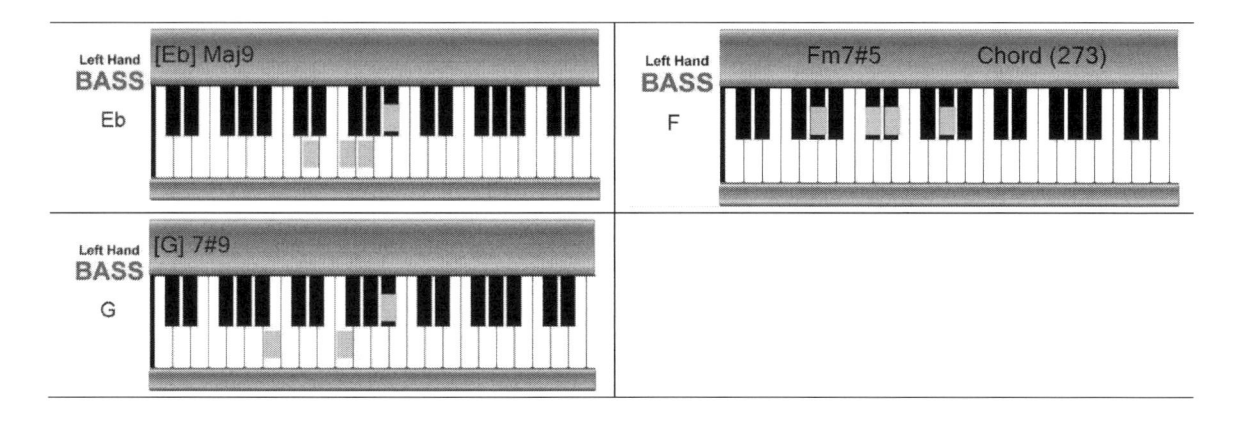

We could have also done this the other way by keeping the (Bb) as the suspension and playing the **m7#5** passing chord that has the (Bb) as the suspension. That first (Eb) chord that we are playing has a (Bb) as the suspension. So the proper passing chord in that case would be a (**Gm7#5**).

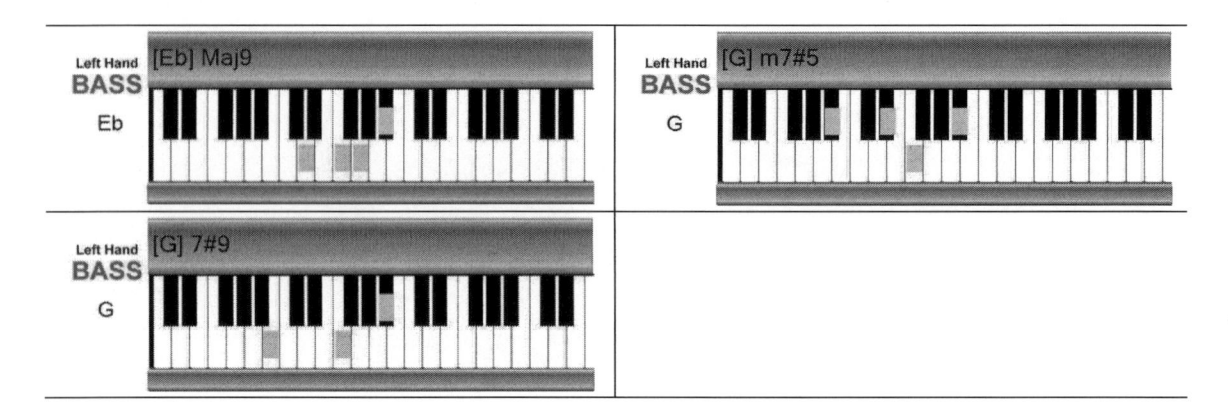

Left Hand [Eb] Maj9
BASS Eb

Left Hand [G] m7#5
BASS G

Left Hand [G] 7#9
BASS G

Look at what you just learned; you now know 12 new passing chords that you can call up at will. You can make this movement at any time and it does not matter what key you are in!

Imagine if you had 10 or 20 more picture chords like this. Any chord can be turned into a picture chord if you simply do the analysis on the chord. Some just lend themselves to be created more easily. You don't need me to tell you how to play a chord as a picture chord. Just look at the chord and see if there is an easy way to create it. Do the visual analysis on it. That's what the pros do. You simply need to stock your mini chord library with all these tricks that you can call up at will.

The reference Adventures in Harmony – Harmonization on the Melody is devoted to suspensions. Every chord in that reference can be used as a passing chord. Simply find the chapter that corresponds to your suspension and every chord in that chapter can now be used as a passing chord for that suspension.

The reference Preaching Chords is also devoted harmonizing on the melody note.

There are many references in this course that are devoted to melody harmonization.

16 Progressions

In this section, you will learn to use the Adventures in Harmony Play by Number System to create your own beautiful progressions. We have already done the hard part for you in selecting voicings for each tone in and out of the major scale.

Think of all of the voicings, in this course, as part of a child's LEGO™ building block set.

This set of over 1200+ building blocks, is everything you need to create your own song or progression in any key. Remember, if you are trying to create your masterpiece in some other key, we told you how to use the number system to utilize these building blocks in the key of your choice. All of the building blocks in this set fit together. It is your job as the creator, to fit these blocks together. There is NO incorrect way to fit these blocks together, because they are all part of the same set.

In this building block set of over 1200+ voicings, imagine that the individual blocks are the actual chord voicings. Also imagine that these 1200+ blocks are in separate buckets, and that there are (12) twelve buckets, one bucket for each one of the notes in and out of the major scale. We are going to give each of the twelve buckets names, and these names are going to correspond to the Roman numbers for the scales that we learned earlier in the course. (Table 16-1) shows the (Db) scale as an example with all the accidentals.

Db Scale												
Note	Db	D	Eb	E	F	Gb	G	Ab	A	Bb	B	C
BucketNumber	I	bII	II	bIII	III	IV	bV	V	#V	VI	VII	MajVII

Table 16-1

A progression is indicated by a series of these Roman Numbers. i.e. (II V I), (I MajVII III VI).

In creating your own progressions; you are simply going to pick a sequence of Roman Numbers. Let me first tell you that there are NO rules in defining the sequence of the Roman Numbers. This is totally up to you! As I said, there are NO rules, but there are suggestions or common transitions or movements between chords that we will discuss.

16.1 Progression Sequence

In traditional Western Music there seems to be a common theme with regard to chord progressions. Progressions tend to want to move towards home. In this context, home is defined as the (I).

In this particular instance, in a (II V I) progression, the progression ended up on the (I). You are going to find it common in praise and contemporary music, for a song or progression to either start, and or end on the (I).

So in creating a sequence of Roman Numbers to represent the progression of your masterpiece, you may select one of the following structures:

(I) → Modulate over available tones (I)-(VII) → (I)

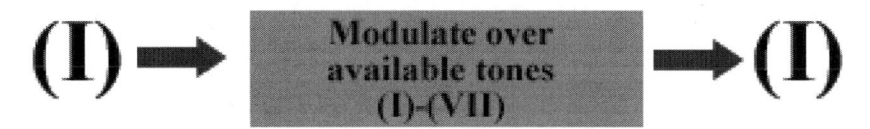

Figure 16-1

Start on the (I), modulate elsewhere, and then end back on the (I).

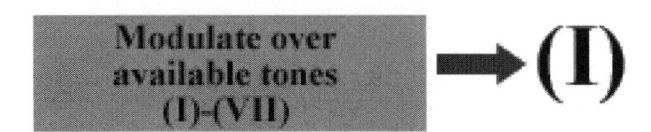

Modulate over available tones (I)-(VII) → (I)

Figure 16-2

Start somewhere and eventually end back on the (I).

(I) → Modulate over available tones (I)-(VII)

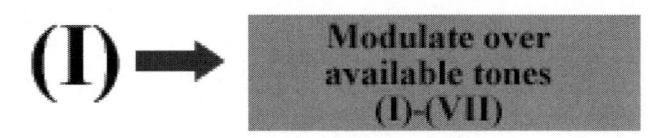

Figure 16-3

Start on the (I) and end somewhere.

16.2 Tone Sequence

Each one of the tones (Roman Numbers) has a preference or tendency to want to move to another tone. Here is a list of the common preferences.

(I) → (IV)
(II) → (V)
(III) → (VI)
(IV) → (VII)
(V) → (I)
(VI) → (II)
(VII) → (bIII)
(MajVII) → (III)
(bII) → (bV)
(bIII) → (+V)

(+V) → (bII)

Using the key of (Db) as an example, the above preferences tells us that the (V) likes to move to the (I), which would be (Ab) moving to (Db). We can also see that the (VI) likes to move to the (II), which would be (Bb) moving to (Eb). Don't worry about memorizing the above movements because you already know them, and probably don't know it. There is a trick to it, if you don't already see it.

The trick is that the next chord is always the (4th) of where you are. For example if you are on (Eb) the next chord would be an (Ab). (Ab) is the 4th of Eb. It doesn't matter if (Eb) is the (I), the (II) or whatever, the trick always works. So if (Eb) was the (V), the chart above says that the (V) goes to the (I). If (Eb) is the (V), then the (I) is (Ab)! If (Eb) was the (III), the chart above says the

Adventures in Harmony – Introduction to the System

(III) goes to the (VI). So if (Eb) is the (III), the (VI) is (Ab)! We get the same answer no matter what. So the quick way to figure this out is to always go to the (4) from wherever you are. If you are on an (C) chord, the next chord would be (F), (F) is the 4th of C. It doesn't matter if C is the (+V) or whatever, just always go to the (4) and you will be correct! Remember the circle of 5th's and 4th's.

In short, we are telling you that whatever chord you are currently playing, the next chord that you can play is always the 4th of where you are. All you have to do is pick a voicing and the movement will be correct.

16.3 Being neighborly

There is also another preference in how the tones like to move among themselves. This movement I will call "being neighborly." It works like this, whenever you are moving to another tone, before you get to that tone, stop and visit one of the neighbors.

For example, if you were going to make the transition

$$(III) \rightarrow (VI)$$

Figure 16-4

Before you get to the (VI), stop and visit (play) one of the neighbors of the (VI). That would either be the (VII) or the (+V).

Therefore you would have one of the following choices available to you

$$(III) \rightarrow (+V) \rightarrow (VI)$$

Or

$$(III) \rightarrow (VII) \rightarrow (VI)$$

Figure 16-5

It's much easier to actually create this movement on the keyboard and actually play it, as opposed to write the Roman Numbers. In plain English, all we are saying is in any chord movement; you can always stop and play the chord that is ½ step below or above your destination.

In the key of (Db), moving from the (III) to the (VI), would be moving from the (F) to the (Bb). Therefore all we are saying is that before you get to your destination, which in this case is (Bb), stop on the (A) or the (B). This is something that you don't need to practice, because you are going to make the decision on which neighbor to visit, seconds before you do it.

An another example, if you were going to make the transition

(V) → (I)

Figure 16-6

Before you get to the (I), stop and visit (play) one of the neighbors of the (I). That would either be the (MajVII) or the (bII).

In the key of (Db), moving from the (V) to the (I), would be moving from the (Ab) to the (Db). Therefore all we are saying is that before you get to your destination, which in this case is (Db), stop on the (C) or the (D).

We are not going to give you any more "rules/suggestions" with regard to how progressions move, because with the little bit that we have told you, you can create millions of progressions. Remember, there are NO rules; these are only suggestions and common tendencies. We are not playing any chords yet because we have not yet picked the quality of the chords i.e. Minor, 11th, Major, etc. We will do this later.

16.4 Build a progression

In this section we will build a sample progression. For this example, let's use the following framework to start building our progression. We are going to start on the (I), and end on the (I), and put some stuff in the middle (Figure 16-7).

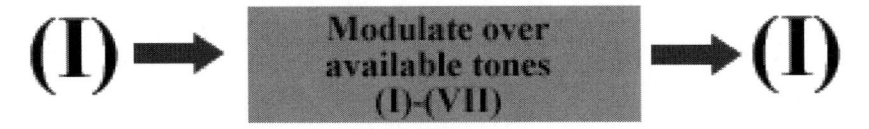

(I) → Modulate over available tones (I)-(VII) → (I)

Figure 16-7

Modulation over tones (I)-(VII) is defined as the playing of other chords based on these tones (I)-(VII). It does not matter how many tones you choose or the order.

We can pick any tones that we want, to be in the middle. There are twelve tones available in the scale. It does not matter which one you pick (Figure 16-8).

Scale											
Roman Numbers	I	bII	II	bIII	III	IV	bV	V	#V	VI	VII	MajVII

Figure 16-8

Let's just pick one, the (III).

Now we have a (I) – (III) – (I) progression, if we wanted, we can just stop right here and call it a day. But instead, we are going to build on this progression so that you may see the infinite possibilities.

16.5 Add to a Progression

To build on this (I)-(III)-(I) progression, we have two places where we can insert more chords. We can insert chords between the (I) and (III) at position (A), or we can insert chords between the (III) and (I) at position (B) (Figure 16-9). How do we decide that chords to insert?

$$(I) \rightarrow_A (III) \rightarrow_B (I)$$

Figure 16-9

At this point, there are many possibilities given the simple "rules" that we have given you so far.

Whenever you have two chords that you are trying to insert a chord between, you always need to ask yourself TWO questions.

1) What chord will allow you to arrive at the destination chord?
2) What chord follows the origination chord?

In applying this to the example above (Figure 16-9), we want to insert a chord at position (A) between the (I) and (III). So we ask the two questions:

1) What chord allows us to arrive at the (III)?
2) And what chord follows the (I)?

If we look back to (Section 16.2) on Tone Sequences, we see that the Maj7 allows us to arrive at the (III),

$$(_{Maj}VII) \rightarrow (III)$$

And the (IV) follows the (I).

$$(I) \rightarrow (IV)$$

Therefore we have two choices, we can insert the (MajVII) or the (IV) between the (I) and (III). It doesn't matter which on we pick. Let's just pick the (MajVII). Now we have the following progression (Figure 16-10).

$$(I) \rightarrow (_{Maj}VII) \rightarrow (III) \underset{B}{\rightarrow} (I)$$

Figure 16-10

You are free to stop now, or you can continue and add more chords to this progression, remember there are still possible chords that we can add between the (III) and (I) at position (B) (Figure 16-10). We can ask ourselves the same questions to figure out what chords we can insert between the (III) and (I).

        1   What chord allows us to arrive at the (I)?
        2   What chord follows the (III)?

If we look back to (Section 16.2) on Tone Sequences, we see that the (V) allows us to arrive at the (I),

$$(V) \rightarrow (I)$$

And the (VI) follows the (III).

$$(III) \rightarrow (VI)$$

Therefore we have two choices; we can insert the (V) or the (VI) between the (III) and (I). It doesn't matter which on we pick. Let's just pick the (VI). Now we have the following progression (Figure 16-11).

$(I) \to (_{Maj}VII) \to (III) \to (VI) \to (I)$
    A   B   C   D

Figure 16-11

16.6 Build Forever

Now that our progression has five chords in it, there are four positions available where we can go through the exact same process and insert more chords. We can insert chords at positions (A, B, C or D) in (Figure 16-11). This process can go on forever and there are an infinite number of possibilities.

Let's add one more chord at position (D), and let's choose a neighbor chord that we learned about in (Section 16.3). We are going to add a chord that is either ½ step above or below the (I). We have two choices to arrive at the (I) (Figure 16-12).

$(_{Maj}VII) \to (I)$

$(bII) \to (I)$

Figure 16-12

Since we already have a (MajVII) in our progression, let's pick the (bII). Now our completed progression is as follows:

$(I) \to (_{Maj}VII) \to (III) \to (VI) \to (bII) \to (I)$

Figure 16-13

Now that we have a progression, the next thing that we are going to do is voice the progression. The Roman Numbers only tell us what the chords are, they don't tell us what kind of chord (i.e Major, Minor, etc.).

16.7 Voicing a Progression

Let's get back to the idea that chords in this course are part of a child's LEGO™ building block set. Remember we said that the chords or voicings are in twelve separate buckets. The Roman Numbers in the progression tell us which bucket to select a voicing from in the Adventures in Harmony Play by Number System.

Each one of the reference manuals in this course contains voicings for the various buckets.

We are going to use these references to voice the following progression that we just made up from scratch:

$$(I) \rightarrow (_{Maj}VII) \rightarrow (III) \rightarrow (VI) \rightarrow (bII) \rightarrow (I)$$

Figure 16-14

There are NO rules for selecting a voicing, but we are going to give you some suggestions that we suggest that you follow initially until you become familiar with the available voicings.

We are going to treat the chords in the middle of the progressions as if they were passing chords. Remember in creating the progression we had the following structural possibilities:

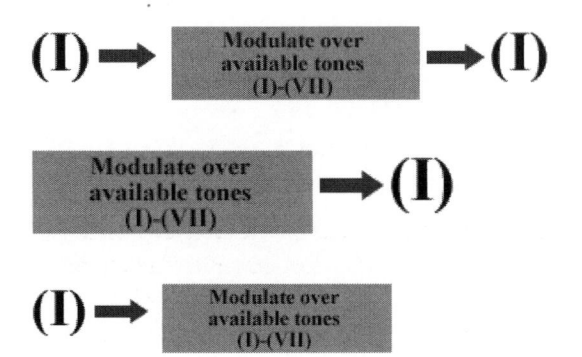

(I) → [Modulate over available tones (I)-(VII)] → (I)

[Modulate over available tones (I)-(VII)] → (I)

(I) → [Modulate over available tones (I)-(VII)]

Figure 16-15

The chords that are represented by the boxes are going to be treated like passing chords with respect to voicing. Remember earlier in the course, we said that the voicings like to move from consonance to dissonance and the back to consonance. We are going to make the following suggestions in selecting the voicing for the first, middle and last chords of the progression.

Adventures in Harmony – Introduction to the System

1) The first chord should not have closed harmony with multiple accidentals.
2) The middle chords should not have open harmony without accidentals.
3) The last chord should not have closed harmony with multiple accidentals.

In simple terms, the first and last chords should not have too much tension, and if there is tension, the chord should be played in open harmony, and the middle chords should have more tension then the first and last chords. These are the most important concepts in creating progressions!!!!

In looking at the entire movement through a progression, (A) is the first chord in the progression, (C) is the last chord in the progression, and (B) are the chords in the middle. These chords should have the following properties (Figure 16-16).

A — CONSONANCE OR OPEN HARMONY DISSONANCE

⬇

B — (NO OPEN HARMONY CONSONANCE) DISSONANCE OR CLOSED HARMONY CONSONANCE

⬇

C — CONSONANCE OR OPEN HARMONY DISSONANCE

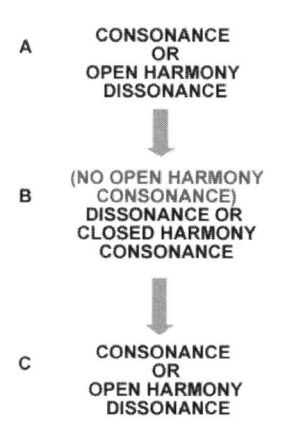

Figure 16-16

When we refer to consonance in the above diagram for (A) and (C), we really mean 'minimal dissonance.' For example, a chord containing the (-3) or a minor chord, has a little bit of dissonance, and that would be fine to start or end a progression on, but a chord with multiple accidentals like a (-3) and a (+5) is probably a little bit too harsh to start a progression. Remember we want to climb up the hill in section (B) to create tension, and then release the tension in coasting down to (C). You may be asking yourself why this is important. Following these suggestions is going to make sure that in your progression, the first chord (A) sounds like a beginning chord, or a chord that you would begin a song with, and it's going to make sure that one of the chords in the middle (B) doesn't sound like you just ended the song, and that the ending chord (C), sounds like and ending chord, and not like you just stopped playing in the middle of a song where one would expect more chords to follow! The figure above also states there should be no open harmony consonance in the middle of the progression (B). The reason for this is that when you play a chord with open

Adventures in Harmony – Introduction to the System

harmony, and there are no accidentals in the chord, the chord sounds like you just ended the progression. For example if you played a F major9 (A) (C) (E) (G) voiced 3 5 7 9, that sounds like an ending chord.

Remember earlier we discussed consonance and dissonance:

The sound of consonance is created by chords that have pure tones as long as those tones are not played in closed harmony. A chord that has pure tones is one that does not have any accidentals. Chords that are made up of only the following tones are usually considered chords that create consonance (1), (2), (3), (5),(6),(7), and the (Maj7). A chord has open harmony when the tones are physically spread wide apart on the keyboard. When the tones start to get physically close together, the chord starts to create dissonance, even though we are using the above tones that are usually considered pure. This dissonance is minimal compared to that which is created when accidentals are added.

The sound of dissonance is created by chords that have accidentals or closed harmony. A chord has closed harmony when the tones are physically close together on the keyboard. Chords that contain any of the following tones are usually considered to be dissonant (b2), (-3), (4), (b5), and (+5).

Use the chart above (Figure 16-16) as a suggestion to voice any progression. In summary the chart is telling us the following:

A) The first chord in the progression can have consonance or open harmony. The first chord cannot have closed harmony dissonance, but it can have open harmony dissonance.

B) The chords in the middle of the progression should have dissonance. They can have consonance, but they should not have open harmony consonance. The sound of open harmony consonance tends to sound like an ending chord. They can have closed harmony consonance, but not open harmony consonance.

C) The last chord in the progression can have consonance or dissonance. However, the dissonance should be open harmony dissonance.

Sections (A) and (C) of the progression are something that you really are going to have to play and experiment with in terms of dissonance. Dissonance is allowed as long as it's not too harsh. For example, playing a chord with a (-3) as the first chord in the progression is ok. The (-3) does create some dissonance, but not as much as if you had a (b5) in the chord. I would say that the following order of alterations have increasing levels of dissonance (-3), (4), (+5), (b5).

Adventures in Harmony – Introduction to the System

The most important thing from all this is that in playing your progression, tension should increase after playing the first chord, and the last chord should have less tension than the middle chords.

The following diagram maps the progression that we just created onto the suggested rules.

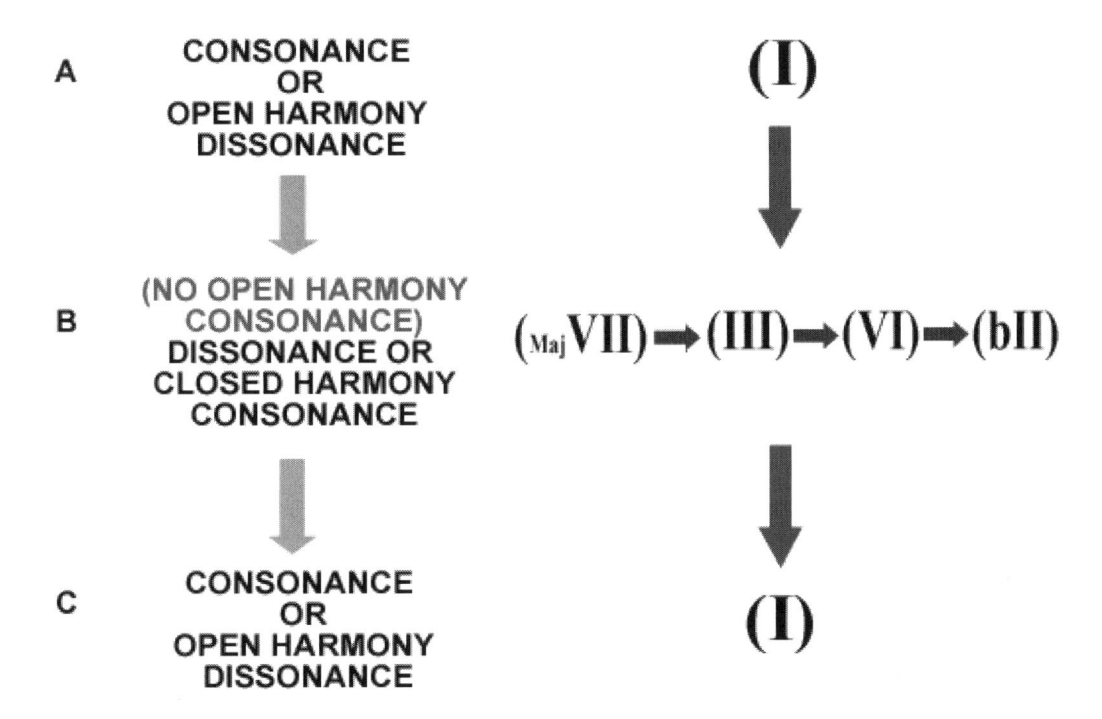

A — CONSONANCE OR OPEN HARMONY DISSONANCE — (I)

↓

B — (NO OPEN HARMONY CONSONANCE) DISSONANCE OR CLOSED HARMONY CONSONANCE — (MajVII) → (III) → (VI) → (bII)

↓

C — CONSONANCE OR OPEN HARMONY DISSONANCE — (I)

16.8 Voice our progression

We are now going to use the course reference manuals to voice the progression that we just made up from scratch. We are now essentially picking the blocks or voicings from the buckets in our "LEGO™" building block set.

The suggested rules above give us some guidelines on which voicings to pick from the different buckets. Remember these are not hard-fast rules, but are only suggestions. Let your ear help you make the final decision!

Now let's voice the progression we created in the last section:

$$(I) \to (_{Maj}VII) \to (III) \to (VI) \to (bII) \to (I)$$

Adventures in Harmony – Introduction to the System

16.9 Voice the first chord in the progression (I).

To voice this [I] chord, open the reference "Adventures in Harmony – In Scale Harmonization - Substitution and Passing Chords" - This reference contains voicings for the [I], [II], [III], [IV], [V], [VI], [VII] and Major VII. Open to the section on the Tonic [I], and select one of the available voicings.

Let's examine the possibilities for this chord:

1) **The Major9 Chord (658)**

    The reference indicates that this voicing has the following tones:

    Maj 7, 9, 10 and 12

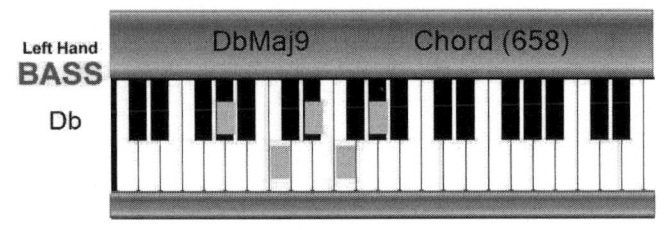

    [Keyboard diagram: Left Hand BASS Db — DbMaj9 Chord (658)]

    Remember, it was suggested that the first chord have consonance, or open harmony dissonance. Well there are no tones that create any dissonance in this chord. So right away we know this chord has consonance. Play this chord and listen to it, you will hear that this chord sounds like a chord you would start a song or progression with. Don't forget to play the base note (Db). This chord would be a good possibility to start our progression.

2) **The Minor 7#5 Chord (694)**

    The reference indicates that this voicing has the following tones:

    (7), (-3) and (#5)

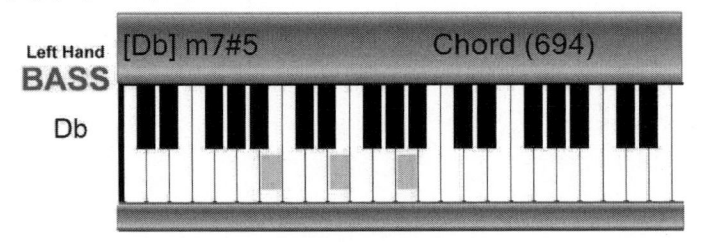

    [Keyboard diagram: Left Hand BASS Db — [Db] m7#5 Chord (694)]

Adventures in Harmony – Introduction to the System

Remember, this first chord should have consonance, or open harmony dissonance. Well it doesn't have consonance because it has a (-3) and (#5) in it. So right away we know this chord has dissonance. But, maybe it has open harmony dissonance. Remember in open harmony we want the notes spread apart, especially the notes causing the dissonance. If we look, the (-3) and (#5) are spread apart. This is open harmony with respect to these two notes. So we have open harmony dissonance. Play this chord and listen to it, you will hear that this sounds like a chord you would start a song or progression with. Again, don't forget to play the bass note (Db). This chord also sounds like it would be a good possibility to begin our progression.

3) **The 6,9b5 Chord (51)**

The reference indicates that this voicing has the following tones:

(3), (b5), (6) and (9)

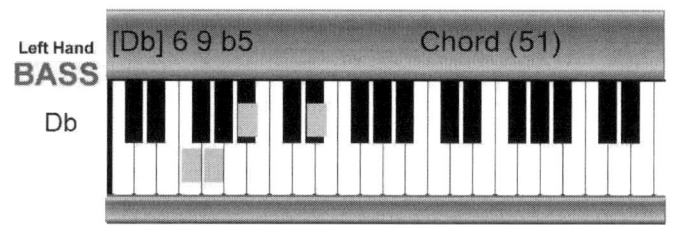

Remember it was suggested that this first chord have consonance, or open harmony dissonance. Well it doesn't have consonance because it has a (b5) in it. So right away we know this chord has dissonance. But, maybe it has open harmony dissonance. Remember in open harmony we want the notes spread apart, especially the notes causing the dissonance. If we look, the (3) and (b5) are right next to each other. This is not open harmony with respect to these two notes. If the (F) were played on top and not next to the (G) we would have open harmony and this could be a possible chord that we could start our progression on. Play this chord and listen to it, you will hear that this chord doesn't sound like a chord you would start a song or progression with. Again, don't forget to play the bass note (Db). This chord would not be a good possibility to begin our progression.

4) **The 6,9 Chord (57) – Voicing 1**

The reference indicates that this voicing has the following tones:

(3), (6), (9) and (12)

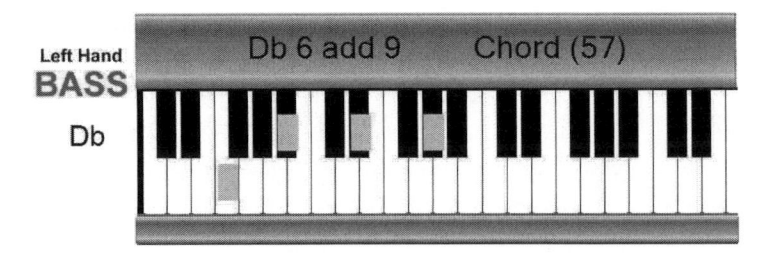

Adventures in Harmony – Introduction to the System

Left Hand BASS Db — Db 6 add 9   Chord (57)

Remember it was suggested that the first chord have consonance, or open harmony dissonance. Well there are no tones that create any dissonance in this chord. So right away we know this chord has consonance. Play this chord and listen to it, you will hear that this chord sounds like a chord you would start a song or progression with. This chord would be a good possibility.

Feel free to try out all of the additional voicings in this section, you might have a different taste then we do. If it sounds good to your ear, feel free to use it. In the beginning we suggest that you take the time to play and hear each voicing.

16.10   Voice the second chord in the progression (MajVII).

To voice this [MajVII] chord, open the reference "Adventures in Harmony – In Scale Harmonization - Substitution and Passing Chords" - This reference contains voicings for the [I], [II], [III], [IV], [V], [VI], [VII] and [Major VII]. Open to the section on the Leading Tone [MajVII], and select one of the available voicings.

Let's examine the possibilities for this chord:

1) **The 11th Chord (679)**

    The reference indicates that this voicing has the following tones:

    (5), (9), (11) and (14)

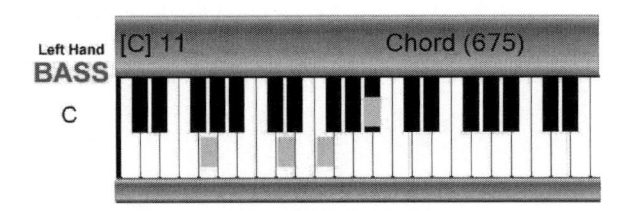

Left Hand BASS C — [C] 11   Chord (675)

Remember it was suggested that the chords in the middle of the progression have dissonance. They can have consonance, but they should not have open harmony consonance. Well this chord has dissonance because it contains an (11). Remember an (11) is the same as a (4). Play this chord, after playing the chord that you previously selected to start this progression. This chord would be a good possibility as the second chord in your progression. Below are the chords that we selected to be the first and second chords in this progression (**Db 6,9** followed by **C11**).

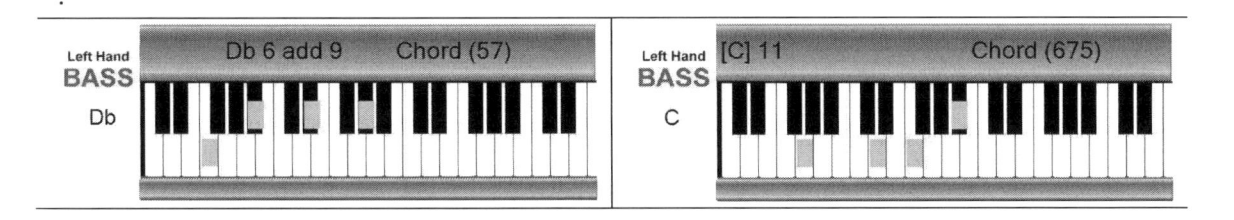

2) **The -7sus Chord (710)**

The reference indicates that this voicing has the following tones:

(5), (7), (b10) and (11)

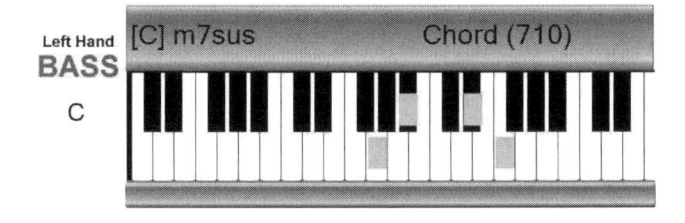

Remember it was suggested that the chords in the middle of the progression have dissonance. They can have consonance, but they should not have open harmony consonance. Well this chord has dissonance because it contains an (11) and a (b10). Remember an (11) is the same as a (4), and a (b10) is the same as a (-3). Play this chord, after playing the chord that you previously selected to start this progression. This chord would be another good possibility as the second chord in your progression. Below are the chords that we selected to be the first and second chords in this progression (**Db 6,9** followed by **C11**).

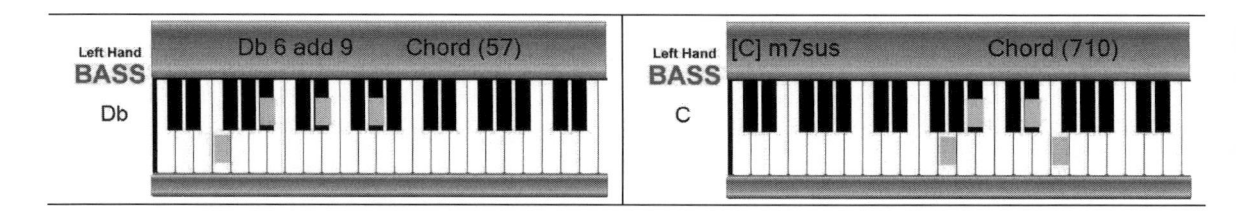

Adventures in Harmony – Introduction to the System

[Keyboard diagram: Left Hand BASS Db — Db 6 add 9 Chord (57)]
[Keyboard diagram: Left Hand BASS C — [C] m7sus Chord (710)]

Or maybe you want to be bold and add both!! Try it out!

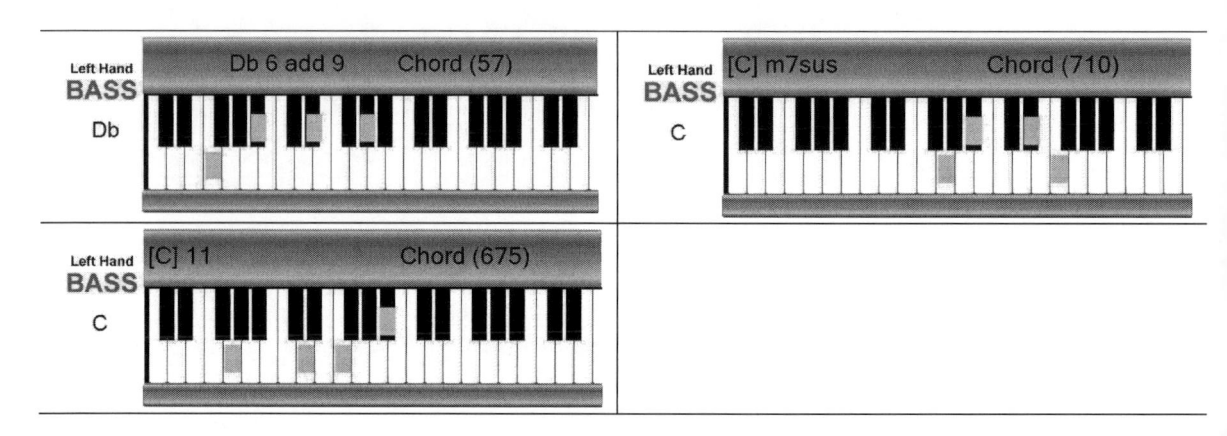

[Keyboard diagram: Left Hand BASS Db — Db 6 add 9 Chord (57)]
[Keyboard diagram: Left Hand BASS C — [C] m7sus Chord (710)]
[Keyboard diagram: Left Hand BASS C — [C] 11 Chord (675)]

And even try it again and reverse the order by playing the (**C11**) before the (**C-7sus**)! Remember this is all about creativity!! Sounds sweet!

Feel free to try out all of the additional voicings in this section, you might have a different taste then we do. If it sounds good to your ear, feel free to use it. In the beginning we suggest that you take the time to play and hear each voicing.

16.11   Voice the third chord in the progression (III).

To voice this [III] chord, open the reference "Adventures in Harmony – In Scale Harmonization - Substitution and Passing Chords" - This reference contains voicings for the [I], [II], [III], [IV], [V], [VI], [VII] and [Major VII]. Open to the section on the Mediant [III], and select one of the available voicings.

Adventures in Harmony – Introduction to the System

Let's examine the possibilities for this chord:

1) **The #9#5 Chord (217)**

   The reference indicates that this voicing has the following tones:

   (-3), (3), (#5) and (8)

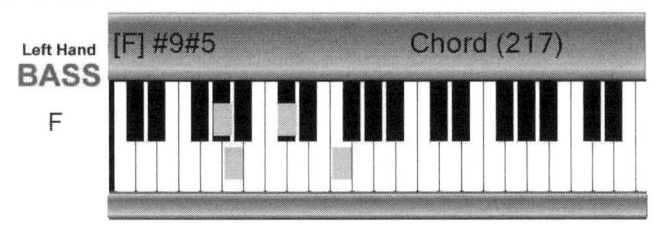

   Remember it was suggested that the chords in the middle of the progression have dissonance. They can have consonance, but they should not have open harmony consonance. Well, this chord has dissonance because it contains a (-3) and a (#5). Play this chord after playing the chord that you previously selected to be the second chord in this progression. This chord would be a good possibility as the third chord in your progression. Below, are the chords that we selected to be the first and second and third chords in this progression (**Db 6,9**, then **C11** and then **F#9#5**).

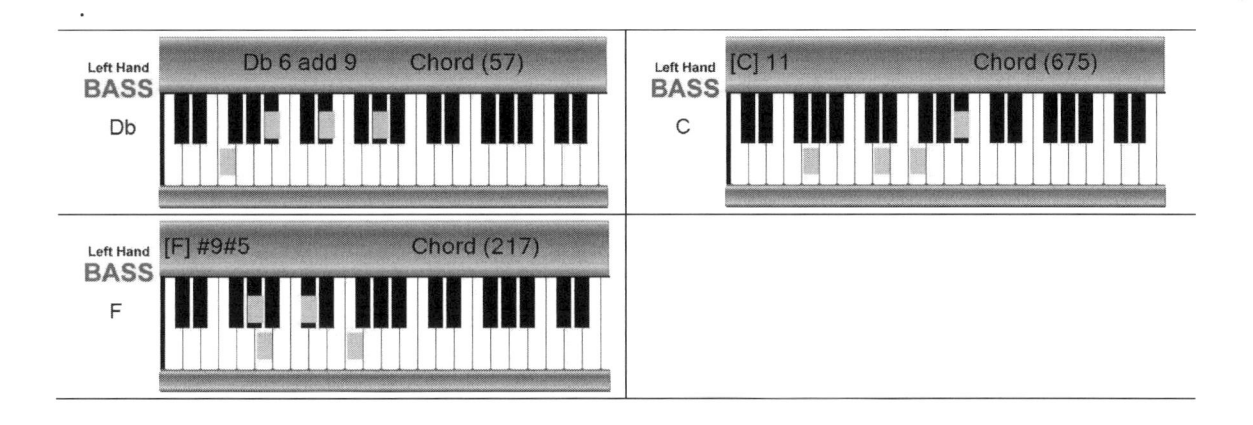

Feel free to try out all of the additional voicings in this section, you might have a different taste then we do. If it sounds good to your ear, feel free to use it. In the beginning we suggest that you take the time to play and hear each voicing.

Adventures in Harmony – Introduction to the System

16.12 Voice the fourth chord in the progression (VI).

To voice this (VI) chord, open the reference "Adventures in Harmony – In Scale Harmonization - Substitution and Passing Chords" - This reference contains voicings for the [I], [II], [III], [IV], [V], [VI], [VII] and [Major VII]. Open to the section on the Submediant [VI], and select one of the available voicings.

Let's examine the possibilities for this chord:

1) **The 7#9#5 Chord (389)**

   The reference indicates that this voicing has the following tones:

   (7), (b10), (10) and (#12)

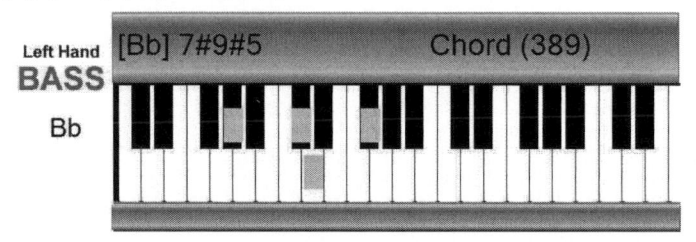

   [Bb] 7#9#5 Chord (389) — Left Hand BASS Bb

Remember it was suggested that the chords in the middle of the progression have dissonance. They can have consonance, but they should not have open harmony consonance. Well this chord has dissonance because it contains a (b10) and a (#12). Remember a (b10) is the same as a (-3). Play this chord, after playing the chord that you previously selected to be the third chord in this progression. This chord would be a good possibility as the fourth chord in your progression. Below, are the chords that we selected so far in this progression (**Db 6,9**, then **C11** then **F#9#5** and finally **Bb7#9#5**).

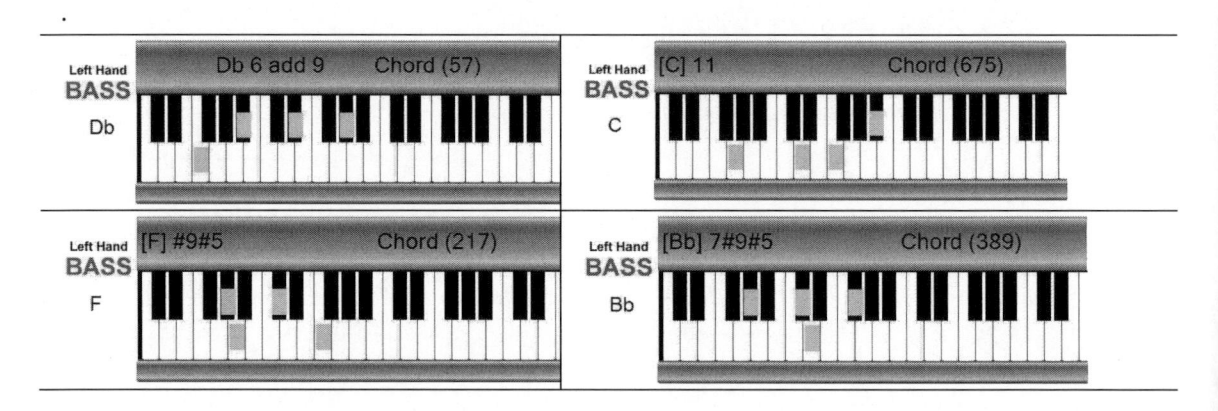

Db 6 add 9 — Chord (57) — Left Hand BASS Db

[C] 11 — Chord (675) — Left Hand BASS C

[F] #9#5 — Chord (217) — Left Hand BASS F

[Bb] 7#9#5 — Chord (389) — Left Hand BASS Bb

Adventures in Harmony – Introduction to the System

Feel free to try out all of the additional voicings in this section, you might have a different taste then we do. If it sounds good to your ear, feel free to use it. In the beginning we suggest that you take the time to play and hear each voicing.

16.13   **Voice the fifth chord in the progression (bII).**

To voice this [bII] chord, open the reference "Adventures in Harmony – Core Reference – Volume – Out of Scale Harmonization - The Tritone and Beyond" - This reference contains voicings for the [bII], [bIII], [bV], and [#V]. Open to the section on the [bII], and select one of the available voicings.

Let's examine the possibilities for this chord:

1) **The 7#9 Chord (579)**

   The reference indicates that this voicing has the following tones:

   (3), (5), (7) and (#9)

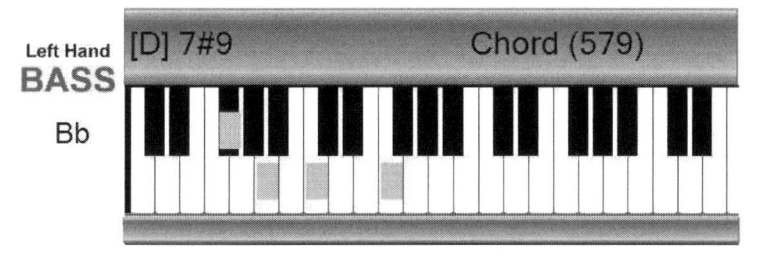

   [Keyboard diagram: Left Hand BASS Bb, [D] 7#9 Chord (579)]

   Remember it was suggested that the chords in the middle of the progression have dissonance. They can have consonance, but they should not have open harmony consonance. Well this chord has dissonance because it contains a (#9), remember the (#9) is the same as a (-3) or (b10). Play this chord after playing the chord that you previously selected to be the fourth chord in this progression. This chord would be a good possibility as the fifth chord in your progression. Below, are the chords that we selected so far in this progression (**Db 6,9**, then **C11** then **F#9#5** then **D7b10** then **B7#9#5** followed by **D7#9**). NOTE: We switched the second chord from the (**C11**) to the (**C-7sus**), remember change it up!

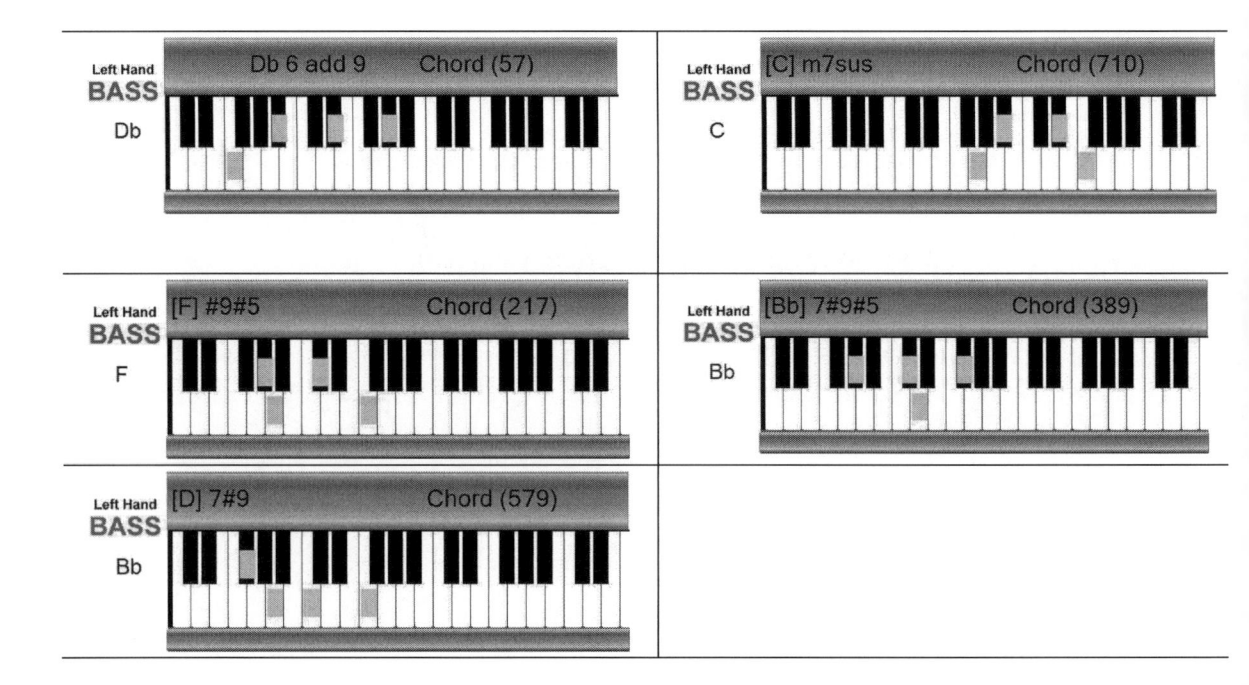

Adventures in Harmony – Introduction to the System

Left Hand BASS Db	Db 6 add 9	Chord (57)	Left Hand BASS C	[C] m7sus	Chord (710)
Left Hand BASS F	[F] #9#5	Chord (217)	Left Hand BASS Bb	[Bb] 7#9#5	Chord (389)
Left Hand BASS Bb	[D] 7#9	Chord (579)			

Feel free to try out all of the additional voicings in this section, you might have a different taste then we do. If it sounds good to your ear, feel free to use it. In the beginning we suggest that you take the time to play and hear each voicing.

16.14   Voice the last chord in the progression (I).

To voice this [I] chord, open the reference "Adventures in Harmony – In Scale Harmonization - Substitution and Passing Chords" - This reference contains voicings for the [I], [II], [III], [IV], [V], [VI], [VII] and [Major VII]. Open to the section on the [I] the Tonic and select one of the available voicings.

All the possibilities that we had for the first chord in the progression, also exist for the last chord. Remember at this point we want to release the tension and we are returning back to the (I) Chord. We selected the following voicing to end our progression.

Adventures in Harmony – Introduction to the System

1) **The Major9 Chord (658)**

   The reference indicates that this voicing has the following tones:

   (Maj 7), (9), (10) and (12)

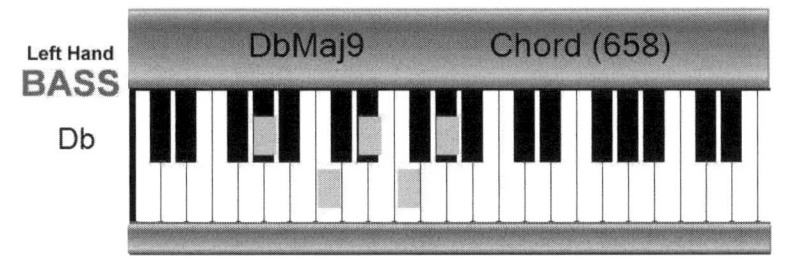

   Feel free to try out all of the additional voicings in this section, you might have a different taste then we do. If it sounds good to your ear, feel free to use it. In the beginning we suggest that you take the time to play and hear each voicing.

   Our progression is as follows

   $$(I) \rightarrow (_{Maj}VII) \rightarrow (III) \rightarrow (VI) \rightarrow (bII) \rightarrow (I)$$

   Our completed voiced progression is written as follows:

   $$(I\ 6,9) \rightarrow (MajVII\ 11) \rightarrow (III\ \#9\#5)$$
   $$(VI\ 7\#9\#5) \rightarrow (bII\ 7b10) \rightarrow (I\ Maj\ 9)$$

   Congratulations!! You have created your own unique progression!! Now, from the Roman numbers you should be able to play this progression in any key.

17 Begin Your Adventure

We are constantly publishing new voicing references for our course. While you are experiencing your Adventure in Harmony, please feel free to experiment with any of the voicing references.

Let me first state that I am a user of my own course material. When I harmonize a piece of music, I go through the same process that is described in this volume. And in going through the process I do many times surprise myself with many of the progressions and sequences that I discover.

Here I will detail one such experience.

My original intent was to re-harmonize the nursery rhyme "Mary Had a Little Lamb" in the key of (F).

```
Mar - ry  had  a   lit - tle  Lamb
(A)   (G) (F) (G) (A)  (A)   (A)
```

in going through the process, I got as far as the chord on the word "HAD" where I found myself blown away by a chord sequence that I stumbled upon in the harmonization process.

As I have said many times, this course is an Adventure in Harmony allowing you to explore and create, and that's exactly what I was doing. I wanted to make a couple of chord changes on the word "HAD", and choices I made surprised me and I just had to share them with you.

The end result was that I was so taken by these changes that I just forgot about the song and wanted to play with the chord changes that I created on this single word.

Just to put things in perspective, here are the first two chords that I selected to harmonize the word "MAR - RY." (**A-7#5**) and (**E7#9#5**).

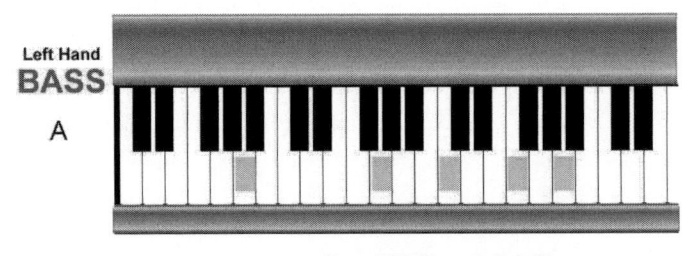

Left Hand
BASS
A

Am7#5 - MAR

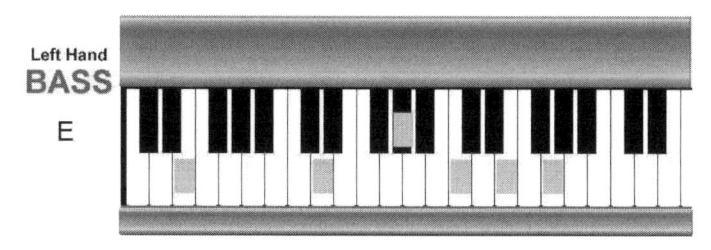

Adventures in Harmony – Introduction to the System

E7#9#5 - RY

Now I move on to the word "HAD" with this G-9 voicing. This is one of my favorite voicings on the minor 9 and I have never seen it voiced like this. Just as an FYI at Creative music we use computers to model chord voicings. This gives us the ability to create voicings that I am going to classify as "undiscovered." I think the following two voicings and chord movements fall into this category as "undiscovered" the minor 9 followed by a **6 add 9b5**.

The **6 add 9b5** is a chord from our newest release "Preaching Chords - Special Edition"

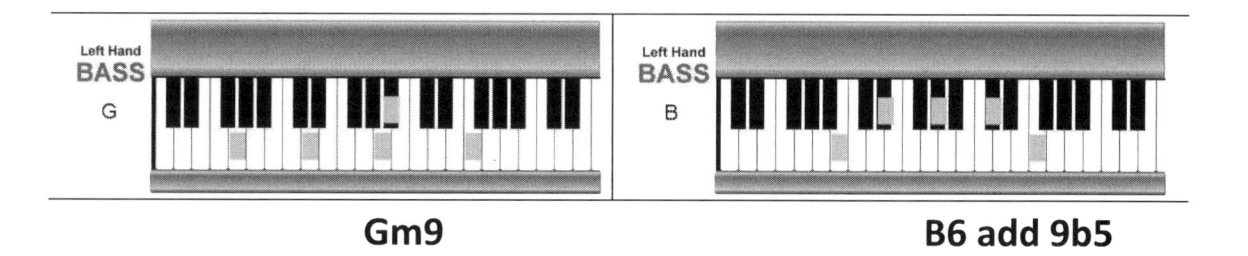

Gm9   **B6 add 9b5**

This movement from the **m9** to the **6 add 9b5** is sweet.

Now continue the sequence with the following chords.

D7#9#5   **Gm9**

The other thing that I wanted to mention is what I will call the "LEGO™ Building Principle" with regard to the chords in our course.

All Rights Reserved - @ Copyright 2009 Creative Musuc Ventures LLC www.gospel-chords.com 9.02.10

Adventures in Harmony – Introduction to the System

Our chords can be put together in ANY ORDER and sound good.

Just try it for yourself.

Take the last four chords and shuffle them around. The order does not matter!

And just for good measure, go ahead and add this chord in the mix.

It's another chord from our volume Black Gospel Chords.

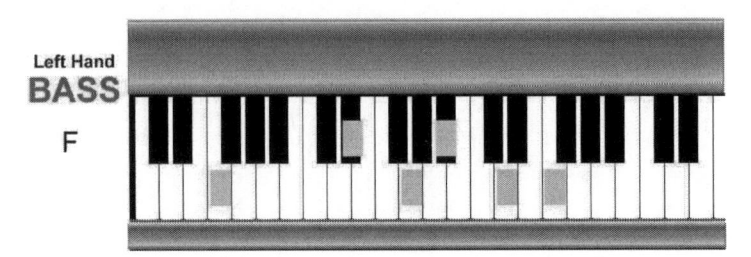

Left Hand BASS
F

F13sus

What you have just experienced in the above chords where the (F) note remains held down while you make chord changes is a very powerful technique where you essentially create a chord cycle progression on the melody note (suspension). You see the chord changes possible are beautiful. You no longer have to hold a single note or chord down for several beats.

You now can always have changes available at your disposal by using this technique.

You can also master this technique in our latest volume "Mastering Chord Suspensions."

All these chords are a result of our computer modeling and analysis when we create chords for our course allowing you to easily create and compose. We are not just a music company. We are a music technology and research company.

Adventures in Harmony – Introduction to the System

18 No Boundaries

You are going to discover that there are no boundaries in this course. The possibilities are endless with regard to harmonization.

This is another example of a partial harmonization of the song JOY TO THE WORLD.

For this example we are in the key of (C).

Before I even started this harmonization, I decided what the chord movement would be. I decided that the chords would move in fourths starting with (Gb).

So the chord sequence would be

Gb - B - E - A - D - G - and then to C.

JOY TO THE WORLD

The choice of chord movement is entirely up to you. The Adventures in Harmony Course will give you the proper voicings so that your creation sounds beautiful.

The chords in this harmonization are from our reference Volume Preaching Chords

So in this example we are going to harmonize JOY TO THE WORLD and play the chords in this order (Gb, B, E, A, D, G) and on the last word of the phrase on the word "World" we will make four chord changes!

The melody notes for this phrase are as follows:

C	**B**	**A**	**G**
JOY	TO	THE	WORLD
I	Maj VII	VI	V

In the key of (C), this corresponds to the Roman numbers [I], [Maj VII], [VI] and [V].

To harmonize this song, all we have to do is open up the reference volume on melody harmonization, and pick a chord that corresponds to each one of the tones (I, MVII, VI, V).

1. For the word **JOY** the note is (C). (C) is a [I] in the key of (C). So open the reference volume to the chapter on harmonizing on the [I], and choose a chord.

2. For the word **TO** the note is (B). (B) is a [Maj VII] in the key of (C). So open the reference volume to the chapter on harmonizing on the [Maj VII], and choose a chord.

3. For the word **THE** the note is A. A is a [VI] in the key of (C). So open the reference volume to the chapter on harmonizing on the [VI], and choose a chord.

Adventures in Harmony – Introduction to the System

4. For the word **WORLD** the note is (G). (G) is a [V] in the key of (C). So open the reference volume to the chapter on harmonizing on the [V], and choose a chord.

   The next page contains the results of our selections.

And remember you can do this with ANY SONG! You can pick any chord to go with any melody note; we have the voicings in our course to make it happen!

And if you do not like our selections, you are free to choose your own and make this your own unique harmonization.

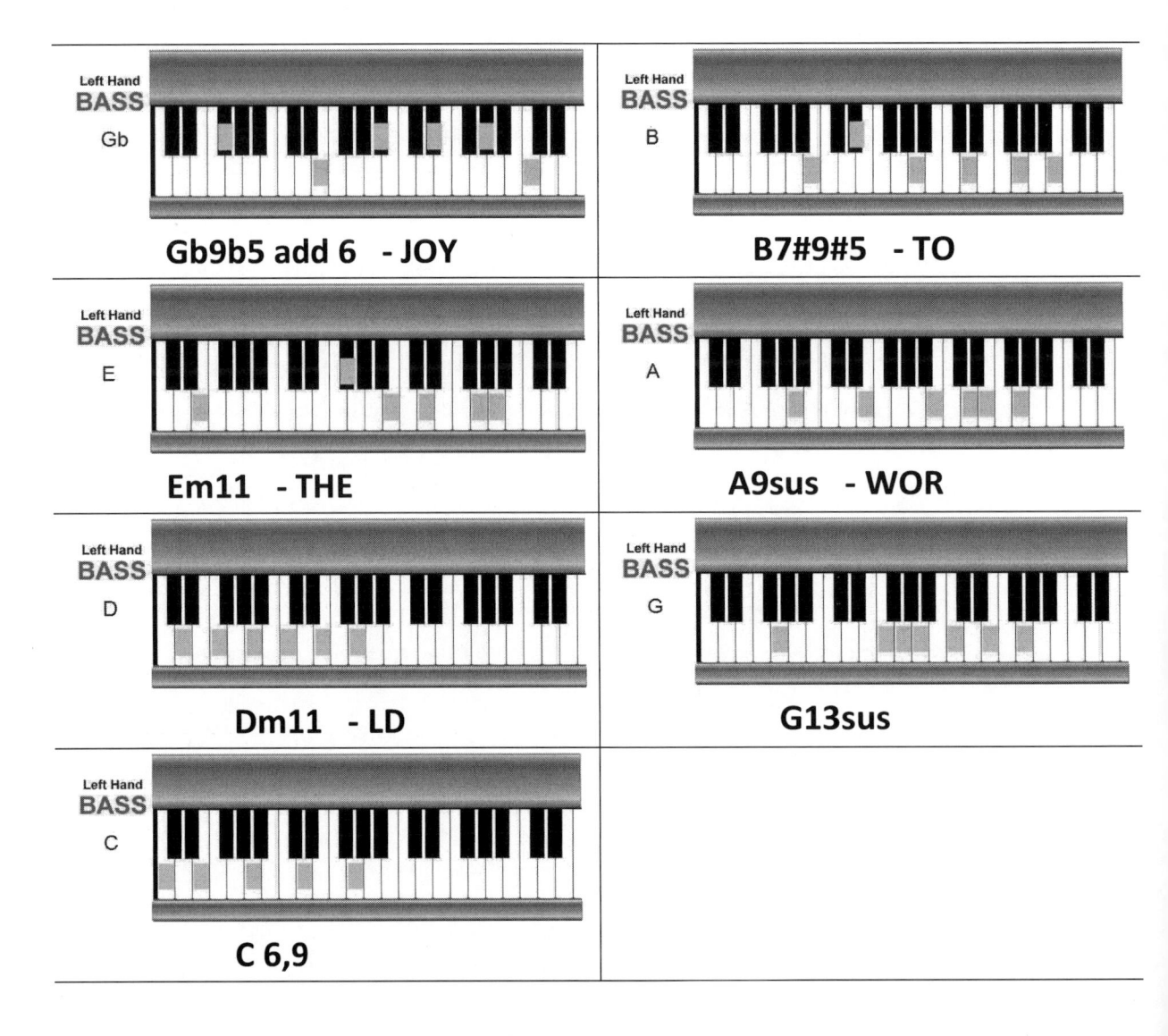

Left Hand BASS Gb
Gb9b5 add 6   - JOY

Left Hand BASS B
B7#9#5   - TO

Left Hand BASS E
Em11   - THE

Left Hand BASS A
A9sus   - WOR

Left Hand BASS D
Dm11   - LD

Left Hand BASS G
G13sus

Left Hand BASS C
C 6,9

All Rights Reserved - @ Copyright 2009 Creative Musuc Ventures LLC   www.gospel-chords.com 9.02.10   Page 170

Adventures in Harmony – Introduction to the System

The chords that we used on this harmonization are in the volume" Preaching Chords", and all we did was harmonize on the melody note. The top note of every chord corresponds to a different melody note in the song and we were able to choose a different chord for each melody note. This is how you get all the color and flavor in your music.

We hope you have enjoyed your introduction to your Adventure in Harmony.

Remember to aid in your Adventure we also have all of our chords available on 4x6 cards. You may use these cards to arrange chords and try out new progressions while sitting at your instrument. The front of the cards contains a large picture of the chords so that you may easily put your hands right on the chord. The back of the cards contains the chords detailed note-by-note in all 12 keys. The cards are available at our website www.gospel-chords.com.

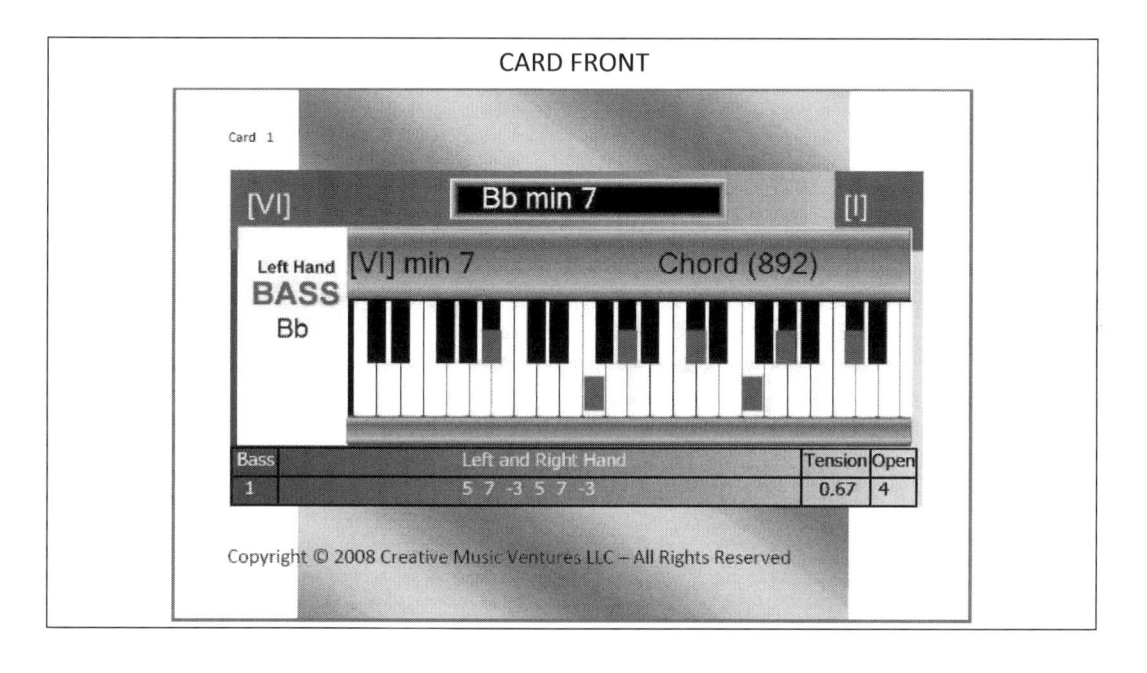

CARD FRONT

Card 1

[VI] **Bb min 7** [I]

Left Hand [VI] min 7   Chord (892)
BASS
Bb

Bass	Left and Right Hand	Tension	Open
1	5 7 -3 5 7 -3	0.67	4

Copyright © 2008 Creative Music Ventures LLC – All Rights Reserved

Adventures in Harmony – Introduction to the System

19 Appendix – Roman numbers – Enharmonic Scale Numbering

19.1.1 Key of C

C Scale														
Note	C	D	E	F	G	A	B	C	D	E	F	G	A	B	C
Number	1	2	3	4	5	6	7	8	9	10	11	12	13	14	15
	I	II	III	IV	V	VI	VII	I	II	III	IV	V	VI	VII	I

19.1.2 Key of Db

Db Scale														
Note	Db	Eb	F	Gb	Ab	Bb	C	Db	Eb	F	Gb	Ab	Bb	C	Db
Number	1	2	3	4	5	6	7	8	9	10	11	12	13	14	15
	I	II	III	IV	V	VI	VII	I	II	III	IV	V	VI	VII	I

19.1.3 Key of D

D Scale														
Note	D	E	Gb	G	A	B	Db	D	E	Gb	G	A	B	Db	D
Number	1	2	3	4	5	6	7	8	9	10	11	12	13	14	15
	I	II	III	IV	V	VI	VII	I	II	III	IV	V	VI	VII	I

19.1.4 Key of Eb

Eb Scale														
Note	Eb	F	G	Ab	Bb	C	D	Eb	F	G	Ab	Bb	C	D	Eb
Number	1	2	3	4	5	6	7	8	9	10	11	12	13	14	15
	I	II	III	IV	V	VI	VII	I	II	III	IV	V	VI	VII	I

19.1.5 Key of E

E Scale														
Note	E	Gb	Ab	A	B	Db	Eb	E	Gb	Ab	A	B	Db	Eb	E
Number	1	2	3	4	5	6	7	8	9	10	11	12	13	14	15
	I	II	III	IV	V	VI	VII	I	II	III	IV	V	VI	VII	I

Adventures in Harmony – Introduction to the System

19.1.6 Key of F

							F Scale								
Note	F	G	A	Bb	C	D	E	F	G	A	Bb	C	D	E	F
Number	1	2	3	4	5	6	7	8	9	10	11	12	13	14	15
	I	II	III	IV	V	VI	VII	I	II	III	IV	V	VI	VII	I

19.1.7 Key of Gb

							Gb Scale								
Note	Gb	Ab	Bb	B	Db	Eb	F	Gb	Ab	Bb	B	Db	Eb	F	Gb
Number	1	2	3	4	5	6	7	8	9	10	11	12	13	14	15
	I	II	III	IV	V	VI	VII	I	II	III	IV	V	VI	VII	I

19.1.8 Key of G

							G Scale								
Note	G	A	B	C	D	E	Gb	G	A	B	C	D	E	Gb	G
Number	1	2	3	4	5	6	7	8	9	10	11	12	13	14	15
	I	II	III	IV	V	VI	VII	I	II	III	IV	V	VI	VII	I

19.1.9 Key of Ab

							Ab Scale								
Note	Ab	Bb	C	Db	Eb	F	G	Ab	Bb	E	Db	Eb	F	G	Ab
Number	1	2	3	4	5	6	7	8	9	10	11	12	13	14	15
	I	II	III	IV	V	VI	VII	I	II	III	IV	V	VI	VII	I

19.1.10 Key of A

							A Scale								
Note	A	B	Db	D	E	Gb	Ab	A	B	Db	D	E	Gb	Ab	A
Number	1	2	3	4	5	6	7	8	9	10	11	12	13	14	15
	I	II	III	IV	V	VI	VII	I	II	III	IV	V	VI	VII	I

Adventures in Harmony – Introduction to the System

19.1.11 Key of Bb

Bb Scale															
Note	Bb	C	D	Eb	F	G	A	Bb	C	D	Eb	F	G	A	Bb
Number	1	2	3	4	5	6	7	8	9	10	11	12	13	14	15
	I	II	III	IV	V	VI	VII	I	II	III	IV	V	VI	VII	I

19.1.12 Key of B

B Scale															
Note	B	Db	Eb	E	Gb	Ab	Bb	B	Db	Eb	E	Gb	Ab	Bb	B
Number	1	2	3	4	5	6	7	8	9	10	11	12	13	14	15
	I	II	III	IV	V	VI	VII	I	II	III	IV	V	VI	VII	I

Printed in Great Britain
by Amazon.co.uk, Ltd.,
Marston Gate.